BACKSTREET
MOM

A Mother's Tale of Backstreet Boy
AJ McLean's Rise to Fame,
Struggle With Addiction
and Ultimate Triumph

BACKSTREET
MOM

Denise I. McLean
AND
Nicole P. Gotlin

BENBELLA

BENBELLA BOOKS
DALLAS, TEXAS

BenBella Books

6440 N. Central Expressway, Suite 508, Dallas, Texas 75206

Send feedback to feedback@benbellabooks.com
www.benbellabooks.com

Printed in the United States of America

10 9 8 7 6 5 4 3 2 1

Library of Congress Cataloging-in-Publication Data

McLean, Denise I.
 Backstreet mom / by Denise I. McLean and Nicole P. Gotlin.— BenBella Books ed.
  p. cm.
 ISBN 1-932100-15-6 (trade pbk. : alk. paper)
 I. Gotlin, Nicole P. II. Title.

PS3613.C576B33 2003
813'.6—dc22

                                                                2003019540

Cover design by Melody Cadungog
Interior designed and composed by John Reinhardt Book Design

I dedicate this book to all the single parents out there struggling day to day with the task of raising their children. I am with you in spirit along your path. As you put forth your efforts to help bring good and honest people into the world remember that each child is an individual. They are only separated by personality and environment. You as parents can never prevent them from making mistakes as they grow. You can only be there for them to help them learn from each one and continue to move on with their lives. This is a difficult lesson for a parent to learn but it is necessary if you want to remain a part of your child's life.

I also dedicate this book to every child with a dream in his or her heart. Dare to become the best person you can and learn to nurture your talents to their fullest potential. Shoot for the stars; they are within reach to be grasped and held on to.

Acknowledgments

THERE ARE TOO MANY PEOPLE who have helped my son and me on the road to success to mention them all in a few sentences. So for those who I have not named, and you know who you are, both family and friends, I thank you from the bottom of my heart. My life on the road and at home is richer for having you all in it.

To begin, I must first thank my son, Alex, and his four adopted brothers for giving me such amazing opportunities during my time with you. You were my inspiration for this book and will always hold a special place in my heart.

To my mom who I know watches over me every day. You gave me the strength in life to go after my dreams and loved me for it—thank you. I love you and miss you.

To my dad for being there to listen to me with patience and understanding and always loving me, thank you.

To my brother, Bill, for his unconditional love and support. I love you and thank you for watching over me. To Darlene for watching over my big brother, thank you.

To Kelly and Bill, a special thanks for your love, abounding energy and help with just about everything through the years.

To Nicole, the daughter I never had. Thanks for helping me keep my sanity for all these years. I love you. Give Max and Doug a kiss for me.

To Andre, my mentor and friend who lived the chaos with me, tip the glass for me and tell Mr. Grumpy Mrs. Gibson's gone to Cleveland.

To Nina and Polsia, your perseverance, professionalism and knowledge has helped both Alex and me achieve our visions from past to present. I love you both as soul sisters. We will do more great things together.

To Judy Segelin, you have seen the best and the worst from the legal side and have remained my friend through it all.

To David and Sue Zedeck and the girls, for your support, love and friendship through the good times and the bad.

To Glenn Yeffeth for believing in my project and me, thank you. I hope we will work together again.

To Jim Dickerson, thank you for your guidance and patience in helping me edit this book. It was greatly appreciated.

And last but not least to the love of my life, Tony. Your support and love on this roller-coaster life of mine has helped me more than you know. I love you with all of my heart and look forward to spending the rest of my life with you.

Contents

Author's Note

I WROTE THIS BOOK with the hope that I could pass along some insight into the business of entertainment for other parents to share with their children. I also wish to help those single parents dealing with the issues of raising a family in this high-pressured world we all try to survive in on a day-to-day basis. I believe that all children have a gift and as a parent it is your job to unwrap it, nurture it and share it forever. The experiences you live with your children are priceless and should never be taken for granted, whether they are good or bad. Save the good ones for memories and learn from the bad.

Introduction

THIS WAS NEVER thought to be a life-long journey. But my emotional and physical travels continue to take me along a path toward peace, success and love for my closest friends and family. This book is both knowledge and truth about my life and the life of my mother. I hope this book finds you learning and living with a better understanding of how the success and friendship of a son or daughter and their parent(s) can be unconditional and everlasting, and /or broken.

P.S. You can live and learn, but you cannot learn to live. So just live.

CHAPTER ONE

Big Poppa Does His Thing

MARCH 1994—Upon our arrival at Jive Records' headquarters in Manhattan's Chelsea neighborhood, we were given a quick tour of the three floors that the company occupied in the twelve-story building. Jive Records was founded by South African entrepreneur Clive Calder, who had an office on the sixth floor.

With its many cubicles the layout of the office reminded me of a company where I once worked, though we turned out telephone systems, not world-class music. I had never seen a music factory, so I didn't know what to expect.

As we walked the halls, saying our hellos to what seemed like an endless number of faces, I couldn't help but notice my son Alex's eyes widen as he looked at the impressive line of gold records on every wall. Originally founded as a small independent label in London in the late 1970s, Jive Records—the name was taken from "township jive," a type of South African music—had by 1994 become one of America's leading hit factories, with an impressive stable of R&B and rap artists, including R. Kelly, Billy Ocean and others.

"Wow, I didn't know Jive had these guys!" Alex said, gazing at the gold records.

Then, moments later, he bubbled over with, "Hey fellas look at this one!"

Alex (you know him as AJ, but he will always be Alex to me) wasn't the only one there who was impressed.

All of the boys—Alex, Nick, Brian, Kevin and Howie—were pretty overwhelmed by what they saw. I could not help but think back to the beginning of all this craziness and marvel at how far we had come. Admittedly, it had taken over two years of blood, sweat and tears to get to that point, but all that suddenly faded away. At that particular moment it was all just so surreal, almost like walking through a dream.

Finally, we were taken to the conference room, where we were greeted by more gold records. The dark-wood conference table, really too large for the room, was surrounded by black-leather chairs. I could barely walk around the table without brushing up against the walls. Windows covered one entire side of the room. At one end of the room, closest to the door, were two more leather chairs, with a small table just large enough for a telephone in between them.

Even though the atmosphere was initially welcoming and friendly, a nervous tension grew as we gathered at the table. I looked around the room, feeling a bit put-off by the odd seating arrangement. The five boys sat together on one side of the table, while their manager sat across from them, next to record-company representatives. Nick Carter's parents, Bob and Jane, stood behind their son. I stood behind Alex.

An invisible line seemed to divide the boys from their manager, Johnny Wright, and group founder Lou " Big Poppa" Pearlman, who started off the meeting by introducing the boys to their attorney, Kendall Minter. We didn't even know the boys had an attorney, so that was the first surprise of the day.

Minter was a thin, distinguished-looking black man with a deeply receding hairline and a pencil-thin mustache. Although none of us knew anything about him at the time, we later learned that he was a Cornell University-educated lawyer from New York who had an impressive client list that included Archbishop Desmond Tutu, Lena Horne, and the Government of Jamaica. He was what other lawyers like to call a heavy hitter.

After a few pleasantries, we were told that Mr. Minter had read all the contracts and, in his "expert" opinion, felt that we now had before us the best deal we were going to get. That was nice to know, but we each reached out and took copies to begin reading.

That was the second shock. We were told that Jive Records had made an offer to the boys. We were not prepared for what was to follow. In our minds we had been led to believe we were there to hear the offer and discuss it as a group; we were not prepared to sign contracts. The idea of listening to an offer and being pressured into signing a potentially life-changing contract are two entirely different things.

As we went through the documents, Lou and Johnny took turns going over all of the paragraphs that they felt were important and, with each line read, questions arose from the parents and the boys.

"In reference to merchandise sales, why does the record company get part of that—and what is the usual amount?" asked Bob Carter.

"Is this the best deal we can get?" asked one of the boys.

Every time a question arose regarding percentages or the like, Lou, Johnny and the attorney left the room to speak to the record company people in private. We were never privy to those discussions. While I might not have understood a good deal of it, I felt as though I was being deprived of having some input on my son's behalf.

Back and forth they went, time after time. We even heard some voices raised a couple of times between Lou and Johnny, but we did not know why. I felt more like a spectator than a participant. The uncertain glances cast between Nick's parents and me during the course of the meeting gave me the idea that they felt the same.

Once the contracts were read through, an awkward silence hung in the air. Lou looked over at the five boys and smiled. That was our signal that the terms had been reached and all was final. There was no room for questions or comments.

Then, from out of nowhere, a lightning bolt struck.

"We'd like our attorney to look over the contract, if you don't mind," said Bob.

As soon as I heard that, I piped in and agreed with the Carters that we should be allowed to take the contracts back to Florida so that we could sit down with our own attorneys to give them the final once-over. What could that hurt? It might delay things by a week at best. Didn't people usually go over contracts carefully before they signed them?

Lou and Johnny seemed stunned by our request. The smile on Lou's face dissipated into a clenched jaw and wrinkled brow. Johnny's eyes widened and he grimaced. Not a word came from anyone. After a moment's silence, Lou's expression softened. "Look, I hired this attorney for all of us," he said. "He is here to get these five boys the best possible deal he can. Don't you trust me? Aren't we all one big family?"

What could we say to that? I could not deny that Big Poppa had opened his heart and his checkbook to us for the last two years. He had practically supported my son and I for half that time. There was nothing he hadn't given those boys—dinners, parties, trips. There was no denying that he had spoiled them. Lou had never positioned himself on the same level as management. Big Poppa was more like a rich uncle who also happened to be a financial backer and producer. More like family.

In fact, Lou had referred to himself as the sixth Backstreet Boy from the very beginning. That was even reflected in the contracts, since his signature was grouped on the same page as those of the five boys. What could we do? Part of me agreed with the Carters, but the reality was that I did not even know a lawyer and, up until now, there had never been a question of Lou's motives.

Again, Nick's parents spoke up with the same argument. At that point things got a bit heated and Lou blurted out: "This is the only deal on the table. It is a take it or leave it situation." My entire body tensed at the sound of his angry voice. I felt Alex's shoulders jerk. I looked down at my son and he turned his head up, his eyes filling with tears. I saw his lip quiver as he pulled up towards me.

"Mom," Alex said, his voice low and pleading. "Please, this is what I want to do. Please sign the contracts for me."

How could I refuse? With weak knees, I asked if the boys, parents and I could have a few minutes alone to compose ourselves and talk this over. Everyone agreed. Soon it was just the boys and the parents alone in the room. I asked Alex if he was sure. Did he realize what this really meant? He answered, yes.

Again he said, "Mom please do this for me."

Nick made the same plea to his parents. What else could we do? At that point, the other three boys had joined in on the conversation. They wanted to do this as a team, as the brothers they had started to become.

Our children had worked too hard for this day to let it end in disappointment, so we called everyone back into the room and signed the contracts. My son was elated, as were the other boys. When we finished, Lou suggested that we all go out to dinner to celebrate.

The Backstreet Boys were on their way.

CHAPTER TWO

Igniting the Spark

I BECAME A SINGLE MOM when Alex was a just a little over two years old. The year before that had been one of the most stressful periods of my life. My marriage to Alex's father had been a mistake from the start, but I was eighteen, rebellious and desperate to leave home. I wanted to experience life and love—the future be damned!

I grew up in a loving middle-class home. However, at eighteen I couldn't bear to be under my parents' thumb a moment longer. I felt smothered, as many teens did in those hippy days. It was, after all, the late sixties—a time of free love, rampant drugs and wild-spirited youth. I never indulged in drugs because I had lost a few friends to that nasty stuff in high school, but in every other way I was a normal young woman of the times.

I did do my fair share of drinking. It somehow made me feel like I fit in better with my peers. Whenever we wanted to have a party, we drove across the state line from New Jersey into New York, where you could buy beer with a fake ID, loaded the car up with beer and then went to someone's house where we wouldn't be bothered by parents.

As a teen, my big vices were drinking and smoking, neither of which I ever dreamed of doing at home. My mom, a little red-headed fireball of

German descent named Ursula, had made it very clear to me that smoking was a big taboo. In her youth, she had been a "social" smoker who only lit up on weekends with her friends. My dad, Adolph, had been a smoker once, but he, too, had given it up. In our home, cigarettes were public enemy number one. Smoking was not the only taboo: Mom was very opinionated and old fashioned when it came to morals.

I was not allowed to date until I was sixteen. Of course, that did not stop me from sneaking out of the house to go to the movies with boys. One Saturday, I asked her to drop me off at the movie theater, where I met my clandestine date after she left. Naturally, she returned early to pick me up and caught me with the boy.

On the way home, she laid a real guilt trip on me for telling her a lie. She must have told me a thousand times how disappointed she was in me. I was—and still am—a pleaser by nature. When she questioned my sense of family loyalty, I listened. Mom knew how to do that all too well.

Dad, a short, handsome Latin man with thick black hair, grew up in a family where his father did not play a major role in raising the children. I only met my dad's father once and that was when I was very young. Dad swore that he would never be like his father and he stayed true to that.

My father was a devoted family man who worked hard to provide for us. Only once did he ever raise a hand to me in anger and that happened when I arrogantly moved out of the house at age seventeen. My parents didn't have to raise their voices to keep my brother and me in line. We knew the "look" well enough to know when it was time to stop our insolent behavior.

Both of my parents had a great sense of humor and we laughed quite a bit in my house, but as I grew into womanhood something changed between us. It seemed as though I saw only the worst in them. I am positive I caused more than one gray hair on both of their heads during my teen years. Pretty soon, there was nothing the three of us could agree upon.

When I was fifteen my parents decided to move away from the winter weather and settle into South Florida. That was where my future husband, Bob, entered my life. We met while I was in high school. To me it was love at first sight. While he was not drop-dead gorgeous, he had a charm about him that won me over instantly. Bob was the little puppy who followed me home. He had a car and that enabled us to tool around after school. The fact that he played in a band made him the ultimate cool boyfriend.

Bob was not very demonstrative. When it came to our relationship, I knew it was up to me to make the first move—and I did. I proposed marriage. Much to my delight, he quickly accepted. My father had seen the writing on the wall where Bob was concerned. In an attempt separate us, he sent me away to my aunt's house in New Jersey for the summer.

That did little to discourage us. Bob and I spoke every night on the telephone and planned our getaway. Since we were too young to get married in Florida, we decided to run away to Tennessee, where we had heard it was possible to get married at the age of seventeen.

Within a month of my arrival in New Jersey, we put our plan into effect. I told my aunt that I was spending the weekend at a friend's house, but instead Bob came up from Florida and we drove nonstop to Chattanooga. We found a room that we could afford and then set out to complete our task of matrimony. Much to our dismay, the information we had about Tennessee was wrong. We were informed that we were too young.

Saddened by our misadventure, we drove to Florida, where we hid out for a couple of weeks in a sleazy motel. The only thing we could think of to do was for me to move into Bob's apartment and live with him without benefit of marriage. A marriage certificate was just a piece of paper, right?

The afternoon before leaving the motel, we were lying on the couch watching television when we heard a knock at the door. Figuring it was the maid or the owner, Bob got up to answer it. To his surprise, he came face to face with my brother, Bill, who had come to take me home.

"Get your things, you're going home with me," he said.

My brother is much taller and larger in build than Bob, so the possibility of a mismatched confrontation between the two of them created an awkward silence that left all three of us staring at each other in shock. When I recovered from my brother's unexpected arrival—and then saw the tremendous anger on his face—I quickly gathered my things together and hurried out the door without another word.

"Mom and Dad were terrified that something bad had happened to you," he said, using a tone of voice that reflected the seriousness of the situation. "They called the police. Then, when they realized that Bob was also missing, they figured out what had happened."

"How did you find us?"

"A trooper spotted your car and got suspicious."

My stay back home was short-lived. I had a huge fight with my parents and my dad told me that I was a disgrace to the family. That was the first and only time that my dad ever slapped me. I stormed out of the house and moved in with Bob and his family.

One year later, on October 18, 1972, Bob and I drove to Miami and got married at city hall. Since I had not spoken to my parents for well over a year, I didn't bother to tell them about the marriage.

I was convinced that we needed little to live on except our love, but I learned quickly that you also needed a roof over your head and some food on the table. Money was tight in Bob's home. His mother Irene was a short, frail-looking, gray-headed woman in her sixties, who had never worked. She survived entirely on the meager Social Security benefits that she received after the death of Bob's father. Bob did odd jobs and played in the band, but his brother, Jim, never left the house.

I convinced Bob that he needed to go to school and learn a trade. He decided on a one-year computer school since it had the most attractive tuition plan. Both he and his brother enrolled in the school and we moved to Miami.

I worked two jobs and took a few classes in the evenings. Most of my income went toward helping Bob and his brother pay their tuition and expenses. After he finished school, Bob interviewed with a few major computer companies and we moved to Boston for six weeks so that he could complete his training. When we returned to Florida, a pile of bills greeted us. Jim had relocated to another state, so he was no help with our expenses. We had Bob's mom to worry about, as well as credit card bills from the trip.

With all of that weighing on us, I decided to put off finishing college and get a full-time job. There was very little money for fun stuff. Most of our time was spent in our apartment watching television and occasionally going out for ice cream or a cheap movie.

Mom and Dad were very upset with me for marrying Bob, but they realized that I was not going to be the first to give in. Mom eventually made the first move and soon we were talking again. They loaned us $250 to put down on our first house. It was only half of a duplex with two bedrooms and a tiny yard, but it was brand new and all ours!

When we first moved in, our neighbors were other nice young couples like ourselves, but as the years passed, the development turned into rental properties and the neighborhood declined rapidly. Many of our neighbors moved, only to be replaced with transients and low-income families. Once, I had to call the health department and report a neighbor who was allowing garbage to pile up beside her house.

Things for us as a married couple went pretty well for a few years. Even so, Bob's hours were hard to deal with. Being the new guy meant that he got all the shifts that no one else wanted. As he continued to rack up more time with the company, his employment situation improved and we began to reap the benefits from both of us working and having a reasonably low overhead. Meanwhile, Bob's brother moved his mom to the West Coast to live with him, which meant that we were able to save enough money to buy a boat and take a nice vacation to the Grand Cayman Islands.

After a few years, we began to talk about the possibility of having a child. By then, my family had accepted Bob to the point where my mom started hinting about grandchildren. We decided to save our money to buy a bigger house in a nice area of town, a process that would take about a year. By that time, Bob was earning enough money so that I wouldn't have to work if I got pregnant. It was time to start our family.

I remember the exact moment I became pregnant. It was a night that Bob had come home late from work. I was a little miffed because I had made dinner and he never called to let me know what time he would be home. He had always been bad about that sort of thing. We had an argument, but then we made up in the usual way that married couples do. When I awoke the next morning, I matter-of-factly said to Bob, "I think we made a baby last night."

"How do you know?" he asked, staring at me in amazement.

"I just do."

I gave it a few weeks and, sure enough, I missed my period. Since I was as regular as clockwork, I was convinced that I was pregnant. Once I found out for certain, the first phone call went to my mom and dad. They were thrilled.

We started looking at homes and soon found a lovely three-bedroom ranch style house in a brand new development. The gods were definitely smiling on us as we sold our duplex in record time. Life was good. The only hitch was that we couldn't move into our house for several months and had to move out of the duplex sooner. As a result, we moved in with my mom and dad.

═══

JANUARY 9, 1978, is a date that I never will forget. At 7:31 that morning, Alex was born at Good Samaritan Hospital in West Palm Beach. I was scared to death when I first saw him. He weighed close to eight pounds, but he was nearly nineteen inches long. He looked so . . . well, fragile!

I was afraid to hold him at first, terrified that I might hurt him. We named him Alexander after Bob's grandfather—and because every time that my brother saw me during the pregnancy, he put his hand on my stomach and asked, "How's Big Al doing?"

By the time we moved into our new house, Alex was four months old. He was, without a doubt, the apple of grandma and grandpa's eyes. My mother could not do enough for that child. He was terribly spoiled. It took a little time for Alex and I to get into a new routine after we

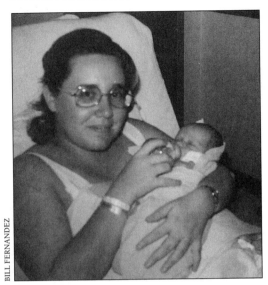

BILL FERNANDEZ

Alex is born

moved, but having a baby did not slow me down for long. He went everywhere I did and loved it. I bought a small, bouncing chair for him before he even could crawl and he moved with me from room to room. We were inseparable.

Unfortunately, his father never really saw having a child in the same way that I did. I truly believe that he was jealous of Alex because of the attention I gave him. After Alex was born, Bob's hours went back to the night shift and he was hardly ever home. On weekends he slept on the couch all day long or watched television. He was tired all the time and never wanted to go out. Before long, he got back into his old routine of coming home later and later and not calling.

Then he started working on Saturdays. When that happened, I started spending more time with my parents so that I would have some adults to talk to. I read to Alex a lot and he became a huge fan of *Sesame Street* at a very young age. He was incredibly bright and learned to walk at eight months. In fact, I really don't remember him ever crawling much. He seemed to go from sitting up to walking. Bob missed out on most of those pivotal moments due to his schedule.

Soon peculiar things began to happen. I began getting phone calls from collection agencies about credit cards I had never heard of. After a while it got really bad and the phone calls got increasingly nasty. Finally, I confronted Bob about the calls. At first he lied and told me that he had no idea why they were calling. Then I began getting letters in the mail outlining credit-card bills for thousands of dollars. Each one had Bob's name on it, so he found it difficult to continue denying it.

I decided to take charge of the household finances before we went broke. Bob had charged all sorts of things that I had never even seen. In addition, he had acquired several gasoline cards that I never knew about. Arguments became a daily thing in our home. By this time, my brother and future sister-in-law had returned to Florida and moved in with us. Darlene, my brother's future wife, was pregnant and I helped them out until they got on their feet financially. They only lived with us for a short time, but they witnessed some of the fights that Bob and I had on a regular basis.

My brother suggested that we get some professional help. I thought that was a good idea, so I found a marriage counselor and we began to see him once a week. This went on for a few months and things actually started to get better. We talked about what was bothering us in the marriage and committed ourselves to work on making it right.

Things were going really well between Bob and me for several months after we got into the counseling sessions, so well in fact that I got pregnant for a second time. This pregnancy was

Alex with Grandma Ursula

more difficult than the first and I suffered from severe morning sickness for the first five months. We soon found out what the problem was: twins! The doctor put me on higher dosages of vitamins and some other medications, and I began to feel better.

Bob took the pregnancy in stride but when he found out about the twins he went into a working frenzy. He took on extra hours to save for the new additions to our family. My parents and family were so excited

for us and happily began to prepare for the coming event.

The eighth month of the pregnancy arrived and I began to feel sick again. My water broke while I was grocery shopping and my brother rushed me to the hospital, where things quickly began to go downhill.

While prepping me for delivery a nurse put heart monitors on my stomach to hear the twins'

Alex with Grandpa Adolph

heartbeats. An odd look flashed across her face and she went to get a doctor, who looked equally startled. He rushed me into surgery; I was to have another cesarean section. I knew something was wrong when I woke up in recovery because the nurses spoke of taking me to the surgical floor instead of maternity. I called out for the doctor, who took me to my brother. He chokingly told me that the two baby girls had been stillborn.

After crying together, I began to wonder where Bob was. Apparently he had been there, heard the news and left. He returned later and tried to comfort me, but he wasn't there when I needed him and never shed a tear over this family tragedy. We went back to counseling to help deal with our loss, and things seemed to get better despite my doubts. We decided to try again on our own after a few months. On our way home from the last counseling session, Bob and I planned a dinner to celebrate our success.

He didn't get home until 11:00 P.M. When he called with the usual excuse of having to work late, I lost it. I told him he had been putting up a false front with the therapist and with me. I was done with it. He kept apologizing, but I was done listening to his lies. I slammed the phone down and began to cry and shake.

I sat quietly, deep in thought for a long time. Then my anger began to build. All I could think of were the countless burned dinners and the endless broken promises. It finally dawned on me that Bob had abandoned me emotionally a long time ago, or at least that was the way I felt. It was time to make a decision about how the rest of my life was going to be. Should I stay in this life? Or start a new one?

I had no job or degree, so I knew it would be tough at first, but I thought my parents would help, so that eased the anxiety a bit. I figured that my parents would probably be glad to help as long as Bob was out of the picture. They never liked him and it would mean Mom could spend more time with Alex. How could that be bad?

DENISE MCLEAN

Alex flirts with his cousin Erin

All I knew was that I needed Bob to be gone from my house and my life. With that realization, a surge of energy came over me and I set out to rid myself of my old life.

I ran into the bedroom and gathered up Bob's clothes. Then I threw every stitch of his clothing out onto the front lawn. I repeated this until every trace of him was out of the bedroom. When Bob called a couple of hours later and gave me some new excuse for not yet being home, I was crying.

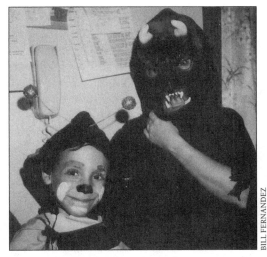

Alex and me dressed up for Halloween

"Don't bother coming back unless it is just to pick up your stuff," I yelled into the telephone. "I want you out of here tonight!"

Bob could not believe what he was hearing. He pleaded with me to listen to him. I refused. Several hours later, he showed up and had a tantrum in the middle of the driveway when he saw his clothes sprawled everywhere. I told him to pick up his stuff and leave. Finally, he did.

Within a year, we were divorced. I got priority custody of Alex, but Bob had visiting rights pretty much whenever he wanted. Soon he started pulling the same old tricks. For example, he would say he was coming to visit Alex on a certain weekend and he would never show up or call. After this happened a few times, poor little Alex became so confused that he started showing signs of stress: sleep problems, nightmares, bedwetting and nervousness. He was dealing with a lot for a two-year-old.

As I watched what this was doing to my son, I became very angry. I tried to make Bob understand what he was doing to his son. It made no impression. I finally stopped telling Alex when his father was "supposed" to come around. His visits became less frequent until one day he just disappeared. I didn't give it too much thought at the time. He often went weeks without communicating. Then the support checks suddenly stopped. When I tried to contact Bob, he was nowhere to be found.

I resigned myself to the fact that he no longer wished to be a part of his son's life. My focus was now on getting on with our lives. When Alex asked about his father, I explained his absence as best I could. As time

Alex and Grandpa Adolph

passed, those questions tapered off until one day all talk of his dad just stopped.

Once again it was necessary for me to find a full-time job. I decided to enroll in nursing school. My mom and dad moved in with us and we pooled our money in order to make ends meet. Alex went to daycare part time. That enabled me to go to school, and it gave him the opportunity to interact with kids his own age.

I had almost completed my first year of nursing school when an experimental class began at the institute I attended. They were looking for volunteers to take some quick lessons on a word processor and then give them some kind of evaluation on the equipment. The only qualification was that you had to type well. I had always done well in typing class and I was intrigued, so I signed up. The evaluation took a few weeks. When it was done, they told me that I had tested well into the high range of technical aptitude. I was shocked. I had never really tried to do anything with computers.

I proceeded with my nursing classes and things began to change a bit as I entered into the clinical end of the course. That meant I had to go to a hospital and work a few hours each week. It was a nightmare. I wanted desperately to go into pediatric nursing, but I quickly found out that I could not deal with watching those poor little ones suffer every day, especially the ones with terminal illnesses.

Then I tried adult patients, but that turned out no better, because I got too

Alex at one year

14

emotionally involved. It had nothing to do with the blood or cleaning them up after an accident. It was just the whole environment of the hospital. I did not blend into the situation at all. It became obvious to me that I wouldn't last and quit soon after that.

After a few months of searching for employment, I decided to try word processing. My dad worked for a company called Siemens, so he got me an interview in their data-processing department. A woman named Linda Watson offered me a job. She was diminutive, but she had a feistiness about her that belied her height. I looked at her as a role model from day one. She would become a lifelong friend.

Never before had I met such a group of people. It was one of those situations where all of us seemed to be going through life transitions of one kind or another. The way we helped support one another was much like what you would expect in a family.

=======

As a single mother, I was presented with the usual problems. I had to make a living. I had to be both mother and father to my son. One of the things that was lacking was a social life. Even though I did not have much time for a social life, I craved interaction with others outside of the workplace.

I decided to try the theater. Ever since high school, one of my passions had been the theater. I wasn't much for acting, but I really enjoyed the behind-the-scenes work. My co-worker and close friend Mimi Trinkner had been involved with a small, struggling children's theater group for a few years. She constantly bent my ear about the kids that she worked with on the weekends.

After I told Mimi about my interest in the theater, she was relentless. Every day she worked at whittling away my resolve. Mimi was determined to get me to join her group. When the Christmas holidays rolled around that year, she pleaded with me to consider helping with their production of A Christmas Carol.

Curiosity finally got the best of me, so I agreed to go with her to the audition. I wanted to meet the people that she spoke so highly of. But I made it very clear that my interest lay purely in either painting sets or taking on a production role. Things went much differently once I got there.

Mimi knew the directors were in desperate need of chorus members. It was the perfect place for me. There was no way that I would be seen or heard as long as I remained part of the group. Okay, I thought, how hard could that be? I had sung in church and that was pretty painless, so why not?

What a mistake that turned out to be! Doc Peterson, the director, asked me to actually read for a part. He was such a kindly older gentleman that I could not refuse him. He was tall and thin, but he still had a head full of blonde hair. Doc just oozed theatrical flair. In addition to being as animated as a cartoon character, he was impossibly charming. He assured me I could do it, so I tried.

Even though the part was minor, it was still a scary thing for me to do. I am not the type to seek out the limelight. After my reading, the director pulled me aside to speak to me. Suddenly I felt a tug at my dress. Trying to remain focused on my conversation, I put out my hand instinctively to my son thinking that he had grown tired of all this and wanted to go home. Again the tug. This time I looked down and said, "Honey, please let me finish and we will go home."

Alex gave my clothes one more tug for good measure. Before I could utter a word, this skinny little six-year-old blurted out in a voice not to be missed, "Mom I don't want to leave, I want to read! I want to be in the play too."

Alex's enthusiasm and persistence prompted the director to speak to him alone. He asked how old he was and how well he could read. Alex perked right up and said, " I know how to read very well. My mommy taught me from when I was little."

Chuckling, the director handed him a script and asked him to read a few lines. Alex obliged. In an instant, his eyes lit up and his voice filled with excitement and confidence. This kid wasn't fooling around! Even at that age, when he had a captive audience, you had better look out, because invariably you wouldn't know what hit you.

Alex gave one hell of an audition. Unfortunately the part he read for was already taken, but he made such an

DENISE MCLEAN

Alex with my grandparents, Oma and Opa Maier

impression on the director that a new part was written into the play especially for him. When the show finally opened, I was amazed. Every time Alex gleefully recited his few lines, he never failed to elicit laughter and applause from the audience. Alex naturally sensed how to charm a crowd.

From the moment Alex walked onto that stage, he never really wanted to leave. The stage, the audience, the footlights . . . all of it became a second home to him. It was a place where he felt comfortable and secure. A place where he was able to leave everything behind and become whomever he wanted to be.

I don't know why any of this came as a big surprise. From the time he was three, Alex had an active imagination. He spent hours creating characters through which he acted out entire stories. He danced and sang for anyone who was interested.

When MTV first came about, Alex watched it for hours after doing his homework. Great pains were taken to copy and perfect the dance moves of some of his idols, especially Paula Abdul. Alex developed a passion for music and he loved to move to every kind of beat imaginable. When old musicals aired on television, he sat glued to the screen watching his favorite stars, especially Gene Kelly.

In addition, Alex always put a spin on the words that sometimes came tumbling out of his mouth. Depending on what movie he was drawing from or what character he was playing on any given day, he would speak like them. If they had a British accent, Alex tried to copy it. If they were older, he lowered his voice. And so on.

Odd child really . . . his imagination was just out there. Oftentimes, I would listen outside of his bedroom door. Had I not known better, I would have been hard pressed to say that there were not two or more people talking to each other. Alex had unusual talents, even at that young age.

Alex and me on his
fifth Christmas

BILL FERNANDEZ

Alex's vivid imagination was not always seen as one of his better traits. In later years, he spun wild tales both about his family and himself. I think part of it was to hide the fact that his father was not present in his life. Alex would tell friends that I had given birth to him while on a skiing trip to Switzerland with his dad. Or that his dad traveled a lot, so that was why he never seemed to be around. This went on throughout his school years and much beyond. His imagination seemed to have no boundaries.

I remember a particular incident when Alex was in middle school. He convinced his math teacher that he was an entirely different person. I'm not really sure to this day how he pulled that one off. The truth finally caught up with him when he failed to turn in his homework. Now, as clever as my son thought himself to be, he had unwittingly given the teacher his real phone number. After several mysterious messages on my answering machine about some kid named Duane, I figured out what was going on.

When I spoke with the teacher, we were both a bit shocked to find out that this Duane was actually my son, Alex. That is when I realized just how damaging his imagination could be when given the chance to run rampant. His practice of "becoming" other people was a portent of things to come.

At about the age of seven, Alex asked me to take him to dance class. He told me he wanted to learn tap and jazz because those were the main steps that Paula Abdul used in her music videos. I explained that girls mostly attended dance classes and he might feel out of place. Alex said he didn't care. He wanted to see what it was all about.

I asked around and found a dance school that my friends all recommended. We went to observe some classes and Alex begged me to let him enroll. I worked it out in the budget so he could take a couple of classes to start. With-

Alex the cowboy at six

in a month, he had caught up to the rest of the class and was having a wonderful time. The instructors told me Alex had a natural rhythm and a good ear for music. My parents and I were amazed at his first recital performance, for he performed a short solo.

In addition to his dance classes, Alex also wanted to learn how to play a musical instrument. Again, through some friends, I found him a teacher, a minister at a local church who took Alex on as a student for piano and organ. Alex loved it! I have videos of him playing the organ and singing along at the same time. Or, as Alex put it so eloquently, cute lisp and all, "simultaneously, at the same time."

That lisp never stopped him from reaching for his dreams. He owes quite a bit to a wonderful lady named Margie Sargeson Richards who became Alex's second mom when he was not with me. In addition to being his English teacher in elementary school, she was also his voice and dialect coach in drama school. Margie was the person responsible for helping Alex to hone both his dramatic acting skills and his animated speaking skills.

The two of them worked closely together on the many plays he performed in from the ages of six to ten. Margie was a huge influence on Alex during that time. She taught him the importance of laughing at yourself when you make a mistake.

Margie also worked with him on his lisp. She taught him to enunciate his words so that everyone could understand him. At the time, she had no children of her own, so there was always extra time for Alex. And he loved her for it. They were quite a pair onstage. She loved to play the villain and he the hero. A perfect match. Margie insisted that he learn Shakespeare, which later paved the way for him to write songs and poetry.

During that time, Alex continued with his dance classes despite the fact that he was one of only a few boys who attended. My son

Margie and Alex

LARRY RICHARDS

was no fool. The ratio of girls to boys was off the charts. It gave him a playing field on which to learn the fine art of flirting. He perfected it to a higher form and flexed his flirting "muscles" every chance he got.

Alex attended a very small, private school for most of his life. Not surprisingly, his classmates were like a family to him. Since Alex did not have the benefit of his father's presence, he developed very close bonds with some of the male teachers in his school. One of them was his coach and fencing instructor, Coach Diaz.

Coach Diaz was a very handsome Latin man with a wonderful outlook and an exciting teaching style. It took a lot to get those young people interested in things like stage combat and fencing—not the typical school sports. Coach Diaz managed to inspire each and every one of them. Alex took to him immediately.

Alex loved the movement and challenge associated with fencing. The coach said his dancing classes had undoubtedly helped him with his form. The rest was apparently just his natural ability. I was amazed. Up to that point, Alex had not really shown any aptitude for sports. I believe it was his coach's teaching style that inspired my son to really want to excel in that sport.

There is no doubt in my mind that the staff in that school, aptly named Unity, started Alex out on the right track. He was given a good foundation with which to start his journey into the real world. At the school, everyone filled his or her role in a loving and respectful way. Private schools are not cheap, but I felt that since my son had so many outside activities it would be easier for him to adjust to smaller classes where he would receive more individual attention. It was not easy to come up with the money and every year the tuition rose. But, as usual, I always found a way.

Alex in fencing class

Alex's promo page at age seven

SINCE ALEX WAS JUST A CHILD, I wasn't sure how seriously to take his fascination with theater. It soon became clear to me, along with the rest of the family, that Alex was in his element. Every time Alex walked onto that stage, whether it was in front of five people or five hundred, the audience took notice. Time after time, our little Alex left his mark on them. I came to believe that mark was made with indelible ink.

Another close friend at that time was Richard Lustig, a local talent agent who produced talent shows that were booked by local bars and nightclubs. He took a shine to Alex right away and included him in the shows. By then, Alex had come to be a celebrity of sorts among the performers and audiences that followed them from venue to venue.

Richard must have been a frustrated singer since he always managed to work his signature song, "Moon Dance," into every show. He was the quintessential master of ceremonies, with his white fedora and classy clothes, and he had a charm all his own. He and Alex hit it off right away. He was totally enamored of my son's talent and the skill with which this tiny boy could grab hold of an audience.

At the time, Alex was heavily into puppeteering. His act included a rendition of several songs from the musical *Little Shop of Horrors*. As part of the act, he performed a "duet" with his puppet. They would move together while lip-syncing to the voices of the lead characters in the show. It was quite amazing really.

The way that Alex showed the different personalities of the two characters by making the puppet come alive proved what a real knack for puppeteering he had. Every time we went to a mall or anywhere that puppets were sold, he talked me into buying him another one to add to his family of friends. Each one had names and personalities. It was one more way for Alex to unleash yet another side of his imagination. He developed otherworldly accents and deepened his voice to create different characters for his stories.

Alex had a briefcase in which he kept a video-game electronic arm and he cut a piece of foam to fit the arm so it did not move around in the case. Sometimes, when we were in the car, he took it out and slipped in onto his arm so he could become "Killer Jack," an evil character who was actually (according to Alex) a good guy. Killer Jack was a super hero of sorts or maybe an anti-hero.

The first time that Alex met my boss, Linda, he was carrying that briefcase and wearing a white fedora, another habit he had developed. He had a large collection of hats and loved developing personalities that fit each one. Upon meeting Linda, he extended his right hand and very formally introduced himself as Alex McLean. She just chuckled and gave him a hearty handshake. Then she asked him what was in the case.

"You really don't want to know," he said.

Linda just left it at that. To this day she still speaks of that meeting and fondly recounts her first encounter with my son.

RICHARD LUSTIG'S TALENT CONTESTS took place every weekend. Alex wanted to attend them all, but sometimes that was impossible. When it was necessary for him to miss a show, he was terribly disappointed. Each show always meant a new routine. Alex was always eager to show off in some new and different way. The talent shows gave him the venue.

However, the one thing that stayed the same was Richard's insistence that Alex do his puppet routine. During one of the shows, Alex surprised me with a dedication that he apparently had worked on for weeks. I was sitting in the audience when out came little Mr. Entertainment, microphone in hand. He announced that he was dedicating the next song to his mom, whom he described as his hero.

"I love you," he said, then launched into "Wind Beneath My Wings," a big hit at the time. I cried as my heart swelled with pride. I think it brought tears to the eyes of most of the people in the audience. It remains a moment I will never forget.

On more than one occasion, Alex won the talent contest, leaving the adult entertainers in his dust. No one ever got angry. He was just so cute and charming that he never failed to win them over as well. And he was only eight years old.

As I look back, I realize that Alex was already developing his charm with women and had a real knack for winning over everyone's heart. The agent ran a series of shows for a couple of months and performers were eliminated week by week. Every time, Alex managed to come in at the top of the running and continue on to the next show. By the time the series was done, Alex had come in first place at many a show.

A few months later, Richard came to us and told us he was getting together all of his winning acts from the past year to put together a television talent show on local cable. He had booked an hour time slot and really needed Alex to be a part of it. Alex and I decided this would be a good idea, given that this agent had done so much for him over the past year. We quickly put together some highlights of past performances. In addition, Alex came up with a couple of dynamite numbers for the show. It was filmed at a local hotel conference room and the budget was small, but it was a fun event and gave Alex a chance to perform in front of a television camera.

Alex was very excited about it. He made certain that all of his props, like puppets, hats and wardrobe, were perfect. The show took place without any problems and aired on late-night television a few weeks later. Nothing ever came of it as a regular cable show, but it gave Alex a new experience in performing. That was the last event I remember doing with Richard. We lost touch after that and Alex returned to musical theater.

———

THE FINAL PROOF OF ALEX'S COMMITMENT to his dream came during the opening-night production of *The King and I* at the Burt Reynolds Dinner Theater. It was Alex's first role in professional theater. I remember sitting at the table, waiting for the show to begin with my heart in my throat. My mom, dad, brother and sister-in-law all sat there with expressions of sheer terror.

As usual, I helped my little actor apply his stage make-up and wriggle into his costume. I gave him a big hug and kiss for good luck, and then he was gone, off to play with the other children in the cast just like it was any other day. It was as if it didn't occur to him to be nervous. In his mind, he was going to be doing what he had done hundreds of times during rehearsals.

Alex with the child cast from *The King and I*

I sat there, frozen in my seat, eyes glued to the stage. My worst fear was that Alex would forget what he was supposed to do, or freeze up once he hit the stage. A hundred "what if" scenarios played out in my head. I was also worried that something would go wrong with the whistling. Alex's character was a whistler, but Alex, despite many attempts, simply could not whistle. For that reason, the director decided to let someone offstage whistle for him. We held our breath as the curtain went up.

I will never forget the look on my family's faces when he walked out onto the stage. Their eyes bulged, their mouths dropped to the table. I joined them in their state of utter disbelief. Alex's stage presence, charisma and confidence were like that of a seasoned performer. He bounded around the stage and recited his lines in a way that made them his own. Joy and exhilaration emanated from his entire body. It was obvious that Alex reveled in being on stage, hearing the audience react to his every word.

From that moment, Alex radiated the same confidence and exhilaration every time he hit the stage. Whatever his personal issues, when he performed he was in total control. After that initial performance, there was no turning back for either of us. His goal was to perform. Whatever form that performance took was of little consequence. I became completely dedicated to helping him make his goal a reality.

Our schedule became more intense, with all the hours of driving to auditions, rehearsals and tapings. The school was very patient with Alex and gave him work to take home whenever we thought he might fall behind. Margie helped with that as well. Since she was one of his teachers, she kept me aware of what areas he needed help with before things got out of hand. We made a good tutoring team for my son. Everyone on the staff at Unity was supportive of Alex and his desire to keep working toward his dream. It was a blessing that he was in a private school during that time.

My mom was also a great help in getting Alex to and from lessons on those occasions when I had to work. We all did our part. My dad helped Alex rehearse his lines at night if I was not there to do it.

Alex really lived a charmed life. Every time an audition came up, he would at least make the final cut, if not get the part. And more than once the casting director changed a role or added one so that Alex could appear. That's how much he impressed people. Alex auditioned for a horror film when he was eight. It was a low-budget independent production, so they hired several local people as extras. Alex auditioned for the child lead in a flashback scene. The director was so impressed with his reading that he cast him on the spot. He even made the adult lead actor change his hair color to match Alex's!

It was quite some time before the word "rejection" ever entered our vocabulary; but, as every performer knows, rejection and disappointment are as much a part of the business as are the ovations.

Alex's first disappointment came at age nine. After winning a pivotal role in a film called *Truth or Dare*, he nailed his part as a young street child with impressive clarity. And the amazing thing was that he never spoke a line in the film. His character lived in an alley under the apartment window of the main character. The lead was a young girl who had run away from home. She resorted to prostitution to pay the bills.

In large part, the story is told through Alex's eyes. In the end, Alex's character dies alone after starving to death in an alleyway surrounded by trashcans. The final scene of the film focused on his battered face and glazed eyes. Even though I knew it was just acting, the scene was too much for me to watch.

Unfortunately, the film was never released. Alex was crushed. The fact that he never got to see the finished product was a real blow. I managed to convince him that it was only the first of many life lessons that would help to make him stronger. My hope was that I had paved the way for him to understand the inevitability of disappointment.

My hopes were realized when I saw how calmly he faced the many rejections that soon came his way, including the one thing that he had his heart set on the most: becoming a performer on the Mickey Mouse Club.

Alex auditioned for that show three times. We

BILL FERNANDEZ

At the Halloween party for *The King and I* at the Burt Reynolds Theater

26

would be there for hours, but Alex would wait patiently with the hope that his name would be called. As the day grew longer and the lines grew shorter, his hopes would rise. He would tell me, "Mom, now it's my turn." But each time we walked away with nothing to show for our efforts, except exhaustion and disappointment. Alex was not discouraged. He never gave up. Every time he heard that a Disney audition was coming to Florida he was ready to go.

After his third and final rejection at the age of twelve, the casting agent approached us and reassured Alex that the reason he hadn't been cast had absolutely nothing to do with his talent. It was just that at the age of twelve, he was simply too old. When I asked what the problem had been the previous years, he responded frankly that at that time Alex was a bit too ethnic looking for what he needed in the show.

He commended Alex's tenacity and advised us to think about moving to a larger city where there were more opportunities. He suggested Orlando and gave us names of contacts there. From what I was reading in

DENISE MCLEAN

Alex holding a fake razor blade in *Truth or Dare, A Critical Madness* the trade papers, Orlando was becoming "L.A. East." The casting director gave us a lot to consider.

I had a house, a great job with a company I liked and friends that I did not want to leave. Alex had been born and raised in South Florida, so he, too, had ties. Then there was the matter of my mom and dad who still lived with us. Would they come with us? Did they even want to move? My dad worked for a good company and we were all pretty settled in. There was no guarantee of employment in Orlando, or even that Alex would be any more successful there.

The truth was that Alex's career had stalled a bit. The last few auditions had been for parts in offbeat films that I knew would never see the inside of a mainstream movie theater. After having acted in all of the major theaters in southern Florida, Alex was ready for a change. He wanted to take some serious acting lessons and try out for more challenging roles in both television and film. Alex was willing to take chances as long as they were pointed in the direction of furthering his career. We talked about him auditioning for roles on Broadway, but that seemed just a bit too scary for me. I had never lived in a big city. The thought of just going out there cold was more than I could handle.

We considered our other options. A few of the single moms that I had been friendly with had moved to Los Angeles and we had kept in touch. I called them and they encouraged us to move out there. My next step was to talk to some of the agents we had come to trust. What was the next logical step for Alex to take? Where did it seem his next big break might be waiting? L.A. and New York were the overwhelming favorites. My agent friends gave me names of contacts in both cities.

I was now more confused than ever. The thought of moving to Los Angeles or New York scared me to death. After many sleepless nights and countless family discussions, we decided to put our destiny in the hands of fate. I put our house on the market to see what developed. Our neighbor just happened to be a real estate agent, so I gave her the listing. We both agreed that with the market the way it was, it would probably take at least six months to sell. I even put the price up a bit high to protect myself. Amazingly, the house sold the same day it went on the market! Fate seemed to be giving us a nudge. The pressure was on.

We decided to move to Orlando. It was a good place to nurture Alex's career, but it was not nearly as intimidating as Los Angeles or New York.

We had forged lifelong relationships that deeply affected us, so it was hard to leave them behind, but I had made a commitment to my son that we would move to a new city and fulfill our destiny.

CHAPTER THREE

A Winning Hand

MOM INSISTED THAT WE MOVE as a family so that she could help Alex and me with whatever we needed. Dad had been working for a while at a good job, but Mom convinced him to leave it and move with us. Dad had never had a problem getting work, so she was sure that he would find something in Orlando that would be just as good as what he was leaving behind.

To tell you the truth, I was relieved that they wanted to move with us. It was especially important for Alex. His grandparents were a huge part of his everyday life. There was a strong bond among the three of them that I was hesitant to sever. Also, we could continue to pool our money and I would not have to find a job right away. I took a chance quitting my job and moving to Orlando. I took one more when I decided to live on the money that I had made from the sale of my house. I hoped that the money would give me a year to get Alex established in his new town.

Mom and Dad helped with the general running of the house and paid basic utility bills. I covered the rent and a few leftover personal expenses. Fortunately, I was able to pay off most of my debts. That allowed me to concentrate on Alex's career and it gave me a jump on achieving my own goals of learning the show-business game. It was really an excellent opportunity for both of us.

We found a cute townhouse on the north side of Orlando in a nice community. It was set back from the main road and was accessible to most parts of town. It was the summer of 1990 and Universal Studios was preparing for opening day. The adventure was just beginning and the excitement on my son's face was hard to miss.

Since school was out for the summer, Alex and I were able to spend all our time researching the "whos, whats and wheres" of Orlando's entertainment community. Temporarily losing the distraction of a nine-to-five job was one of the smartest things I ever did for my son. I would never have been able to devote the hours necessary on a daily basis if I had still been working. I became, for lack of a better word, Alex's "manager." That became my job seven days a week.

I set up a makeshift office in the back bedroom of our house and I made up new resumes and press kits for my son. Headshots, press clippings and show reviews were copied and collated. The object was to pack maximum information into the smallest amount of space. By this point Alex's resume was pretty well-rounded. I just hoped Orlando would agree.

When the press kits were done, the phone work began. One of my very first calls was to the Mickey Mouse Club casting director who had originally suggested that we move to Orlando. He gave me the names of several people who would be able to help Alex break into television and other commercial areas of the industry.

The next order of business was to find a talent agent to represent my son. I searched the phonebook and combined my findings with the list I had gotten from the casting director. I sent out several media kits and resumes that first month. The responses came in quickly, but I had to check each one out and that took time.

Finding Edna Byers was one of the most positive things that happened when we first moved to town. Edna had a great rapport with all the casting agents for film and television in the state. She helped put Alex's resume in front of everyone who mattered. Right from the start I could tell that Edna was a very hard worker. During our first "get-to-know-you" meeting, she was on the phone nonstop talking to casting companies. She was impressed with Alex and felt confident that she could find him work.

Alex and I both had a good feeling about Edna, so we signed a nonexclusive agreement that gave her the standard ten-percent commission on any work she procured for my son. Edna put Alex on track with a career plan for movies and commercials. She sent him on casting calls and auditions for a couple of years. We owe our ongoing relationships with Disney and Nickelodeon to the fact that Edna got us in the door.

Alex soon found work in all the major theme parks. He filmed a travel video for Disney that required him to ride a roller coaster. He was scared to death, but made it through with only one or two "Oh, sh-t's!" that had to be edited out. It was actually pretty funny to watch, because you could see the white knuckles as he clenched the lap bar. Even so, Alex kept his cool throughout.

Alex met the first love of his life during that filming. Stephanie was the director's niece and she was a cute, brown-haired teen who looked younger than her age. They were both thirteen when they met. At the time, her parents were going through a divorce and she talked to Alex night after night about that. He thought he could help since he had grown up in a household of divorce, but we had been a mom-and-son team for so long that he really did not know any other life.

Since she was in Florida only to visit her uncle during the summer, their friendship got costly when she returned home, since they spoke often on the telephone. The relationship went along pretty smoothly for a while. Stephanie came to Orlando on weekends and holidays to visit Alex. Those trips were probably good for her since they enabled her to get away from the stress associated with her parents' divorce, but I began to realize something was not right with the situation when Alex confided in me about their conversations, which sometimes ended in fights.

At that point I stepped in and told her uncle that Stephanie and Alex were having problems. Alex has always avoided conflict whenever possible, so he really didn't know how to deal with the situation. After a while they did not speak at all.

———

ONE OF ALEX'S MOST FAVORITE ROLES came his way about four months after our arrival in Orlando. He landed a supporting part in a new sitcom that Nickelodeon was producing called *Hi Honey I'm Home*. It was a spoof with a fifties theme about a modern-day single mom with a couple of kids who move next door to a family that appears to live back in the black-and-white television era.

As the younger brother of the lead son, Alex's character was called "Skunk." He had to have a rat-tail hairpiece put in, as well as a blond streak that ran down the middle of his head. At the time, Alex was attending a Baptist middle school. Needless to say, a rat-tail and yellow stripe down the middle of his head was not part of the dress code. I had

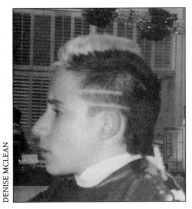

DENISE MCLEAN

Alex with "Skunk" hairdo

to get special permission from the headmaster for him to keep his hair that way.

Alex loved being an entertainer, but he often had to put up with a lot of ridicule from his schoolmates. The new hairdo did not help. One day, my mom, Alex and I were at the mall near where they were shooting the pilot, when some teenagers walked past us and made some really nasty comments about the way Alex looked.

Mom took off after those boys like a bat out of hell and gave them a major talking to. She was so enthusiastic that I was afraid the teens were going to call security. As I pulled her back, she told Alex not to be bothered by them since they were all just a bunch of losers.

It took a few weeks to rehearse and finally film the pilot. Alex had fun with his rebellious character. Between his outlandish hair and his tooling around the set on his skateboard, he was hilarious. The director, cast and crew were pleased with his performance, which made Alex beam with pride. He eagerly looked forward to continuing his work with those same people on the series. We thought it might be the big break we were looking for.

DENISE MCLEAN

When we learned that ABC Television had picked the series up for one season, we nearly jumped out of our skins. A wrap party was held at the studio a few days later. It was a blast. We expected to get the details that night of how filming would

In full "Skunk" regalia

proceed. Alex and I were so excited I think we would have boarded a plane right then.

Nothing was said that night about the plans. The next day, the phone rang with devastating news. We were told that Alex had been replaced by the producer's nephew. Alex had worked hard and had put up with so much. The teasing in school. His friends' jealousy. He was so hopeful that his big break had come.

I did my best to explain the realities of show business. I think he grasped some of what I was saying, but it was still hard for him to understand. After all, when you put your heart and soul into something, it hurts when you get smacked in the face. I think he would have accepted the decision better if they had told him he was not right for the part or that he was too old. It just seemed very unfair. Curiously, it all turned out for the best. When the series finally aired, it was a flop. If we had left Florida at that point, Alex's true destiny would have been lost forever.

Although it seemed a big setback at the time, another opportunity quickly presented itself. I read an ad in the local trade paper about another pilot being produced in Orlando. This one was for a news show that targeted children. They were looking for animated young people around Alex's age to be the show's anchor team. The great coincidence was that the writer/producer, a man named J. Michael Hicks, was also looking for an office manager.

It turned into a two-for-one deal for Alex and me. He got the part he auditioned for and I got the job of office manager. I thought that would give me an inside track on learning what it took to produce a television show. He could only pay me a small salary, but he was willing to give Alex singing lessons for free.

Soon it became clear that J. Michael needed much more than my office skills to stay afloat. He was running out of money for the pilot. After some thought, I agreed to take stock options in the company instead of a salary. It was not a hardship for me since I still had some money saved. It was enough to enable him to complete the project.

Over the next several months, I learned an enormous amount about television production, script writing and fund-raising. We worked for hours refining every episode into the mirror image of a network newscast. I was proud of what we had accomplished and excited at the prospect of being a major contributor to a hit television show.

Once all of the episodes were written, we started looking for our actors. We auditioned candidates from local agents and found what seemed to be the perfect mix. We had Alex, the animated funnyman with energy to spare. Jennifer Pena was a beautiful, petite, young lady with an olive-toned complexion and piercing dark eyes. Jennifer's father was understandably protective of his daughter, but he still encouraged her to develop her talents. Tommy Cariera was the son of a local couple who owned two successful Italian restaurants in the area. He had dark-brown hair and eyes, a dazzling smile and a great sense of humor. Amber Benson (later of *Buffy* fame) was a statuesque beauty with stunning eyes and long, lustrous, blonde locks. Finally, the youngest was Rachael Stump, who had a fabulous singing voice and elfish charm.

The kids worked as a team from the start. It was nice for Alex to finally have some kids in the industry that he could really relate to. He and Amber had the most experience when it came to acting. They took the majority of the speaking parts and assumed the roles of the anchors. The other kids aptly played the parts of field reporters who contributed their stories throughout each episode.

It was also a nice change for me. I had finally come across some parents who looked at the business in the same way that I did. All of us had a skeptical eye. We watched out for each other and for our children.

The cast of the children's news show pilot, including a young Amber Benson

After the first few episodes were filmed, we concentrated on finding a way to sell the series. The perfect opportunity came along when we heard about an upcoming convention in New Orleans. It was one of those once-a-year deals where television producers and network executives get together to pitch their wares.

We booked ourselves a tiny space at the convention and built a small, portable set to take with us. We costumed our cast in bright, eye-catching garb and creative hairstyles. If nothing else, they would be noticed!

We flew to New Orleans, along with a camera, light and sound crew, a few days early so that we could finish filming and editing our pilot. The city had just completed a huge new aquarium and park on the Mississippi River, so we shot some scenes there.

Alex and Amber did a great piece about the rain forest. The simulated set of lush foliage provided the perfect backdrop. You could hear the rain falling and see the mist all around them. Next came Alex's piece about the albino alligator. He was less than thrilled when he found out that the two-foot reptile was not stuffed, but rather the real thing with its mouth taped shut. You could see the nervousness on his face as he recited his lines and held the gator. I highly doubted he would ever want to try that again.

That week we worked our butts off. We did everything we could to convince the television movers and shakers that we had a hot product, but, in the end, we were disappointed once again. After almost two years of hard work, the pilot was never picked up. J.

Alex with Richard Kiel, James Bond's "Jaws" in New Orleans

DENISE MCLEAN

35

Michael ran out of money and I ended up nearly broke. The only thing we had to show for our efforts were some industry contacts and some useless stock in a company that was going nowhere. I knew there were risks going into the venture, but it all seemed like such a good idea. When J. Michael and I parted ways, I was devastated.

During that time, J. Michael and I had become very close friends. Alex adored him. At one point, I even recall J. Michael professing deep feelings of affection toward me; but as the money grew tight and tempers flared I became bitter and felt used. I vowed never again to work for someone unless they paid me a decent wage. Never again would I be so quick to lend my time and loyalty to someone without knowing exactly what I was getting myself into.

I lost more than my money in that experience. My self-esteem took a nose-dive as well. I felt as if I had failed my son. I was heartbroken. My savings were dwindling away. I didn't know how much longer I could exist without finding a job. One thing I realized after living in Orlando for almost a year was that I needed to be located in another part of town. My commute to the agents and people I needed to see meant that I had to travel across town to attend meetings.

Our lease was coming up for renewal and there had been a couple of problems with some of the appliances breaking down, so we moved into a brand-new apartment that was located in a good school district. The rent was cheaper and it had some features that all of us liked—a swimming pool, a gym and Alex's favorite, a billiard table.

Once we were moved and settled, I updated my resume and started looking for a job. As I searched and interviewed I found myself really unmotivated. I lost focus and became depressed. In the past, when I found myself at a crossroads, I sometimes reached out for spiritual help. One of the good things that came out of meeting J. Michael was that he re-introduced me to something that would become very important in my life: spiritual readings.

Not long after we first met, he drove me to a small town about forty-five minutes outside of Orlando called Cassadaga. It was a small community populated mostly by psychics. They had their own church and post office. There was a small hotel and some bookshops that sold metaphysical materials, but people didn't go there to shop, they went to get psychic readings. The services offered ran the gamut, from Tarot cards to numerology. It was a very interesting place.

My first experience there was with a spirit-guide reading. It was very strange since the psychic who read for me hardly looked at me throughout the hour. She introduced me to my spirit guide, an uncle named

Andrew Reinhardt who had passed away several years before. She spoke with him and then relayed the information to me. She looked out the window at "Uncle Andy" most of the time, but I did get some guidance and thanked him for watching over me.

The next time, I had a more traditional, tarot-card reading. The psychic told me of things past, present and future and used a set of picture cards that I shuffled and she cut into three piles. Each pile represented a different time frame. Again, it was helpful.

Even though I was raised in the Lutheran Church, I have never really been one for organized religion. It is difficult for me to buy into the whole idea of one specific interpretation of the Bible. Organized religions seem to make up too many rules about what you should not do and they don't stress enough the things that you should do.

I have attended many church services and I've even gone to a few temples. I once considered converting to Judaism since it seemed to be the closest belief system to my own. I look at myself as a follower of the spirit rather than a follower of any specific organized church. I just try to be a good person everyday.

Upon my return to Cassadega, I got an appointment with E. Matthew Sekunna, the son of the head of the psychic community. He started with a palm reading and told me that many great things lay in wait for my son and me. It became clear that my son's life path and mine were to be entwined in a number of ways for many years to come.

Matthew told me I would meet a man in a big white house. He described him quite vividly: he was a large man with glasses, light-colored hair and eyes, and he had a jolly attitude and warm personality. In addition, he told me to beware of two women associated with this man. The part about the two women was a bit vague.

The description Matthew gave of the big white house was so clear that I could see it in my mind's eye. It was on a large plot of land that you could see from the road. It was a contemporary-style, one-story home with a tile roof. There was a circular driveway with a fountain in the center. When he finished that reading, he asked if he could do a numerology reading for Alex. I thought that odd since Alex was not with me. I told him he was very young and there was probably not much to tell yet.

Matthew disagreed. He said he felt strong vibrations coming from me with regards to my son. There seemed to be a very powerful force of royalty around him. I acquiesced and he proceeded with his reading. That was the first time that I had seen a numerology reading and it proved to be quite interesting.

From just his birth date and time, Matthew was able to tell me a lot about my son. He informed me that Alex had been some kind of king in a former life. His path was destined for fame and fortune. Again, he went back to this big man and how we would both meet him in the next few months. Matthew kept coming back to one main point throughout every reading: this large man in the big white house would change our lives forever.

Not only did I feel better about myself after that encounter with Matthew, I also felt better about the decisions I had made in my life up to that point. It took a lot to get over my depression. I was using up my savings every month and desperately needed to find a job. Thankfully, that came about rather quickly.

I was relieved when I landed a really nice job that I enjoyed. I started working with children ages three and up in a franchised computer school. It was great fun. This was in 1991, when most public schools were just getting into computers and not many families had them in their homes yet. Since the starting salary was low, I ended up supplementing my income by tutoring some students privately on the weekends or in the evenings. I found the job very fulfilling and it provided a much-needed change from the entertainment industry.

Life seemed to be getting back on track for us. My dad was still working so that was a big help during the rough times. Neither of my parents ever complained or criticized me for my decision. Of course, they were disappointed when the television show ended up being a bust, but we all moved past that and continued with our lives. I eventually pulled myself

Alex's graduation from Denn John Middle School

BILL FERNANDEZ

out of my depression by working with the children and by doing fun stuff with my son on the weekends.

Around that time, Alex tried out for a new Star Search series. His audition went badly. He failed to even get a callback. I began to worry in earnest. The jobs were getting few and far between for him. He couldn't help but be discouraged. I could not bring myself to admit defeat to Mom and Dad, so I kept plugging away.

Alex started classes at his new school and began to work with his drama teacher, who helped Alex get into some local theater productions. It was then that I felt as though he had come full circle back to his roots of musical theater. It kept him busy and he learned from each role.

I was saddened that I could not become involved with the new group, due to the long hours my job required. I was lucky to even make it to the shows. However, he understood my situation. There was no way I could have kept him in those classes had I not been working extra jobs.

Finally, Alex found an opportunity that excited him.

It began with an advertisement in the local newspaper for an upcoming Latin talent festival. Alex was intrigued by the ad because it called for a teen that could sing and dance to all different types of music. Stretching the fact that Alex's grandfather was of Latin descent, we went to the audition.

Upon entering the hotel room where the audition was taking place, I stopped dead in my tracks. A man with a video camera greeted us. That was it. No assistants. No other people whatsoever. My initial response was to bolt, but Alex insisted on staying. He walked up to the man with his hand outstretched and introduced himself.

After a few minutes I felt a bit calmer. Luckily, the man did not ask me to leave him alone with my son. We talked for a bit and he explained what was needed to enter the talent show. He also mentioned that the first prizewinner would receive one thousand dollars. That did the trick with Alex!

After Alex finished singing, the producer remarked that he was a bit overwhelmed to hear such a deep, booming voice coming out of this pipsqueak of a thirteen-year-old. He hired Alex on the spot.

"Okay, what exactly does that mean?" I asked.

I was told that Alex had to devise a forty-five minute one-man show, which he would perform every few hours over the course of the carnival. That was fine with Alex. It would give him an opportunity to show off his talents and someone in the audience might notice. Alex wanted to showcase all of his talents, from singing and dancing to rock, show tunes and pop songs all the way to the big finale of his puppet show.

We had about a month to get ready for the event. With my schedule I did not know how we would do it, but I really didn't want to disappoint Alex. The first task was to find enough music to fill the time. Alex feverishly went through hundreds of cassette tapes in a search for the right songs.

Once we had the music timed out, remembering to allow for costume changes, we put together a wardrobe. Alex decided on one basic costume, with a couple of changes toward the end of the show. One was pretty simple, just a cape, mask and white gloves for his *Phantom of the Opera* song. He had always loved singing "Music of the Night." Now he wanted to do it for an audience. For some reason, Alex had become enamored of magic tricks. He learned a sleight-of-hand routine that he could do while setting off pyrotechnics. It was harmless really, just a puff of smoke.

We worked so hard on the project that I decided to dig up some dollars to hire a professional video company to shoot a couple of the shows and edit them together for a video resume. It was a good move given the fact that the performance really did end up showcasing all of Alex's talents.

The carnival weekend started out very slowly. That was all right with us because it gave us the opportunity to work out some of the bugs, as well as get a few good video shots in from different angles without getting in front of an audience. By late afternoon on the first day, word had spread about Alex's show.

One of the people who kept coming by was Tony Donetti, a young man just out of junior college. He had a handsome Latin complexion and a sweet personality. I spoke to him for a few minutes and he told me that he was performing in another part of the carnival. Tony did a dance routine with a partner, using mostly Latin-style music.

After Tony headed back to his partner, I told Alex about my conversation with him. He said he recognized him from the singing classes they had taken a while back. If he remembered correctly, Tony had been at a couple of the same auditions at the Nickelodeon studios. Suddenly, Orlando was becoming a smaller town.

For the rest of the weekend, Alex put on show after show. It didn't matter if there were five or fifty people in the audience, Alex just kept on singing and dancing for anyone who would watch. This time his efforts paid off. He beat Tony and everyone else for the thousand-dollar grand prize. He was beside himself when they announced his name as the winner. If I remember correctly, Tony ended up with second prize and congratulated Alex on his winning performance. Little did either of

them know, but they were both destined for much, much more and very soon.

We were all so proud of Alex and how well he had done. I took him to the bank and he opened his first savings account. I made a photocopy of the check and had it framed for him to keep as a reminder of his first sweet victory in Orlando.

Top: Alex displays his puppetry skills at the Latin Carnival

Right: Alex wins first place at the Latin Carnival

IN MARCH 1992, shortly after Alex turned fourteen, I read an ad in the local trade paper calling for young men between the ages of twelve and eighteen for a five-member vocal group. I called the number and got all of the information from a very pleasant young woman named Gloria Sicoli. She told me that a local businessman was looking for young men to form a pop singing group that he could sign to his record company.

When I told Alex about the ad, he was thrilled and said he couldn't wait to go. I told him that he had to be able to sing two songs from the New Kids on the Block album and perform a five-minute dance routine. That made Alex even more excited. He asked if we could go to the record store right away so he could find the music and begin practicing that night. Alex had never been a big fan of the New Kids, but he was familiar with both of the songs. Alex practiced every day, until he knew all of the lyrics and had his dance routine down pat.

On the day of the audition, we followed Gloria's directions to a well-known golf community that I had heard of but never visited. When we pulled up in front of the house—a large, white structure with a circular driveway and a fountain in the front yard—my eyes widened in shock.

Alex looked at me and said, "Mom, what's wrong? Isn't this the house?"

"Alex," I said in a calm voice, "this is the exact type of house that the psychic described to me in the reading I told you about."

I suddenly felt as if I was in a dream. All the words the psychic had said to me about the house came rushing into my head. As we pulled into the driveway, the front doors opened and a large man with glasses and light hair stepped out and quickly walked up to the car. I was speechless.

"Hi," the man said, opening Alex's car door and extending his hand. "I am Lou Pearlman and this is my house. Please come in."

As we made our introductions, Lou walked us into his house. He was very warm and relaxed, dressed casually in a sports shirt and slacks. After entering the house, he led us down a small hallway with three rooms off to the side. I noted that the combination of eggshell-colored carpeting and tile made for a crisp and clean impression.

The furniture was patterned in tropical colors and shapes. A couple of solid pastel side chairs accented the room. Next to the living room was a nicely appointed dining area. Six high-back chairs surrounded a large glass-topped table. There were lots of large potted plants scattered tastefully throughout the rooms. We continued until we reached a small sitting area adorned with two brightly-colored loveseats and a coffee

A.J. McLEAN
D.O.B.: 1-9-78
HAIR: BROWN
EYES: BROWN

Alex's promo page when he auditioned for Lou

table. On one side was a guest bath, on the other was what appeared to be a sunken bedroom.

The next room we entered stood out in stark contrast to the others. We walked down a couple of short steps and into a room that would be any guy's dream. It was a large game room complete with a pool table and an old-fashioned Coke machine. Everywhere you looked there were all sorts of movie memorabilia and toys. It was like a mini museum. There was also a long bar that curved around the side of the room. The barstools were chrome and black leather.

To the right was a group of couches in front of an entertainment center; behind that was an atrium with plants and a small pond. The walls were covered with gold records and plaques. Other than the gold records I saw nothing that had anything to do with the music business. It made me wonder what line of work this Mr. Pearlman was in.

There was such a diverse collection of things in that one room that my head was spinning. Alex was in awe. The look on his face was priceless. He had the wild look in his eyes of a small child who wanted to touch and try everything. Instead, he held back and stood with his hands folded in front of him.

We were asked to sit in the entertainment nook, where I noticed a video camera set up on a tripod. Lou disappeared into a back room and then an attractive young woman dressed in a nice suit entered. It was Gloria. Her face seemed of Italian descent; she had dark-brown hair and eyes. She conducted herself in a professional manner as she explained that Lou wanted to form a singing group fashioned after New Kids on the Block. He planned to form his own record label in order to back them financially.

At that point, she asked Alex if he was prepared to sing and do his dance routine. Alex said yes and we all sat down to wait for Lou. When he emerged from what appeared to be an office, he asked Alex to sing.

Alex gave it his all that day. When it came time for the dancing, Alex did a split and then popped back up. He had those moves down! When he finished, Gloria asked us several questions about what types of roles and shows Alex had done during his career. Alex told them about his musical theater background going back to the age of six.

Alex then told them he had always dreamed of being in a group like this and he was very excited to be auditioning for it. That was news to me! Alex had never mentioned this to me before, so I had no clue that he had any interest in this type of thing.

I just sat and listened to my son go on and on about himself, his career and his dreams of becoming a pop star. It was all very revealing to me. When Alex was through we were told, "Good job. We'll call you soon."

Those words had rung in our ears so many times before, with nothing coming of it, that I could see the disappointment in my son's eyes as we left to get into the car. On the way home he confessed that he had a very good feeling about all of this. I tried to be just as positive, but I was very confused about the whole situation. My mind kept going back to the reading and the psychic telling me how this man was going to change my life. I just kept praying it would be sooner rather than later.

After a few anxious weeks of waiting, Alex convinced me to call for an update. Gloria informed me that Alex had definitely been chosen for the group, but had to wait while they continued their search for the rest of the members. At that point I felt it was necessary to have a serious talk with my son. We had to decide if this was going to be a genuine opportunity or just another dead end.

I told Alex the good news about the phone call with Gloria but then asked him to think long and hard about the direction he wanted his career to take. Up until now his goals had been on theater and his dreams had been Broadway bound. Alex thought for a moment and then looked me straight in the eye as he told me how it had always been his secret desire to dance and sing on MTV, just like all his pop idols. "The theater is a nice goal," he said, "but music has always fascinated me in ways I can't really explain."

Alex said that being in a group with other guys like him would be like having the brothers that he never had; it would be an extension of our little family. At that, my heartstrings gave a tug. Alex was as serious as I had ever seen him. He wanted to do this more than anything. It was almost like he instinctively knew what was ahead of him. I got a very weird feeling about that conversation. It was like the feeling I got when we drove up to that big white house.

CHAPTER FOUR

Reality Check

SEVERAL FOLLOW-UP PHONE CALLS with Gloria revealed a bit more about the mysterious Lou Pearlman. He was cousin to pop legend Art Garfunkel, but the references were so vague that we never knew for certain. For years Lou had written music with the hope of breaking into the industry, but with no success. Luckily, he had another passion: airships, commonly known as blimps. With the help of a financial backer in Germany, Lou had built a successful airship company.

Originally from New York, Lou and a few childhood friends moved to Orlando to start up a billboard business that used airships. They worked with theme parks and large companies until the company began making a profit. Despite that accomplishment, Lou's real dream was to enter the music industry. Before we met him, he had spent much of the previous year researching how the New Kids had become such a household name. It was obvious to him that a winning formula was at work. All he needed to do was copy it.

In his opinion, the timing was right for a new boy band. Lou did his homework and decided to pull in some shareholders to front him the money he needed for the venture. Most people were skeptical. It was hard to believe that this man, a titan in the airship industry, could deliver the next teen sensation. But he was persuasive and managed to raise the initial capital he needed.

After learning about Lou and his dreams of stardom with this boy-band idea, I decided not to quit my day job just yet. I continued to plug away with my kids and computer classes. Alex kept up with his acting and singing lessons. Not much changed until the next time I spoke to Gloria. She said they had held more auditions and were pretty much set on a boy named Tony Donetti.

Gloria asked me if I knew him and I told her about the Latin carnival. She asked if we had any contact information for Tony, as she had misplaced it and Lou really wanted him for the group. I told Gloria that I would do my best to locate a telephone number or address. When I asked Alex, he said he thought that Tony Donetti was actually his stage name. I got in contact with Alex's old voice teacher, who also had worked with Tony, and he told me that Tony's real name was Howard Dorough.

By April 1992, Alex had become the first Backstreet Boy. It would be another year before the final five members were in full swing. That was our first introduction to the well-worn mantra of "hurry up and wait." All we knew for sure was that, with the addition of Howard Dorough, there were now two members of this boy band.

Alex and I went through the anticipation-elation-frustration cycle many times over the course of that year. Each time the phone rang, Alex got his hopes up about being called to start rehearsals. I checked in periodically with Gloria for updates. However, as time passed, I got the impression that there was a stumbling block in the way.

Doubts again clouded my mind. Had we done the right thing by moving here? Was this the best way to go with my son's career? I had come to realize that my son had developed very good instincts as well. Even with all the doubts that I was suffering he never seemed to flinch. He kept insisting this was the right thing to do. Not entirely convinced, I called some friends in Los Angeles to see if their children were faring any better. They told me that a few parts had come their way, but nothing substantial. Maybe moving again was not the right thing at that point, but I was getting antsy and needed something to break. Some light at the end of the tunnel. A crumb . . . anything! Then the call came. Sadly, it was not the one my son was hoping for.

Gloria called to ask for my help once again. Lou wanted to hold a final casting call to search for the remaining group members. They both felt that if the call were large enough they would find who they were looking for. Putting my reservations aside, I called all of the contacts I could think of. My list included talent agents, casting directors and even former acting coaches that Alex had worked with over the past couple of years.

Then Lou, Gloria and I sat down and made up an ad to place in newspapers and trade journals. We enlisted the help of talent agents Jean Tanzy and Sybil Galler, with whom Alex had been taking classes for a few months. They had never actually gotten him any work, but they talked like they knew a lot of people in the industry. At that point, I figured we could use all the help we could get.

Lou cleared out a blimp warehouse for us to use as a temporary stage and holding area. I helped design some forms for the kids to fill out when they got there. Lou, Jean, Sybil and Gloria made up the panel to evaluate the talent. We got video equipment and sound equipment set up. Alex choreographed a dance routine for the candidates to try. All we needed were the bodies.

As I worked more closely with Gloria I asked her what the hold up had been. She told me that Lou had decided to go with seven young men instead of five—and for two reasons. First, he wanted to make sure he had a backup if it turned out that the commitment level of the boys ever wavered. Second, he wasn't completely sold that five was the magic number. For some reason, he had it in his head that six boys would round out the harmonies better.

I wasn't too happy about that as I felt it would really slow down the process. Finding five boys who could sing together was going to be difficult enough. Now we had to choose seven young men who sounded great together and two of them were going to have to settle for being used as "backup." Based on my son's growing trust in Lou, I decided to stick with it.

Once word got out, the phone calls started rolling in. We tried to do some screening over the phone to make sure that the boys knew exactly what they were getting into. Finally, after days of preparation, the weekend arrived and it was time to begin the auditions. Thankfully, the weather cooled off somewhat. That was a blessing since the warehouse was not air-conditioned.

We all got there early to set up our tables, chairs and equipment. I could tell from the long list of names that Gloria had collected that we were in for a long weekend. One after another they came. They danced, they sang, they left. It seemed endless and some were not very easy to listen to. Finally, after two days of auditions, Lou announced that he had the group that he wanted. Waiting for the next step was torture.

ABOUT A WEEK LATER, we went to Lou's house to meet the other boys. Alex barely slept the night before. Watching him, it was hard for me to not get enthused as well. As we approached the "big, white house," it dawned on me that the holidays were upon us. The coming year could be one that I would never forget. But was I getting too excited?

Lou's faith in the project had never wavered. He was always encouraging and he stayed focused on his goals. He was one of those people who made you feel like family from the first moment you met him. He had a knack for making you believe in him and his dream. It was no wonder that he had convinced the airship shareholders to invest in the group. I could tell by talking with Alex that he was developing a deep respect for Lou and what he had accomplished so far in his life. That growing respect made Alex very passionate about becoming a member of the group.

Despite all our warm-and-fuzzy feelings, the question remained, did this man that we had come to trust have the ability to make my son's dream come true? Whenever I discussed the project with friends and agents, it was clear to me that they were skeptical. More than once I heard about just how fickle the music business could be. Countless bands each year tried to make it and failed.

But every time someone condemned the project, I found myself defending it. Maybe it was the trusting glow I saw in my son's eyes. Throughout my life I have had premonitions about things. Gut feelings that I learned to follow after many years of learning to read them. This was definitely one of those times. I sensed that this was the beginning of something big. I thought back to the reading with Matthew. He had been so emphatic about how this man would change our lives.

All of those things flashed through my mind as we got out of the car and began the walk into our future. I just kept praying this was the right decision. I remembered watching Alex at the auditions as he worked with the other boys. He demonstrated enormous confidence and seriousness as he showed them the dance moves they had to learn. He had patience when they made mistakes and worked with them over and over until they felt good enough to try it on their own.

When we walked into the house there was a lot of tension in the air. Gloria looked nervous, sort of edgy. She greeted us hastily and led us into the game room, where there were a lot of people sitting around. I recognized some of the boys from the auditions. It appeared they were all with their parents. Not everyone looked happy. I wondered what we had missed. The scene did not look promising and Lou was nowhere to be seen.

We introduced ourselves to everyone. The boys seemed to hit it off right away and greeted Alex with hearty handshakes. The introductions finished and I found a seat. Suddenly, Lou's office door opened and he stepped out with a mother and son that I remembered from the auditions. I found out later that Lou had been torn between two of the boys and wanted to speak to them both before we started our meeting. It was at that point that one boy and his mother left the house. I couldn't really tell from their expressions what had taken place but that was all to be revealed soon enough.

There was a small electronic keyboard in the room that was not there the last time we came. I wondered if they were going to be using it today. Lou walked into the room and called the boys over to him. He introduced himself again and told them how happy he was to finally have his new family there with him. As he beamed with delight, Lou told the boys about the music he had been writing. He wanted them to hear it. After grabbing an acoustic guitar from the other room, he sat down to play.

I quickly understood why he had never pursued a singing career of his own. His voice was okay, but it was also undeniably weak. He could carry a tune, that was about it. The boys watched and listened. All of a sudden, one of them started to sing along. Lou just smiled and kept going. Before long all of the boys were singing along with Lou. Then they started experimenting with harmonies. We parents looked at one another in amazement. Something really incredible was taking place right before our eyes. All we could do was smile as the group and Lou continued singing.

When they were done, they shook hands, gave high fives and jumped around the room like they had just won a championship ball game. I must admit that it was pretty cool to watch those six boys join in without trying to out-do or out-sing each other in any way. They just seemed to blend naturally.

Once the room settled down, Lou outlined his master plan for the group. He told us he had decided on six boys instead of seven. He also said he had come to terms with a pair of local talent agents who had agreed to take the boys under their wing for rehearsals and singing lessons. This was the team of Jean Tanzy and Sybil Galler, who had helped with the auditions.

Jean smoked heavily and had chiseled features that looked older than her years. She had long salt-and-pepper hair and a very husky voice. Sybil was the opposite of Jean—a short, young woman with well-kept blonde hair who was always dressed nicely. She had a perky attitude and was usually smiling. I suppose they complemented each other.

Alex and one of the other boys, Nick Carter, had been signed with Jean and Sybil for acting lessons. I had never heard them speak about any experience in the music business, but apparently Jean had done some singing professionally in the past. She told Lou that she had contacts in New York who could help with getting the new group a record deal. That confused me a bit since Lou had always spoken of starting his own label in Orlando.

After the little sing-along session, Lou showed the boys some videos of performances by the New Kids. He explained how he had met their manager and picked his brain about how to form a boy band.

We all got to know each other a bit that day and the tension that had greeted us when we arrived eventually disappeared. I was able to breathe a bit easier. Our holidays were fine, spent with the family as usual. I think both Alex and I were eager to get them over with that year so that we could see what was going to happen next.

At the end of December I got a phone call from Gloria telling us that Lou wanted to throw a birthday party for Alex on the ninth of January at his home. That was great news! Given the fact that Alex's birthday came around right after Christmas I was usually strapped for cash. My son invariably got a raw deal. Typically, people purchased one gift for him and said that it was for both Christmas and birthday.

Journal Entry, January 9, 1993: *Lou had a cake for AJ's birthday today— what a great guy! Alex's fifteenth birthday and last night was the first gathering of the Backstreet Boys. Jean, Sybil and Lou picked seven boys at first. There was a decision to be made between Damon and David. After a long time behind closed doors both boys appeared with about the same amount of confidence and nervousness. We were to find out the next day that Damon had been picked over David. So, Saturday morning David and his mother left to return to Miami and the rest of the boys began rehearsing and continuing to get to know each other. Names in order of age youngest to oldest are: Nick, AJ, Damon, Burk, Howard and Sam. Damon was chosen as the alternate later that day. He was not very happy about that and I would not be surprised if he eventually drops out of the group.*

WITH THE INITIAL ANXIETIES out of the way, the boys began rehearsing and learning the words to the songs that Lou had written for them. It quickly became clear to me that the two partners Lou had enlisted to help with the boys and their schedules lacked organizational skills. It appeared to me that the boys needed some assistance with the daily tasks. Having a written schedule of rehearsals, school and homework would be very helpful to the parents. I spent some time banging on my trusty word processor and worked up some ideas for forms that would fit the bill.

When I showed the package to Lou he was impressed. Since I was the one who would be bringing Alex back and forth, to and from rehearsals, why not put me to work? It appeared that I was the only parent to come up with such a plan. No sooner had Lou approved it than I set about putting my organizational skills into motion.

Not long after that, Lou called me and asked me to gather some background information about the boys. We needed to write bios for the press packet. I was thrilled! The weekend of Alex's fifteenth birthday had been one of the most enjoyable weekends for me in a long time. I *finally* felt like something was beginning happen.

My son and I were a part of it. I could not help but think that going back to work on Monday would be difficult. I did not relish the thought of returning to the same day-to-day grind. On the bright side, I did have the following weekend to look forward to. And so my role with the Backstreet Boys began to take shape.

———

IT DID NOT TAKE LONG for me to figure out that there were problems that had nothing to do with organization. There were problems with parents, contracts and egos. Damon, the alternate, became angry when he was told that he could not perform in the first show that Backstreet landed. That caused a major argument and after several closed-door sessions with Lou, Damon quit.

More problems arose with Burk. I don't know exactly what happened there, but Lou and Burk's mother had some terrible shouting matches. Whatever the reasons, he also ended up leaving.

Lou went back to his audition-tape vault and found a young man named Charles. Unfortunately, he did not last very long either. He had a hard time staying on key with the other boys and had been in an auto accident that left him with scars across his chest. The fact that the boys at some point may have to bare their chests for a photo shoot was a reality. It was a sad day when he was let go.

All of us so desperately wanted the group to work that we chalked the problems up to the obvious age differences that existed, along with the differences in the boys' family backgrounds. It was our hope that the problems would heal themselves.

Unfortunately, that didn't happen. One day, moments before they went on stage at a small nightclub, Sam decided that the group could not sing a song that he had written. Tempers flared and another member was gone. To our surprise, Lou reacted very calmly. Later that night we found out why. In the audience was a young man that Lou had been priming for the group. His name was Kevin Richardson.

When Kevin sang with the other boys, it was clear that he was just what we had been looking for. He was tall, dark and handsome. With his chiseled looks and a model's build, Kevin was just the ticket to drive the older teen market crazy.

With his high-cut cheekbones (that would make any woman jealous) and Tom-Cruise-like good looks, it was no wonder that he had spent some time playing Aladdin over at Disney. Topping off his muscular frame was a head full of silky dark-brown hair.

If you ever found yourself deep in conversation with Kev, he would fix his piercing eyes on you and make you feel as though you were the only one in the room. He was intense for a man of his age, but he had been through a lot in his young life and never took his good fortune for granted.

When the smoke cleared, there were four boys left: Kevin, Howard (who we called Howie), Alex and Nick. Lou deliberately set out to have each member of the group appeal to a certain demographic. The way he envisioned it, there should be something for everyone, from preteen to adult.

Alex had grown into a rather gangly young man of five-foot-seven. He had very thick dark-brown hair and inky black, long-lashed eyes. There was no denying his Latino background. It was the same with Howie, but in a more mature way. Even though he was shorter than the other boys, Howie made his mark with his huge smile and the charming way he had with the ladies. Where Alex had straight hair, Howie's was curly, creating a nice contrast among the four boys. And then there was Nicky.

Immediately tagged as the baby of the group, Nick Carter was only twelve when he joined the other three boys on their strange and wonderful journey. He was your typical tow-headed blond with big baby blues. Since he had not yet hit puberty, Nick was able to hit the high notes with relatively little trouble.

Much to everyone's dismay, even though we seemed to be back on track, something was still missing. It was an intangible something at first, but then it became quite clear. There had to be five members in the group. Everything that had been written for them thus far consisted of five-part harmony. And so it began . . . the desperate search for that fifth member.

The next few months were a blur. We once again went through audition tapes, and held new auditions with the hope that someone who fit the part would materialize. The pressure was on as the deadline of their first show approached.

The boys rehearsed the best they could. It had been a very emotional few months for all of us. It had been really disheartening to have three of the original members leave, with no backup in sight. It was only after Kevin talked to the boys one night after rehearsals that our spirits picked up a bit. He told them about his cousin Brian who was in his last year of high school back in their home state of Kentucky.

Kevin explained that Brian could sing gospel and soul like an angel. Being blond and fair-skinned with bright blue eyes, he also had a good "look" to add to the group. Up until that point, the dark-haired outnumbered the fair-haired, three to one, with Nicky being the odd man out. It seemed worth a shot.

Kevin said Brian was your typical "boy next door." Since the idea behind the group was to bring about a new image for mothers and daughters to swoon over, that seemed like a good fit as well. So with the boys' blessing, Kevin made a phone call home. The die was cast for what would ultimately culminate in the grouping of the final five members of the Backstreet Boys.

━━━

ON MAY 16, 1993, the pieces finally came together. The day began like any other. We got up, got dressed, brushed our teeth and were out the door. We went through the motions like we had done so many times before. We had no way of knowing that by day's end, things would be infinitely different.

As day turned into night, the sun set, the moon rose and a plane touched down at Orlando Airport. Aboard that plane, a fair-haired young man unbuckled his seat belt, stood up and took a good long stretch. His journey from Lexington, Kentucky, had been fraught with excitement and anticipation.

As he made his way off the plane, he followed the signs to the tram that ultimately would lead him to baggage claim. His steps noticeably quickened as he made his way through the narrow passage lined with brightly colored advertisements.

He was jolted into reality as the tram stopped and the voice above directed him to baggage claim. Operating now on nothing but sheer nerves, his mind wandered back to the phone call that had pulled him out of class only two days earlier.

"Do you think it would be all right for you to miss a couple days of school?" asked Kevin.

"I guess so," said Brian. "Why?"

"So that you can sing for this group of guys I'm singing with."

"Sure," said Brian.

"There'll be someone at the airport to pick you up."

After that, it was all a blur. Suddenly, he heard his name being called. As he looked around, he saw a man holding up a small white sign. Before he could reach for his bag, the man muscled his way through the crowd to the conveyer belt, confirmed with a nod that the suitcase he was about to grab was the right one—and whisked it away.

The man introduced himself with a strong handshake and motioned for the fair-haired boy to follow him to the car. Moments later he found himself sequestered in the back of the longest, darkest, fanciest car he had ever seen. His stomach was in knots.

All of us had gone out to dinner with Lou and then to a small ice-cream shop that he owned a few miles from his house. We waited eagerly as Lou got the call that Brian had landed and was on his way. Kevin could barely contain his excitement at the thought of seeing his cousin again. I could read the nervousness in his face as the limo approached.

We all ran out to greet the limo as it pulled into the parking lot. When the back door opened, Brian Thomas Littrell emerged. He was small-framed with short blond hair. As he turned to meet us, we were blinded by his sparkling blue eyes and great big smile. All at once he was enveloped in the arms of his older cousin. Laughter and hasty introductions flew through the air, mixed with tears and hugs. The other boys greeted him like a long-lost family member. Brian's face beamed for the rest of the night.

We all jumped into the limo and headed for Lou's house. When we first heard Brian speak, with his Kentucky accent raging at what seemed to be 100 miles per second, we had to contain our chuckles. However, upon hearing him sing, we all shut our mouths and opened our ears to one of the most angelic voices we had ever heard.

Lou had rented a house for the boys to rehearse in and a couple of them lived there as well. Since none of the boys were being paid, the older ones with apartments were forced to give them up. The rented house was a nondescript, three-bedroom, two-bath box-like structure that was located in a small subdivision. We called it the band house. Working within a tiny budget, we furnished it with just the essentials, which we supplemented with some motherly love and occasional home-cooked meals.

Once the initial excitement of Brian's arrival wore off, everyone went back to the band house, where we all did our very best to make Brian feel at home. While I might have started out being there for my son, I soon realized that each boy had his own special needs. Nick's parents lived a few hours away so they tried to be there as much as they could.

I soon became cook, maid, seamstress, nurse and sometimes just general sounding board when necessary. I didn't mind since, to me, they were all still children.

Once it was official that Brian would be staying, he and Kevin moved into the band house. Nick sometimes stayed there on the weekends. None of the rooms in the house were big enough to rehearse in, so the boys took to the driveway and literally "pounded the pavement." It was the middle of the summer and the heat was excruciating. From the moment they walked outside each morning, until the last step was perfected each night, the sun beat down on them relentlessly.

They started out fully clothed in the morning, but by noon layers were shed and by dinner they would have liked nothing more than to have been dancing in their birthday suits. Luckily, they settled for shorts, sneakers and sunburned skin. Nicely bronzed shoulders and necks became beet-red and sensitive to the touch.

Even their physiques began to change. Alex had been thin to begin with. Actually none of the boys were very beefy and the intensity

DENISE MCLEAN

Alex performs at Lou's temple

of those rehearsals shaved even more weight from their frames. Thank goodness their appetites were good. We made sure that they ate well and we pumped them full of vitamins and drowned them in aloe.

After a month of rehearsals, the boys were asked to perform at Sea World Grad Night in front of seven thousand middle-school students twice a night for two nights. A live performance in front of teenage girls from all over the state! It was a demographic dream. I don't know who was more nervous—Alex or me!

To give them an edgier look, we dressed them in leather outfits that had a bit of a biker feel to them. There was chaos from the moment those five boys hit the stage. Alex ran into the crowd a couple of times and dropped to his knees to sing to the swooning girls. The crowd reaction was like something out of an old Elvis Presley movie. They screamed and jumped up and down. The vibe was intense and the boys loved it.

A COUPLE OF WEEKS BEFORE the Sea World show, Lou took the boys, myself and Nick's parents out to dinner at an Italian restaurant, where we dined in the privacy of a small room in the back. Lou used the occasion to introduce us to Johnny and Donna Wright, a married couple that he had met several months earlier.

Johnny, an articulate and personable man in his mid-thirties, was the New Kids' former road manager. Donna, an animated woman with long,

DENISE MCLEAN

The boys in the early days

dark hair, was a publicist who had some experience organizing teen-club dances. They seemed to have opposite personalities, but they complemented one another rather well.

Donna, Johnny and Lou

Johnny spoke openly to the boys about what they had to look forward to in their careers. He painted a pretty picture, but he made it clear that they would have to be prepared to do a lot of hard work to make it a reality. He seemed to be well versed in the music business, more so than Donna, who seemed to be the more creative partner. It was clear that they were both worlds ahead of Jean and Sybil in their overall experience.

So we met, we ate and we talked. The boys sang for them and afterwards we all went our separate ways. At that point, it was not apparent why the meeting had taken place. That became more obvious when Lou arranged a second meeting with the Wrights to discuss what they could offer the boys in terms of their contacts within the industry. After a few more meetings, we were told that Donna had booked a performance for the boys at a fund-raiser for the Ronald McDonald House in Fort Lauderdale. It was a formal sit-down dinner, so we got to dress up a bit.

The evening started out well enough. The boys sang with their usual energy and style. Not surprisingly, the crowd loved them, especially the girls. However, once the boys came back to the table, things began to heat up a bit.

I was not at the table to witness it, but later my son explained that Johnny and Donna had a confrontation of sorts with Jean over the booking. Jean and Sybil had already parted company, but Jean still considered herself an integral member of the team. From what we were told later, Jean confronted Donna about not going through her with regards to scheduling and an argument ensued. Since neither Jean nor Sybil had ever officially been given the title of managers for the group, no one thought Donna's booking would be a problem. Apparently, to Jean it was.

Lou met with both parties. For the good of the boys, he decided to hire the Wrights and let Jean go. Since Jean had been there from the start, we felt badly about her departure, but Lou assured us that he would take care of everything. He said that everyone would end up happy. Naturally, we believed him.

Meanwhile, I started working in the management office, creating the tools we needed to broaden the fan database. Things like merchandise, pictures, cassette tapes and the like. I tried to come up with a way we could start collecting names of potential fans as the boys ventured out into public for performances at malls and the like.

The next challenge was to figure out how Nick, Alex and Brian could keep up with their schoolwork and their rehearsal schedule. They had to be available almost all the time for appearances since public exposure was the key to getting them known. The countless hours spent on performances, photo shoots and appearances meant that we had to find an alternate method of schooling.

The school principal had called me several times about Alex's absences during the last few months. Nick attended a middle school in Tampa, which meant that he had to be driven back and forth about a hundred miles a day for rehearsals. Brian was in his last year, but his school in Kentucky was willing to accommodate his career. It was a nightmare. The toll it was beginning to take on the boys scared me.

Lou was reluctant to advance money for tutoring, but with the help of the other parents we managed to convince him that it was necessary. We found a local tutoring company called Education In Action. Owned by a lovely lady named Susan Horton, it provided on-set schooling for young actors and actresses while they worked on movies and television shows in Orlando.

Since each boy was at a different educational level, we had to deal with the boys on an individual basis. Brian was the easiest because he only had to finish out his senior year and keep up his grades. We hired a tutor through Susan's company who would travel with him when necessary or come to the band house. Nick had to be tutored as well, but at middle school level. Again, we were able to hire someone to travel with him when necessary. Sometimes it was the same person who worked with Brian.

Alex was another story. His high school did not want to cooperate. Their policy was that once Alex exceeded his sick-day limit, he either had to drop out or get bumped back a year. Neither option was acceptable. Susan and I tried to convince the school board that Alex wanted to finish high school while pursuing his career.

That debate continued for weeks. Finally the school suggested that Alex be enrolled in an experimental school that had been set up to help high-school dropouts from underprivileged families continue their education while also working full time. Most of those kids had to help their single-parent households financially.

In order for Alex to attend that school, he had to become a dropout. Go figure. The school system made him quit so that he could attend the special program rather than work with our qualified tutors to maintain his classes. Neither Alex nor I understood that logic. When I sat him down and told him what his options were he was amazed. He kept telling me that all he wanted was to graduate with his class no matter what it took. His principal was good enough to agree to that.

I filled out the paperwork for him to drop out of school. Then we went to sign up for the Challenger Program as it was called. What a difference it was working with people who understood our situation! They were so helpful and understanding that I could barely believe it. Susan, Alex and I worked for days with the administration and staff of the Challenger School to come up with an appropriate program for Alex.

State guidelines said that every student had to attend a minimum three hours of classes each day. When we were at home that was no problem, but when we traveled it required some creative juggling. We had to make sure that three hours were set aside each day for tutoring—not an easy task when you had managers who were desperately trying to get these boys seen everywhere at once.

The music business is like a hole that sucks you inside and grows larger with each success. It allows no room for the real world. It is comprised mostly of fantasy and the promise of all things shiny and bright. Not too much reality there! That might be fine if you are an adult with a mind of your own, but if you are an impressionable young boy of fourteen or sixteen or even eighteen, you have zero defense against that fantasy world.

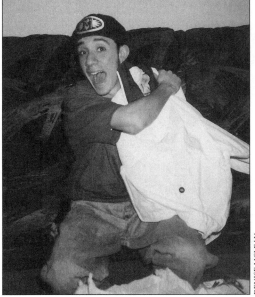

Alex on his sixteenth birthday

DENISE MCLEAN

Lou unintentionally contributed to that fantasy by telling the boys that when they became famous they would always ride in limos and private jets and eat in only the best restaurants. He backed that promise by displaying his own boyish toys—limos, boats, planes and airships. He took the boys on shopping trips and to fine dining establishments.

At the time, it all seemed okay, given how hard the boys worked. But, little by little, they lost touch with reality. Alex was not too bad at first. None of the boys were really. They were so wide-eyed and new that it really didn't affect them right away. It took years for that to happen.

As the tour grew closer, Susan and I prepared the schedule the boys would have to follow during the summer months for their classes. Already, they had gotten behind. The one saving grace to this new schedule was that they could actually bank hours. On those days when they couldn't put in the necessary class time, we simply withdrew the needed hours from their "bank."

The summer came and went rather quickly. Before we knew it, the time had come to hit the road for a tour of middle schools and high schools from Florida to Ohio. I had quit my job and started working in the management office months before. My former boss came to a couple of mall appearances to check the boys out. He relished telling me that my job would be waiting for me when I got back from this little adventure.

"The odds are against you, you know," he said.

For Alex's sake, I looked at it as an opportunity that I could not pass up. Ten years down the road I didn't want to be explaining to him why I didn't let him give it his best shot. Whether he succeeded or not, at least he was giving it his all.

Leaving for that first tour was only the beginning. Mom never did get used to our being gone so often. The phone bills rose considerably when the boys were out of town, but it was worth it because it gave Mom and Dad peace of mind to know we were okay.

We used a bus that once belonged to a traveling airship crew. As we lumbered along the hills and valleys that took us to the middle schools and high schools of America, we learned why the bus had been so generously bequeathed to us. The engine had problems on an almost daily basis. We spent many an afternoon playing football beside the road while the bus driver worked on the engine.

On a trip through the Midwest during late November, the bus's heater went out as we were on our way to attend a 10:00 A.M. school assembly. We bundled up in every article of clothing we had, but that wasn't enough to keep us warm. Still shivering, we drove from fast-food restaurant to fast-food restaurant, drinking cup after cup of hot tea, cocoa or coffee in order to stay warm. We did not want the boys' voices to freeze up on stage. Our efforts paid off. The show went without a hitch.

As far as having roadies to do the grunt work, let's just say, "You're looking at 'em!" Our roadies consisted of the five boys, one manager, one soundman and me. Whether it meant setting up or breaking down equipment, or lugging wardrobe cases, we did it all. It really was about teamwork in the early (as well as lean) days.

The number of hats that I wore seemed to increase on a daily basis. As I worked my way into becoming an integral part of the team, I reveled in the creative freedom I was given. No longer was I merely in charge of the boys' clothing. I was assistant soundman, hair and make-up girl and miniature merchandiser, all rolled into one.

Being virtual unknowns meant giving away more stuff than we sold. I kept busy handing out free cassettes of their first single, a song titled "Tell Me That I'm Dreaming," which they recorded for Lou's Trans Continental Records. The fans that we picked up along the way gave us a substantial fan base. To this day, we still get phone calls from people who say that the Backstreet Boys once played at their school.

After that tour, it was back to Florida for a brief rest before heading to New York City for a showcase at which we hoped to impress record executives. According to Lou this was necessary for the boys to get the promotional backing of a major label. I was a bit unsure about the whole thing. It seemed pretty scary to put the boys on such display. With the schedules they had been keeping, I feared they might get sick or have stage fright.

None of the boys (with perhaps the exception of Nick, who grew up in upstate New York) had ever been to New York City. Our excitement began in earnest the moment we climbed out of our cavernous limousine. That, by the way, is no exaggeration. That limo was a monstrosity. As we took a moment to soak up our surroundings, an obviously very swank and ritzy hotel loomed in front of us, seemingly larger than life. It wasn't just any hotel: it was the Plaza Hotel.

Alex hopped around like the Energizer Bunny. I think the only words uttered from any one of the boys were, "Oh my God!" or "Yes, we're really here!" There they stood, those five young men, a few of them still just kids, all decked out in pristine white shirts and perfectly knotted black neckties. Their blue jeans were so new that they still had creases running down the front.

The Plaza had always been a landmark to me, given the fact that I grew up not too far away (just across the bridge, in New Jersey). It brought back memories of trips to the big city when I was growing up. My grandmother took me twice a year—once during Easter to see the show at Radio City Music Hall, and then again at Christmas to see the trees and lights at Lincoln Center. During those visits, I probably felt the way I felt as an adult: like a kid going to pick out her new holiday clothes.

After checking in, we were introduced to the two people who would remain with us for the duration of our stay. They were the first bodyguards the boys had ever known. One was a young, very tall, dark and handsome off-duty street cop named Mark. We found out later that he apparently did part-time work for Lou whenever he came into the city. We were never quite sure what the second man did. He was a short, very Italian-looking young man who always dressed in shiny suits and sharp shoes. We were immediately reminded of Joe Pesci, so that is what we called him.

We got to our rooms and settled in for the night. Alex and I shared a room. I think we just talked ourselves to sleep that night. I asked him if he was nervous about the showcase. He told me not really since they would be doing the same songs they had done all through the summer tour and so it was no big deal.

"I am kind of nervous about signing a record contract," Alex said.

"Don't worry," I told him. "Nothing will be finalized during this trip."

Getting a record deal was . . . well, a big deal. I couldn't imagine any record company hearing a group and then making an offer on the spot. Commitments of that magnitude required a great deal of thought and research. All too soon I would find out just how naïve I was about the music business.

The next morning, I went down to the main lobby without Alex to have breakfast. I was enjoying a cup of coffee when I heard a voice that I instantly recognized.

"Mom, Mom," the voice said. "I can't find my jeans or sneakers."

I turned around and saw Alex standing in the lobby, wearing only his boxer shorts, white socks and a big smile.

The next day was a long one. The boys sang and danced hour after hour for anyone who showed up at the showcase. I was a little disappointed at the small number of record executives who accepted our invitation to meet the boys. Based on the responses we had gotten from the school tour, along with the feedback from everyone else that had heard the boys sing, I assumed that they would be knocking down our door.

It was just a bit hard to watch the boys' faces when they were told that they had received no offers, but Lou gave them a pep talk and made sure they understood that this was only the beginning. He made it clear that he had no intention of giving up. That made all of us feel better.

CHAPTER FIVE

Jive Talk

LESS THAN SIX MONTHS AFTER THE SHOWCASE, we returned to
New York City, where we met with executives at Jive Records. It was
actually the second record company to make an offer. As Lou had pre-
dicted, a record contract did come through following the showcase. The
boys were signed to Mercury Records.

However, as the weeks went by, it became obvious that Mercury had
no intention of picking up its option to record the boys. They let the
offer expire without ever sending the boys into the studio. As luck would
have it, the Mercury executive who signed them subsequently resigned
and took a position with Jive Records, where he found co-workers that
believed in the Backstreet Boys as much as he did.

All of which landed us in the conference room of Jive Records. There
we sat gathered around the negotiating table, hacking through mounds
of legal mumbo-jumbo with an attorney that Lou had hired for us. As
the saying goes, "If I only knew then what I know now," that scene
would have ended quite differently.

I learned a few very important things as a result of that meeting. Never, ever sign a contract without having your attorney look at it and without having a complete understanding of the document. Never allow

yourself or your child to be bullied into something without having all of your questions answered. By that point, we had put all of our trust in Lou. He had taken a big risk financially and, by that time, we felt that we owed him so much. On more than one occasion, Lou told the boys how he was going to make them into millionaires. The way he lived was the way we all wanted to live. Nice house, nice car, fame, fortune. What parent would turn that down for their child?

After we signed the contracts that day at Jive Records, we went out on the town to celebrate. The celebration lasted well into night. It began with a wonderful dinner, after which we went to the Copa Cabana and then strolled through Times Square. It was a night I will never forget. The boys stopped in front of Virgin Records and began harmonizing right there on the street. Lou grinned ear-to-ear as passersby formed a crowd around them.

When they finished singing, the crowd applauded.

With that, one of the boys yelled out, "There will be more to come from Jive's newest recording artists, the Backstreet Boys."

Once the record company took over, life became a whirlwind of performing, recording and "imaging." The main goal was to have that wholesome boy-next-door look at all times. They were expected to adhere to that image, even on their days off. The Jive stylist helped us a great deal when it came to the look and feel they wanted to portray. However, the task of running from store to store with the boys, hemming pants and putting buttons back on, still lay with den mothers like me.

From the word go, Alex wanted to be the odd man out when it came to wardrobe, hair and personality. He wanted to be the bad boy. Every time we went into a store there would be an argument between him and Kevin. Why did Alex need that extra piece of clothing? Why didn't he want to wear the same colors as the other boys? Whatever the case seemed to be, those two repeatedly knocked heads. It was a sibling rivalry of sorts. In the end, they either compromised or Lou was called in to make a decision.

Even as a child, my son had a wonderful sense of color and style. As I recall, Alex didn't even own a pair of blue jeans until he was about twelve years old. That was pretty unheard of for his generation. He preferred the preppie look of polo shirts and cotton trousers to jeans and T-shirts. By the time he turned six, I had very little say about what he wore every day to school. He was very opinionated about his attire.

By the time Alex turned sixteen, he had become a bit of a rebel when it came to his clothing. He was the first of the boys to get his ears pierced. At first, the style was for one earring, but soon after that he decided on both. That caused a problem with his grandmother and me. We felt it was a bit too feminine. Even some of the boys were against it. But, in the end, Alex's stubbornness won out.

It was around that time that the boys received their first payment from the record label. The amount of money they advance is geared to how many CDs the record company thinks it will sell.

When Lou told us that the record company had given the boys a $25,000 signing bonus, we had no idea what that meant. It did seem like a low amount, but Lou said that neither he nor the Wrights took their percentage, which seemed to us, at the time at least, to be a generous gesture. That meant that each boy received $5,000.

From that point on, the new accountant that Lou hired kept track of every penny that he spent on the boys. What he did not list as an expense, the record company did. The word "recoupable" became an integral part of our vocabularies that year. We learned very quickly just how much Lou had spent on getting those boys where they were at that point in their careers because once the "signing bonus" was paid, the boys started getting bills from Lou's office.

DENISE MCLEAN

The Backstreet Boys backstage at Sea World

I had known all along that time would come, but none of us were prepared for what we saw. It was absolutely staggering. I had never seen so many zeroes on one piece of paper before in my life. It was downright shocking what we owed that man. All the dinners, limo rides, plane trips, parties, clothes, etc. were itemized for each boy. Alex and Nick incurred a larger bill than the other boys due to the years of tutoring they had.

Of course, none of us were able to begin paying any of it off. As I looked at the bill, I realized how little the boys would actually make over the coming years. I felt like I would be in someone's debt for the rest of my life. Once again those little demons perched themselves on my shoulders and started picking away at my brain.

Had I done the right thing for Alex? Sure, he seemed to be having a great time traveling, shopping and coming into his manhood with the other boys. There was a lot of good stuff happening here. Was it worth the huge price tag? That question gnawed away at me unrelentingly.

―――――

THE BOYS' FIRST VIDEO SHOOT took place at a small nightclub in Orlando. I had been handing out flyers for weeks at every appearance, trying to get young girls to show up at the club. To direct the video, Donna had hired Ken West, a young man she had met a few months earlier while attending film school. When we first met, I thought he was a bit quiet and reserved. Once he went to work, his personality changed and he took command of the shoot. It was obvious that he knew what he was doing.

I actually felt a bit sorry for him after a while. Donna seemed to give him more direction than he needed. Ken took it in stride, but by the time the shoot was done, he seemed relieved. I heard him say that he had to get the equipment back at a certain time and was running late. It might have been true.

Since that video was strictly for promotional purposes, we didn't have a big budget. We searched the boys' wardrobes for some hot outfits. They had been wearing quite a bit of black and white lately as it seemed to be a crowd pleaser. Crisp, white dress shirts, black jeans and black quilted vests served them well.

The stage was small, which made it difficult for the boys to do most of their choreography, but somehow they managed not to fall off of the stage. I found it very interesting that the girls in the audience never tired of hearing the same songs over and over that day. In fact, as the day went on, they memorized the words and began to sing along. Alex had taken to sitting at the edge of the stage and holding a girl's hand as he sang his piece of the ballad. Once again I saw just how comfortable he was in his surroundings. He reveled in the screaming adoration of the girls.

The reaction by the audience was all very encouraging, considering that the girls were not paid for the shoot. They were just given a quick fast-food lunch. The fact that they stayed hour after hour, screaming so genuinely at the boys was a sight to see. It was the first time I saw the phenomenon that was the Backstreet Boys take hold in earnest. Some were in love with Nick, some with Howie and some with all the others at the same time. It was really difficult to imagine hordes of girls going so crazy over my little boy. Heart-warming, but a bit scary at the same time. He was in his element, so how could it be bad? I would not find the answer to that question for a long time.

No sooner had the video wrapped than it was time to pack our bags again. This time we were off to Seattle. It was our first trip with an actual bodyguard along. Randy Jones was a very large black man with a shiny, bald head. The boys fell in love with him from day one. Randy had spent many years as a bodyguard for New Kids on the Block and he knew what to expect out on the road. Though he looked fierce on the outside, he was a real pussycat through and through. That seems to be the rule for most of the men who travel with pop stars. I mean, really. How threatening do you have to be to ward off a screaming fifteen-year-old girl?

Alex and I had never been to Seattle, so I was looking forward to a bit of sightseeing. The next day the boys were not scheduled to rehearse until nine at night. That gave us the whole day to play. Once up and showered, Alex called all of the boys and Randy to see if we could go on an outing.

We had a great time walking along the Farmer's Market. As we walked, Howie took videos of everything. It had become his trademark. In fact, you had to be careful when someone knocked on your door at night. There was a good chance you would open it to a video camera with Howie behind it.

━━━━━

IN AUGUST 1994, the boys sang their first nationally televised anthem during a Predators football game in Tampa. The anthem had been added to an already hectic schedule at the last minute, which meant that we had to travel by private jet. The boys made it onto the field just in time and the crowd loved them.

I think the excitement of the football game, coupled with the non-stop rush of the day, infused their voices with electricity. The boys' stamina never ceased to amaze me. I was worn out and did not want to stay to watch the game, but I was outvoted. As it turned out, their performance never aired on television because the game was blacked out.

As the school year approached, Jive decided to put the boys on another cross-country tour of middle and high schools. The tour was backed by Macy's, which meant that when they weren't performing the boys were expected to go to malls to sing and then hold autograph sessions at Macy's stores.

The tour got off to a rather bad start. The touring company didn't have a clue what the boys needed in the way of equipment. I don't know if the budget was again too small or what, but the first few shows were disasters because of the sound. To top things off, Donna had run-ins with the touring company. Things went from bad to worse.

It took a least a week for everything to get organized. Finally, the shows began to go well. The boys went out there and did the best that they could with what they had to work with, but it wasn't easy, given that they never knew what to expect from the equipment. Suddenly, in the middle of a song, the sound might just stop. When that happened, they stopped dancing, huddled together to find the note, and then continued on a cappella. The young girls in the audience didn't care whether they were singing or not. They screamed anyway.

The shows often began on a tepid note, since most of the students had never heard of the Backstreet Boys. Once they proved to the audience that they could sing and dance, the excitement levels increased, especially among the girls. Fueled by this enthusiasm, the boys showed off. Sometimes they went into the audience to sing to a particular girl. Other times they pulled up their shirts just enough to flash them a bit of skin. Alex and Howie did that the most. Nick, Brian and Kevin were a bit shy with their movements on stage, but eventually they got the idea.

Typically, they gave two shows at the schools. By the time the second show began, word had gotten out about the boys. The second shows usually began with the girls already frenzied. It was a phenomenon that I did not understand. The only thing that I could relate it to in my youth was when I watched the Beatles perform on the Ed Sullivan Show. The audience's reaction in the studio, and my reaction in my own living room, were the same: uncontrollable screaming during every performance.

In school after school, the reaction was the same. Sometimes the girls ran outside after the boys and followed the bus out of the parking lot, yelling each boy's name. Once, as we left the parking lot, the boys stuck their heads out the windows and waved at the girls. When the girls saw that some of the boys had water bottles in their hands, they begged them to toss the bottles to them. The girls cried and hugged the bottles as if they were gold. After that, we sometimes marked the tops of empty bottles with the boys' initials and threw them out the windows as we left the schools.

SUSAN HORTON SENT A NEW TUTOR out on the road with us, a young woman named Kim Anaszewski. Alex really liked her because she tried to make his lessons more fun. She took him on field trips and had him write reports, instead of making him sit every day for three hours with his nose in a book.

By that time, the school had realized the amount of work that Alex was doing on the road. Susan helped work out a method by which he could get academic credit for his stage performances. She made the school understand how his life experience was worth a lot in terms of things like public speaking. They also came up with a special credit for dancing. Over time, Alex and Kim were able to find enough free time to go on outings and still manage to keep up with the academic program.

The boys at a pep-rally show in Indiana

A couple of times during this period, when we were alone at night in our hotel room, I asked Alex if he was still having fun. Quite emphatically, he would answer yes. He loved what he was doing and didn't seem to care whether there were two kids or two hundred watching.

Occasionally, record company representatives joined us out on the road, primarily to see if the stories they were hearing about the boys were true. They soon discovered they were. That made them even more determined to put them back into the studio to finish their album. It was time to get the Backstreet Boys out into the marketplace.

Once we returned to Orlando, I worked in the office ordering more merchandise and entering names into the database that I had created for the boys. To gather names, I handed out postcards for the fans to fill out during the autograph sessions. Some of them filled them out right there and others mailed them back to us.

By then, Donna had hired an assistant to help with the mounting office duties. Nicole Peltz was a spunky young college graduate who had recently moved to Florida from New York. She was very organized and eager to learn the business.

When we got home, Nicole, who had been manning the front office, had boxes of postcards everywhere. Along with the postcards came the fan mail. Mostly, it was girls writing to their favorite Backstreet Boy, telling him how much they loved him and asking when they would see them again. Always they asked when their album would be released. It was a question we often asked ourselves.

———

THE BACKSTREET BOYS had their coming-out party in, of all places, Kuala Lumpur, Malaysia. That was because Jive's distributor, Bertelsmann Music Group (BMG), had a conference there for its worldwide network of sales reps and buyers. BMG, a much larger company than Jive, owned several record labels, including RCA Records. With our wardrobe cases, makeup and hair supplies and our best finery, we flew from Orlando to New York (two and a half hours), New York to Singapore (sixteen hours) and Singapore to Malaysia (1hour). With plane changes, layovers and delays, it took us over twenty-two hours to reach our final destination.

When we arrived in Malaysia, none of us had the faintest notion what time of the day it really was. After going through so many time zones, we were completely turned around and jet-lagged to the max. The humidity and heat hit us like a wall when we walked off the plane. We were met by two transportation vehicles, neither of which had air-conditioning. The ride from the airport to the hotel seemed endless.

Nick and I sat in the back of the mini bus, sweating terribly. We seemed to be more affected by the heat than anyone else. Suddenly, I felt sick to my stomach. I knew I would not make it to the top of the mountain road we were on without throwing up. The twists, turns and bumps did not help my already nauseous stomach. Finally, I could stand it no longer and yelled for the driver to stop.

"Mom, what's wrong?" Alex asked.

I was so sick I couldn't even answer him. I scrambled out of the van and onto the street, where I lost whatever I had eaten that day. Right behind me was little Nick, in the same condition. He went to the other side of the van. The boys kept oo-ing and ah-ing and saying things like, "Oh boy!"

Alex jumped out of the van and grabbed a hold of me. I must have looked like I was going to drop. He helped me back into the van and insisted I sit up front with him. My problem turned out to be motion sickness. I should have realized that possibility when I got into the van, but the long hours of travel had affected my thinking.

Nick and I breathed a sigh of relief when we finally reached our destination and our air-conditioned rooms. It was all I could do to drop to the bed and crash. Alex was exhausted as well. Later, a ringing phone awakened us. It was time to hit the showers and get ready for the day.

When it was time for the boys to dress, they came to my room. That left me little privacy, which meant that I had to make sure that I was showered, dressed and ready to go before they arrived. They dressed and primped and fooled around until it was time to leave. It reminded me of five women who were dressing for a date. It followed a pattern that ended with the hair spray and questions of "How do I look?"

That evening, their performance took place during the dinner hour in the main ballroom. The stage was very small, but the boys had worked out their choreography to accommodate a smaller space. Before they took the stage, Jive showed a short video of the boys that was comprised of scenes from the school shows. Then came the boys' turn to show the audience what they could do. The performance was full of energy and sounded terrific. When they finished, they were given a standing ovation. It was a magnificent start for the boys.

The more those industry executives and reps were psyched, the more they would sell the boys to the world. It was their mission to help the Backstreet Boys become a household word in any language. I was so happy, tears came to my eyes as I watched it unfold in front of me. Parents have many times in their lives to be proud of their children. This had to be at the top of my list.

═══════

WHEN WE RETURNED HOME, a mere twenty-four hours after we had left for the conference, everyone was psyched. We were sure that the reaction they had received in Malaysia would prod Jive to release an album quickly.

But every time we asked about the album, we were told that the boys were not yet ready to record the album. In our minds, that was not true. All you had to do was see the reaction of the girls to know that we had something real and true. We had thousands of names in our database from the last tour alone. How could they not be ready?

Finally, in June 1995, Jive decided to get serious about the boys going into the studio. The problem was that none of the songs that had been pitched to them by American songwriters seemed right for the boys. As a result, they contacted Swedish songwriter/producer Denniz PoP and invited him to submit songs. PoP and his writing partner, Max Martin, reworked a song titled "We've Got it Goin' On" and sent it to Jive. The A&R department liked it so much that PoP was hired to produce the single.

When the boys arrived in Sweden, they discovered that PoP and Martin had written two additional songs for them. They liked them so much that they recorded all three songs: "We've Got it Goin' On," "I Wanna Be With You" and "Quit Playing Games (With My Heart)." The sessions went remarkably well and they returned to the States filled with enthusiasm.

We felt some encouragement when Lynda Simmons, Jive's head of video production, came to Florida to prepare the boys for a video that the label wanted to make available to MTV when their first single was released. They decided to film it in Orlando. As the shoot progressed, I could see the excitement in Alex's eyes as he sang for the camera. I was amazed that he could withstand the Florida humidity, with temperatures in the nineties, wearing leather pants, a denim shirt and a leather vest, singing his heart out for every take. I kept waiting for one of the boys to faint from heat exhaustion, but it never happened. They just kept singing for take after take.

After production on the video was completed, the boys did another Sea World Grad Night show. This time they were actually paid and allowed to perform as headliners since most of the students now knew who they were. This performance was a bit different in that security wanted barricades put up so that the girls would not get hurt rushing the stage.

Rushing the stage? I did not like the sound of that. There is an area between the barricades and the stage called the pit. From that point on, that's where I positioned myself during the boys' shows. I taped shows with my video camera, talked to the fans, and handed out black-and-white photos.

That was not my only job, though. It now included costume changes between songs. The boys had thirty seconds to get almost naked and re-dressed in the dark. I became very good at holding a penlight in my mouth, while helping my son change wardrobe. Since Alex always had to have a different "something" to wear, he would invariably ask for a bandana or a tank top or different sunglasses at the last second. Depending on how far the dressing room was from the stage, I did a marathon run to find him what he needed. Those moments always made me nervous because I worried about them getting back on stage in time for the next song.

The end of the show was always the best. By that time, one or more of the boys was bare-chested or wearing only a tank top. It drove the girls crazy whenever they saw skin. If the boys lifted their shirts, that made the girls even crazier. Alex relished the cries of adoration. He never tired of hearing his name screamed over and over again.

DESPITE THE SUCCESS of the Malaysian trip, Jive could not decide where or when to release the boys' first single. We were all getting very anxious and discouraged at the record company's inability to make a decision. After numerous changes and postponements, it was finally decided that it would be released simultaneously in the United States and Europe in September 1995.

Fortunately for the boys, all the behind-the-scenes people (sales, promotional, marketing) had continued to work feverishly to get the boys' name out there even without a record to back up their efforts.

At around that time, I had begun to feel a bit out of sorts. Management was already benefiting from the boys' efforts, while the boys and their families were still in debt. We owed Lou and we owed Jive. Things were a bit tight financially, despite the fact that I had managed to save some money from the per diem I received while on the road.

Management didn't seem to be under that type of stress. When the boys signed the record deal, one of the things that Johnny got for his efforts was a brand new BMW convertible. The boys were very impressed with the new wheels. Then they found out how it was paid for. It was at that point that we began to ask for monthly statements from the accountant. That was tortuous. Excuse after excuse came back to us as to why the statements were not ready or why we really didn't need to see them.

Lou again raised the trust issue. However, this time we were undeterred. Some of the other parents and I wanted to devise a plan that would enable us to find out how long the boys would have to be paying out money instead of bringing it in.

The expenses had been enormous over the past few years. I knew that the number was not going to be a small one. At the very least, I wanted an itemized list of things to look over before I began to pay them back. That issue became an ongoing battle between the parents, Johnny and Lou for the next few years.

In September, we listened to the radio obsessively, waiting for the boys' single, "We've Got it Goin' On," to hit the airwaves. One day Alex and I were on our way to rehearsals, when he screamed out of nowhere, "That's us! That's us on the radio!"

We stopped at a traffic light and he jumped out of the car.

"Turn on your radio!" he shouted to every driver within earshot. "Our song is on the air! Turn on your radio!"

When we got to rehearsals we immediately called Mom and Dad. They were so excited when they heard the song that Mom cried tears of joy. It seemed to all of us that success was just on the horizon.

CHAPTER SIX

The Grand Tour

ON AUGUST 31, 1995, the Backstreet Boys began their first Radio Promotional Tour in Miami, where they were joined by record company reps, whose job it was to introduce the boys to the program directors in each city. They were the people who decided which records received airplay. Heavy schmoozing was the order of the day.

We quickly learned that when the program directors saw and heard the boys, it made a world of difference. Initially, several of the stations that we visited were not interested in the boys. That all changed once they met the boys and heard them sing.

Quite a few stations asked the boys to come back to sing on the air and to answer some call-in questions. While we were on the radio tour, we received exciting news from Orlando, where a radio show called "Survival of the Freshest" had been playing the single every night. The show's format was to play new music, then to ask listeners to call in to vote for their favorite songs. The boys won three nights in a row, beating out John B. and even Boyz II Men, by votes of seventy to eighty percent.

Traveling from town to town was a bit scary for us because we could never be sure what the reaction would be from the different radio stations. Radio people are very demanding. For example, some of the DJs quizzed the boys about having girlfriends and playing around all the time—partying, drinking, money, all the vices that come with the territory. The boys handled the off-color and inappropriate questions pretty well most of the time, but they were still a bit green when it came to the media. When things got out of hand, the Jive rep broke in and bailed them out.

Sometimes, if the DJs didn't get any dirt on the guys, they made things up right after we left. In the beginning, that was really distressing to the boys, given that they had worked so hard to keep up a clean-cut image. With experience, they found those situations easier to deal with.

I came to understand how celebrities could grow sick and tired of being hounded by photographers and journalists. Regardless of how hard you work to maintain a good image, inevitably the media will put their own spin on things to make it more interesting for their listeners or readers. They don't seem to consider the negative ramifications of what they say or write about the celebrities and their families.

Despite the overall success the boys had with the radio stations, their record was not added to many playlists. The only radio stations that played the boys' music were in Tampa and Orlando. They found little support across the rest of the country.

Some people said that the timing was not right for the type of pop music that the boys wanted to do. Others said that the large number of radio stations owned by corporate chains make it difficult to break new artists. Program directors for chain-owned stations often have very little discretion about what they can add to playlists that have been put together by corporate programmers.

It does not matter how hard you try, or how charming you might be, if the radio people don't have the power to add your record to their playlists—or if they simply don't believe in you and your style of music—you don't stand much of a chance.

We finished visiting the radio stations on our list, then traveled across the country to Seattle, where the boys performed at the Washington State Fair. Kevin got his shirtsleeve grabbed by a girl in the front row; security had to pull her off.

After that show, we jumped on a red-eye flight to Chicago for a Cubs game. From there we went to Cleveland, then Indianapolis and onward to Roanoke, Virginia, where the boys performed two shows. With each city we visited, the audience reaction was bigger and better than the last. Word was obviously spreading about the Backstreet Boys.

Once that leg of the tour was done, we flew to New York to meet with representatives for BMG. Along the way, we picked up some press people who wrote for the top European teen magazines. It was amazing how quickly the boys learned to manipulate those reporters.

The charming way that Alex had with female reporters constantly amazed me. It made me proud to see how well-mannered and professional he was with industry people. He took to that side of the business like a flower to rain.

AS THE TOUR CONTINUED, issues with management began to unfold. Johnny and Donna bickered over everything. Nothing was ever agreed upon without a heated discussion. Add to that Lou's insistence that we refer to him as the boys' producer, which meant that he put his two cents in at every turn, and you can see the dynamics of our little group. The saving grace in all of this was that most of the time, Lou agreed with Johnny because he was the one with the music business experience. Normally that would pretty much shut Donna up.

Our setup was a bit abnormal since Lou got his percentage from the management side and held part of the company, so he definitely had the power to influence management decisions; but on the other hand he was also recognized as a sixth Backstreet Boy, so he had the power to sway votes on either side. He told us to never refer to him as the boys'

The boys with Lou and Johnny

manager. He suggested that we call him their producer, the sixth member of the group, or "Big Poppa." We thought it odd at the time, but we didn't make an issue out of it because we naturally assumed that he knew what he was doing.

As if we needed more drama, Donna's daughter Marisa set her sights on Alex. Marisa was a very cute girl, not too far apart in age from my son. She, too, had grown up in a broken household, the result of her mother divorcing her father and marrying Johnny. Marisa was petite, with long, dirty-blonde hair and a huge smile that was identical to her mother's. In fact they looked very much alike.

Marisa lived with her father in the Northeast and visited her mother occasionally. When she and Alex met at rehearsals, I saw the look in my son's eyes right away. He liked what he saw, a fact that was apparently not lost on Donna, who seemed to have a special antenna that allowed her to detect people's weaknesses.

We started out as friends, but, with time, I saw some traits in her that I wasn't too fond of. She told me story after story about all the people we had come to know through the boys and she always had dirt on them. A few times, she even tried to play me against Nick's parents and vice versa. Her game would be to tell me that they had said something negative about me or Alex. If I responded, she would go running right back to them. What Donna did not know was that Bob Carter talked to me all the time. The two of us knew exactly what was going on.

Donna once told me that one of her goals was to take my son away from me. She was very jealous of my relationship with my son. This was a way for her to try and push us apart. That is when I decided to keep my relationship with Donna strictly professional. But as the relationship between Alex and Marisa grew, that became very difficult.

Alex filled me in on the details of Marisa's childhood. While he may not have really understood the situation very well, it answered a lot of questions for me. After Donna left her husband for Johnny, her family ties became very strained. When she tried to bring her children back into her life, there was an enormous amount of resentment in her family. It was all very sad.

I always regarded the closeness that Alex and I shared as something that began on the day that he was born and grew out of the fact that his father and I divorced. There were a lot of times when I felt like it was really Alex and me against the world. Even though we did have my parents for support, there were still situations that the two of us confronted on our own while out on the road. He and I could always talk honestly to one another about any subject. We had no secrets. Every time Alex tried to keep something from me, I always found out—and not through any digging on my part. Rather, because everyone who knew us, and knew how close we were, would come to me and tell me if they thought Alex was doing something weird.

My fears about people's "agendas" became heightened after conversations with some of the other parents regarding the boys' management. It seemed obvious to some of them as well that Donna was trying to manipulate the boys. I was not sure if this was due to some insecurity on her part, given that she was not as experienced as Johnny, or if this kind of behavior was just her way. Soon it mushroomed into a bigger issue.

The fact that Donna went out on the road with us for the duration of the United States tour did not help matters. That presented a lot of problems for everyone concerned. In addition to Donna's management style, I also had a problem with her attitude toward expenses. She gave parties for radio people at the drop of a hat and sometimes the boys were not even present to do any type of promotion. It irritated me, not only because it was wasteful, but because I knew that it would eventually end up on the boys' tab.

Perhaps the most disturbing thing of all was the way she dealt with other people. She embarrassed the boys and me on more than one occasion with her vulgar mouth and short temper. Unfortunately, I was not in any position to really say too much. It became necessary for the boys to speak up for themselves. They would talk to Johnny or Lou and sometimes they would pull me aside. I just tried to keep the peace since we all had to live together for the time being. That strategy worked for a while.

━━━━━━

IN THE END, AFTER OUR SKIRMISHES on the road with radio program directors, we lost the battle because there was no market for our sound. The single went nowhere in the United States. Europe was a different story. There "We've Got It Goin' On" shot up the charts like a rocket, taking everyone at Jive and BMG by surprise. They quickly put together a promotional schedule for England, Germany, Austria, Switzerland and the surrounding countries.

As much as we were excited about the possibility of traveling to Europe, Alex and I were apprehensive about leaving the country while the single was still being played. We quickly learned that when you turn your future over to a record company, you have to put your blind faith in their judgment.

Years later, we found out that this was the first time Jive Records had ever attempted to promote a pop group here or in Europe. With the help of BMG, they were given a crash course in Pop Star 101. BMG had plenty of experience with groups like ours throughout the world. It made us feel better to know that we were in good hands.

Our only saving grace on the Jive side of things at that time was a lady by the name of Nina Bueti. She was the head of all markets outside the United States. Nina had been involved with the Backstreet Boys since they broke in Europe. Nina was a tall, very Italian-looking, young woman who knew how to get what she wanted. She was extremely professional and knowledgeable in her work

Another hurdle to be overcome was the fact that both Jive and management were giving me a hard time about the added expense of tutors and guardians traveling abroad. I steadfastly held my ground for two reasons: I was not going to allow strangers to be solely responsible for Alex's welfare, and I had made a promise to my son that I would continue to make sure that his education was a priority.

It took days for that battle to be resolved. Finally, I said, "Look—either the tutor and I both go or Alex does not." Ultimately, we came to terms.

Having already assumed the roles of wardrobe mistress and makeup artist, I also took on the jobs of fan club organizer and meet-and-greet coordinator. Since we were all starting from scratch, everyone on the record company side was open to creative ideas. I worked very closely with the boys to find out their likes and dislikes with regards to their appearance whenever they were in public. My involvement with the project quickly morphed into quite an interesting career.

Eventually, we developed a system. Management in Orlando received requests from Jive or BMG for the lists of attendees. They were then passed down to me to carry out. That doesn't sound too difficult, but when you have to get five boys up and running at the same time for every meeting it can (and usually did) create some unique challenges.

That's when security came to the rescue. We would have meetings every night with the bodyguards to go over the schedule for the next day. They were responsible for setting the wakeup calls, as well as arranging for our transportation. It was also their responsibility to make sure that each boy was up and moving each morning. Alex was the only one who wasn't an issue. We usually shared a room and I knew where to find him.

Boys at Chateau Marmont Hotel

Alex graduates with his high school class

A beautiful shot of Alex looking very AJ

Alex's 24th birthday at Tutu Tangos

Johnny No-Name Charity Show

I'm interviewed by Connie Chung!

Alex with "NO-NAME" band at charity show at Hard Rock Live, Orlando

Alex with the RCA Victrola Dog

Johnny No-Name on New Year's Eve

Alex at Nicole's wedding

Alex and I go through letters of support he received while in rehab

OCTOBER 9, 1995, was the first day of the boys' European tour. When we arrived in England, after an eight-hour flight in coach, we were happy to find unusually warm weather, a balmy seventy degrees. The sunshine was a pleasant surprise since we had been forewarned as to just how terrible the weather in London could be.

A delegate from the record company greeted us and gave us a very warm welcome. When we reached our hotel, the first thing on our minds was a nice nap before dinner. Alex was so excited he had a hard time relaxing. He had slept most of the flight, a pattern that would continue until the present day. He got into that habit because he really dislikes flying, especially in small, private planes. Alex falls asleep as soon as the plane takes off and he doesn't wake up until he feels the bump of the landing.

That evening, we had a nice dinner with the Jive reps. Radio had been playing "We've Got It Goin' On" in Europe for a few weeks and it was doing very well. England is historically a very hard market to break into, but the boys were climbing the charts steadily. Having them there in the flesh to charm the right people might just push the single to the top of the charts.

Our first battle with the television stations came when they realized that the boys wanted to sing live. Apparently, live television performances are frowned upon there because of the technical difficulties involved. When the boys arrived for the first show, an argument ensued as to whether or not they would be allowed to sing live at the taping. Johnny got in the middle of that argument and, thankfully, we won. Everyone was thrilled with the outcome.

Not surprisingly, the boys won the hearts of the audiences and threw all of Europe into a complete tizzy. The effect that television and radio had on the teens there was amazing. It was so different from home. Obviously the kids had been waiting for something or someone new to arrive on the scene. Talk about being in the right place at the right time! When Lou heard the good news, he quickly joined us in London.

Despite the work involved, we managed to have some fun times during our stay in London. It was there that I met photographer Andre Csillag, a man who would become a lifelong friend and traveling companion. He did his first photo shoot with the boys on that trip and really made an impression on all of us. Andre was the only photographer the boys had met who actually tried to make it fun for them.

By then the boys had done so much publicity that they were beginning to get a bit buggy. Journalists asked the same questions so many times that I could have done the interviews in my sleep. I felt sorry for the boys—all they really wanted to do was sing and dance. They were full of energy for the television shows. They loved it. The more frenzied the fans became, the more the boys gave back.

The interviews and photo shoots, however, had become quite tedious for them. It was the same scenario every day: a conference room with drinks on the table, reporters armed with tape machines and an occasional camera, and the inevitable barrage of uninspired questions, asked over and over again.

That is why Andre was such a breath of fresh air for the boys. This small-framed, gray-haired proper English gentleman from Hungary gave us a completely new perspective on what a photo shoot should be about. He began by planning an outing for the boys. He wanted them to have fun seeing some sights around London.

We went onto a private boat and took a ride up the River Thames. We saw Big Ben and the London Bridge and all sorts of things along the way. The boys had on red, white and blue jackets. They looked great. The five of them hung from the boat at every angle, allowing Andre to get lots of fun pictures for the magazines.

Our intrepid photographer, Andre Csillag

DENISE MCLEAN

From England we went to Germany, where we encountered a whole new level of fan hysteria. The first show we did there is one I will never forget. I remember it so well because it was the first time the fans actually held up signs with either the boys' individual names or "Backstreet Boys" written on them. I saw one that had Alex's name on it, with a big, red heart and the words, "I love you." I cried when I saw the expression on Alex's face as he watched the fans wave the signs in unison with the music.

Later that night, a small incident occurred back at the hotel with my son. When we arrived, the lobby was filled with fans. Alex stopped to sign autographs and to pose for pictures with a member of another band. I stopped to speak to a few "regular" moms that I had become friendly with. When I looked for Alex to go upstairs, he was nowhere to be found. I started to worry and went up to our room. Still no sign of my son.

I called Randy and asked if he had seen Alex. He said no, but he immediately started looking for him. I was beginning to panic now. I was instructed to wait in the room until he called me back. On pins and needles, I waited, and waited, and waited. After a couple of hours, I could not stand it any longer and I called the other boys' rooms to see if he was there. No luck.

Now here was what was going through my mind: First time in a foreign country, fans everywhere in the hotel . . . naïve, young man on his own with an older artist from another group. What was I worried about? Plenty! After a few more hours, Randy finally called. He had found Alex in a room with the same artist he had been with in the lobby.

As it turned out, I did not have to chastise my son for making me worry. Randy did it for me. He impressed upon Alex the importance of communication between the artist and his security. Randy told us a tale of how one of the New Kids was almost kidnapped right after a concert. He managed to escape because he refused to get into a car with a driver he didn't recognize. That story made a big impression on my son and he never wandered off again.

On October 30, the boys got a real taste of "fan fever" when they went to one of the largest radio stations in Berlin. More than fifty girls greeted them upon their arrival. Since the studio was on the second floor, they could be seen through the glass windows by the girls downstairs, who sang the chorus of "Jam On."

Given the fact that they couldn't pronounce "jam" too well, it kind of dropped off at the end. It was very cute. The real fun began once the boys left the studio. By then the crowd had grown to over one hundred girls. They had been waiting so long that they were frantic by the time the boys came out of the studio. It was necessary for our security team (to which we had added a tall, blond drink of water from Kentucky named Keith) to clear a path.

Security didn't have much luck with those girls, for they were on a mission to get as close to the boys as was humanly possible, security be damned! They managed to push their way up the stairwell to the studio door. You can only imagine what happened from there. It was unbridled chaos. Security realized that they would have to find another way to get the boys into the van.

Luckily, Randy found an open window behind the stairwell. The boys were asked to climb through the open window into the van. It was the only conceivable way that they would make it out of the studio in one piece. Unfortunately, they still had to climb through the girls to get there. The moment that Nick and Howie came out of the studio, they were attacked.

In all the craziness, Nick tripped and proceeded to fall down the stairs. He lost his scarf and some girl grabbed it. Brian used some fancy basketball footwork in an effort to try and dodge the girls that were crowded

NINA BUETI

The boys with Lou and Johnny in London

around the doors. By the time the girls realized where he was, he had been shoved into the van by security.

At that point, everyone was piled into the van. Or so we thought. Suddenly, Nina, our Jive rep, realized that Howie and Alex were not with us. So she screamed for security to set out and find them. Apparently, some girls had trapped Howie, and Alex had gone back to help him. It was Howie's backpack that had gotten him into trouble. It weighed like two tons. To this day I still don't know exactly what he carried in it.

Johnny with Brian, AJ and Kevin in London

Certainly whatever it contained it was not the best thing to be dragging around when you were trying to make a quick getaway through an open window! The only casualties of the day were Nick's scarf and Brian's hat. It was both a good (and bad) experience for the boys. At the very least, it gave them a glimpse of the future.

———

WE SPENT THE REMAINDER OF 1995 promoting the single throughout the United Kingdom and Europe. Our bus was a seated bus, not a sleeper bus, which meant that we had to learn to sleep sitting up. As we did in the States, we went from radio station to radio station. The boys sang a cappella every chance they got.

During that time, the fan count in each city and at each hotel increased twofold. One of the really high points occurred at the beginning of the trip and helped the boys' careers immensely. We found out a day or so after arriving in London that the current reigning boy band in Europe, a group called Take That, had just announced that they were breaking up so that some members of the group could pursue solo careers. In a statement to the press, they proclaimed that the Backstreet

Boys were the only group that could take their place. That act of generosity was a major coup for the boys.

Typically, when we pulled up at our hotel there would be twenty girls waiting to greet the boys. Within hours that number would more than double. As time passed, the fan phenomenon grew. The amount of time the girls spent following the boys was an ongoing topic of conversation among the boys, security and myself. The only logical explanation we could come up with was that apparently there were a lot of rich moms and dads who enjoyed living vicariously through their children. They took great pleasure in enabling their kids to trek across the country in the family Mercedes.

There were girls in the lobby, girls in the stairwells. Girls running up and down the hallways in desperate search of the boys. Oftentimes girls would reserve rooms in the same hotel as the boys. The girls who couldn't afford to do that camped out in the lobby. Sometimes they would even

ANDRE CSILLAG

Alex comes alive on stage

sleep outside the front of the hotels. Oddly enough, this did not seem to bother the hotel management.

Girls were a usual occurrence in the lobby around the clock. Sometimes the boys paired off and took nightly trips to the lobby to say hi, sign autographs and pose for pictures. They made themselves accessible to their fans. That type of behavior played a big role in the boys' popularity and the fans' loyalty. To this day, some of those fans still wait in lobbies around the world to give the boys a wave hello.

A silly incident occurred in Cologne when Alex and I foolishly went out for a few hours of shopping. Most of the malls in Germany were not enclosed and the boutiques are very small and quaint. One thing that Alex and I always had in common was shopping. We liked to window shop for hours and dream about what we might be able to afford someday should he become famous.

Since Alex's grandmother was born in Germany, he thought it would be nice to buy her something that he could take back on the plane with him. She had always loved crystal figurines and pewter statues, so we looked for them wherever we went.

Since the local kids were still in school, we did not think we would have a problem with fans. However, when you shop, time can fly by. We stopped in several stores and looked at clothes, crystal for grandma and the like.

While we were in one of the stores, a couple of girls walked by and recognized Alex. I did not think that would be a problem, but as we walked out of the store, I noticed that the girls were not far behind us talking wildly on their cell phones. It started out with two, then it went to four—and then ten. Soon twenty-five girls appeared from nowhere.

We ducked into a burger place and sat down to have a quick meal, but we were quickly surrounded by an army of young girls, both inside the restaurant and out. They didn't say anything at first. They simply stared. Then it began. They started calling out his name and asking for autographs.

I finally just stood up and said, "Look, can you please just let us eat—and then he will gladly take pictures and sign anything you want, OK?"

That seemed to calm them down. But then, after a few minutes, the girls seemed to buzz with subdued chatter. I knew that couldn't be good.

"I think we should make a run for it," I whispered into Alex's ear.

We both pretended we were heading for the restrooms, then, with the help of the restaurant staff, we quickly slipped out the back door. As we ran down the street hailing a taxi, we saw a small group of fans fall in behind us and do the same.

Once we got a taxi and drove off, I saw that we were being followed by three taxis. I directed the driver to go to the nearest hotel and stop. I did not want him to go to our real hotel for obvious reasons. We went into the hotel, called Randy, and asked him to rescue us. Even though Alex seemed to enjoy the excitement of it all, he later told me that he had been a bit nervous in the burger place. He said he was glad that I had been there for him.

By the end of 1995, the Backstreet Boys had reached a new level in their career. Everywhere they went in Europe, the fans received them warmly. The other groups seemed to be a bit afraid of the new "U.S. Invasion." By that time, the boys had achieved a measure of success that affected them both positively and negatively. On the positive side, their stage performance was tighter and they had built up a considerable fan base throughout Europe.

On the negative side, they had become big-headed when it came to the success they had achieved. I think that way of thinking rubbed off on them from the other boy bands they had encountered. Oftentimes those groups came from very small countries. Once they achieved the slightest bit of success they were quite happy to sit back and ride the wave. They were not of the mindset that worldwide success was attainable.

Journal Entry, December 12, 1995: *My son has definitely gone through some heavy-duty changes over these past years. Not all for the better, I'm afraid. The one major factor in my son's metamorphosis has been the influence of outside people coming into his life. Particularly, management and Lou. Lou has tried to be a positive influence on Alex but unfortunately he has spoiled him too much. He seems to suffer from the same personality flaw as Nick, meaning he expects things now and does not wait to be asked. I have tried to keep him grounded but for all of my love and sacrifice of time I get only sarcasm in return. Now I realize he is a teenager and this sort of behavior comes with the territory, but in his case it is kind of out of proportion. Alex has always been one to learn things the hard way, even though he is smart and usually ends up making the correct decision in the end. He just takes a very long and winding path to get there.*

By the time the boys left Germany at the beginning of 1996 it had become increasingly difficult for them to get out of the hotel and do normal everyday things. The realization that they were losing their anonymity began to set in. Alex discovered that he could no longer escape to McDonald's, one of his favorite refuges. Girls followed him in droves.

If he asked them to allow him to finish his meal, they would simply stand there and stare at him until he was done. Then they would pounce on him the minute that last French fry was gone. He took it in stride and remained polite and friendly.

═══════

FROM GERMANY, the boys went to Stockholm, Sweden, to continue work on their album with Denniz PoP. We arrived at the airport with fans waiting to take pictures and receive autographs. It took three cars to get all of us, including our twenty-four bags of luggage, to the hotel. The boys had no clue about how to travel light.

When we arrived at the hotel, there were about fifty or so fans waiting. After quickly dropping off the bags at the quaint little hotel (with no luggage carts or bellman and an elevator that only went up to the fifth of six floors), we grabbed the wardrobe and headed out to the local teen club where the boys were scheduled to perform.

Jive's Swedish record division had done only a small amount of publicizing, so we really didn't expect a huge turnout. But about two hundred girls showed up and they were screaming their heads off most of the time. By the time we returned to the hotel, the number of fans there was on the rise.

Apparently, Alex and some of the other boys played games with some of the fans while going back and forth from the recording studio to the hotel—and the girls were not very happy about that. By that, I mean they went into the lobby and took a few choice picks with them back upstairs. That left the remaining girls most unhappy.

When I asked Alex about it, he insisted that they just talked to the girls, with no funny stuff going on. But the fans did not see it that way. Soon after that we started getting hate mail. One of the letters was pretty funny. It was an unflattering character sketch of the five boys that depicted Nick with four girls behind him on leashes and Alex with a nose long enough to drag on the ground. Whatever really happened, I knew that my son could not get into too much trouble since he had to return to my room to sleep. And he always did.

All of the other boys shared rooms at that time. One night our room was next door to Howie and Kevin. We heard girls giggling most of the evening. Then, suddenly, we heard a different sound, like many more girls screaming, so we went to investigate and discovered that Howie had opened the window that faced the street where the fans were standing outside. As usual, he brought out his video camera and encouraged the fans to sing, scream and whatever else he could think of. Finally, we got him to send the girls home so that everyone could get some sleep.

That particular trip was eventful for me because it was the first time I was asked to do a television interview. They asked me a lot of questions about what it was like to travel with Alex and an up-and-coming band. I was very proud and hoped that I said all the right things.

Once the recording session wrapped, we went out on the road again to Cologne, Dortmund and Mulin. Along the way, things began to get more out of hand with the fans. They became more aggressive at each hotel. One of the things I could not understand was the attitude of the girls' parents. It was like the mothers were living vicariously through their daughters. They were in the lobby morning, noon and night. No matter what hour we got in, they were waiting. Didn't those people have other lives and children and husbands to contend with?

It baffled me as to why those mothers would condone and encourage such behavior in their teenage daughters. My German friend, Doris Schulte, once told me that it was a very high honor in Germany for a parent to have their daughter become pregnant by a pop star. They think the family will be set for life and will never have to work again.

Once I heard that, I went directly to Nina and told her that the game the boys were playing had to stop. She agreed and held a meeting with them. Nina tried to make the boys understand that that kind of bad publicity, before they were even a big name, could end all of their careers. Once they heard that, they became a bit more level-headed, for a while anyway.

Halloween Day in Germany was a day from hell. First, we had to reserve seats on an early morning flight to make a date in Hamburg. That was not in the cards. The Berlin airport was fogged in and the flight was delayed for hours. Finally, at 12:30 P.M. we left on a chartered prop plane. None of us were too happy about that, especially in the fog.

From the time we left the hotel that morning, Kevin had complained of stomach pains and diarrhea. It sounded a bit like indigestion to me, so I gave him some antacid and it seemed to make him feel better. Even so, Nina called ahead to the Jive rep and asked him to have a doctor waiting when we got to our hotel in Hamburg.

On the airplane, Nick asked Kevin if he had ever had appendicitis. We all just laughed and said come on, it was probably just something he ate. Kevin was always willing to experiment with different types of food, so it did not seem alarming for him to be a bit under the weather.

Once we arrived at the hotel, we all went to our rooms, while the doctor followed Kevin upstairs to examine him. What a shock we received when we got back downstairs and learned that Kevin had been taken to the hospital. The doctor suspected that he might have appendicitis—and he was right!

Needless to say, we were all very upset. The next day, Lou caught a flight to join us, but by then everything was fine. Kevin rested comfortably in the hospital after his surgery and the other boys breathed easier that it had been taken care of so quickly. The only downside was that a reporter sneaked into Kevin's room and took a rather unflattering picture of him in his hospital gown. The picture ended up in every newspaper across the continent.

By the time we had to move on to our next destination in Munich, Lou had arrived and stayed with Kevin in Hamburg. Randy spoke to Johnny about hiring more bodyguards for the boys. Randy knew of a couple of companies that hired out large guys for just that type of work. The number of fans was growing and we needed enough manpower to protect the boys. To this day, I believe that someone at Jive was letting the girls know where we would be staying during our tour. The fans just knew too much, too fast. It was beginning to get really scary.

As Kevin took a few more days off to heal, we proceeded with interviews and shows in Munich. While there, we all took a day off to visit Dachau, the former Nazi concentration camp located outside the city. It was a very humbling and memorable experience. I felt blessed to be able to experience something like that with Alex.

By the next day, Kevin was on his way to meet us in Frankfurt, where the boys were scheduled to perform in their first arena and then later sign autographs at a large electronics store. They were eager to check out the arena in advance, so we set out early to try and fit everything in. There was another pretty popular boy band performing that same night. All of the boys wanted to find out what the competition would be like. They were totally psyched at the thought of blowing those other guys away.

Our final day in Germany found me in a reflective mood. I could not help but think about the effect that this lifestyle has on a family. In Brian's case, his mom and dad had to deal with separation from their son very suddenly when he was only eighteen years old. He was still in school and looking forward to his prom, dating, getting a job. You know, all of the normal things that eighteen-year-olds do. Well, that was not in the cards. His life changed when he became a Backstreet Boy. The way Brian's mom, Jackie, tells it, Brian left home a boy and returned a man.

After what was deemed a smashing success in Germany, we were ready to head home. All of us missed good ole home cooking and never-ending refills of coffee and soda (not one of the perks of Europe). The German promoter threw us a lavish party after the show. To end the trip right, Nina and I smuggled some champagne back from the party to our hotel. After waiting about an hour for the boys to get snuggled in for the night, we ran through the hall like commandos, banging on each boy's door until he opened it. Then we treated each boy to a champagne shower. After all, moms and record company reps need stress relief, too!

After several heady months in Europe, we returned to the U.S. What a difference! The Backstreet Boys were total unknowns in the United States. Even Mom and Dad's constant bragging to family, friends and anyone who was listening did not help. We dubbed the U.S.A. "NFL"— No Fan Land.

CHAPTER SEVEN

Fan Frenzy

THE SUCCESSFUL RELEASE of the Backstreet Boys' first album in Europe got them signed as an opening act for a well-established European pop star. Since they would be performing for a longer period of time on stage now, that meant they had to lengthen and tighten up their show. However, one pesky little thing kept popping up and getting in the way of their learning the new material: daily meetings with Big Poppa to straighten out management problems. Trouble had been brewing for months.

Every time Donna was out on the road with the boys, ugly incidents occurred. Her battles with record company reps had become famous. She had arguments with the boys over press issues because she made decisions without consulting them. Whenever her authority was called into question, she responded by throwing a tantrum, sometimes in public. Donna's use of foul language in front of the boys and members of the press was a constant embarrassment. She was extremely hot-tempered and unpredictable. We never knew when or where she might blow up.

In addition to everything else, Donna and I had very different ideas when it came to raising children and that created tension between us. It was almost as if she felt she had the right to stick her nose into every facet of each boy's life and career. When it came to Alex, I felt that she should keep her advice to herself. Unfortunately, he was still infatuated with her daughter and that didn't leave me too much leverage, a situation that only widened the gap between my son and me. That was due in part to his being a teenager, but it was aided by Donna, who pulled him away whenever she could.

I sometimes found my son having secret conversations with Donna in her hotel room while I was working. When Alex and I tried to have discussions about Marisa, or his attitude, I heard things come out of his mouth that I knew were direct quotes from Donna. Things like, "It's my life and I am almost eighteen, so I can do what I want."

Donna did her best to promote the relationship between her daughter and Alex. Even the other boys saw what was happening and did not approve. It was clearly not just me being a typical, overprotective, paranoid mom. It was a real problem.

======

FINALLY, THE GROUP CAME TOGETHER at Lou's house to review what could be done about several pressing issues. Only the five boys and Lou were present. From what I was later told, several valid points were brought up and incidents were cited about Donna's behavior on the road. For example, Alex told me that she had bought him drinks when they were in hotel bars and tried to get the other boys to join them.

The final straw occurred during an important dinner on the West Coast. Donna and several Jive reps apparently had a bit too much to drink. They started singing and got very loud and obnoxious at the dinner table in front of the guests, which included several radio personalities. The boys were horribly embarrassed.

After everyone at the meeting had his say, they reached a consensus: Donna would have to be fired. They decided to call a second meeting, to which Johnny and Donna would be invited, but before that happened Johnny requested a formal business meeting with Lou and the boys so that he could introduce them to some potential employees. They decided to use Johnny's meeting as a forum for discussing Donna's future. Lou was much better at doing things kind of sideways like that. He never wanted to look like the bad guy. Having Johnny call the meeting played into Big Poppa's hand.

A few days later, the meeting took place in Lou's office, with everyone present, including myself. Lou brought someone to the meeting to take minutes so that everything would be properly recorded. That was a first for him. The meeting began on a good note as Johnny explained why he wanted to hire some new people to help with the workload. In fact, it seemed to play right into the plan of phasing Donna out.

As the meeting progressed, Donna became more defensive as each boy told of how he felt she had acted unprofessionally and had invariably wound up embarrassing him. With each testimony, Donna's eyes flared. She was boiling! Finally, the last incident was cited. It had something to do with her and a Jive rep sneaking off before a show to have some drinks. Several people saw her, including one of the other boys' parents.

At that point, Donna jumped out of her chair and stormed out of the room, shouting a few choice words as she left. We sat there in shock for a minute, then just continued with our meeting. Suddenly, there was a knock at the door. Nicole poked her head in with a look of astonishment on her face.

"What happened?" she asked.

"Donna just quit," someone said.

"Donna went into her office and started tearing the boys' pictures off the walls—I didn't know what to think," Nicole said. "Then she started throwing papers all around the room. When she finished with that, she yelled out that she was quitting—and she bolted out of the office."

We asked Nicole to get some help and start cleaning up Donna's office. By that time, Big Poppa was fuming over the incident. To make it official for the minutes, the boys all voted unanimously to let Donna go and it was done. I felt a great sense of relief. Now I could try to salvage some shred of relationship with my son without fear of Donna countering me at every turn.

With all of that behind them, the boys focused their attentions on getting ready for the new tour. That meant we needed a larger and better-equipped rehearsal space. Once again, we turned to Lou for help. Unfortunately, his solution merely moved the boys from one bad situation to another.

Lou put them in a warehouse that had been used to store his airship equipment. However, the word warehouse does not in any way describe that steam box of a room. It had no windows, no air conditioning or ceiling fans. To circulate air, they opened the door and put a large fan there, but that merely moved the hot steamy air from one side of the room to the other.

The noise generated by the huge blades made it nearly impossible to think. Now add to that troublesome situation sound equipment generating its own heat, five boys dancing, one manager, one soundman, a choreographer and who knew who else might show up. That is where the Backstreet Boys rehearsed for the next two years!

Yet despite those sometimes dismal conditions, the boys kept going hour after hour. They guzzled down water. They wiped their brows and continued to learn each dance step until it was pure perfection. Fatima Robinson, the choreographer, did not make it easy for them. She was tireless and relentless when it came to her work. She had worked with stars like Michael Jackson and she was on her way to becoming very well known in Los Angeles dance circles. The boys were grateful to have her working with them. They felt that Fatima's creative dance moves gave them an edge.

While the rehearsals were in full swing, Jive decided to do a video shoot, so the boys took a break for a week to do that and then got ready for another trip to the United Kingdom. That only left us a couple of days at home to regroup. I kept busy washing clothes and making sure Alex had his schoolwork ready to go. He was excited about completing high school.

Marisa spent a lot of time at our house during that time. She had apparently had a falling out with her mother and was trying to decide whether to stay in Florida or return to Boston to live with her father. Alex wanted her to stay, but he realized that she had to make some important decisions about her future. Marisa confided in me about her growing up years and I felt a bit sorry for her. She was desperately looking for a home and a family to belong to. She felt misplaced and unloved.

To this day I have a soft spot in my heart for her. When her mother left her father for another man, she felt totally abandoned. Apparently the time she spent with her mother was not always happy. Making matters worse at home was the fact that Donna was no longer a part of the boys' career. That was a lot for a young girl to deal with.

I tried to help her as much as I could, but I also had Alex to think about. The reality was that I truly felt that the last thing he needed at that point in his life was a girlfriend with so much baggage. It was a hard place for me to be in, given that I had so much sympathy for Marisa.

At that point, it was time to leave for London. Marisa still had not made up her mind about what she was going to do, so Alex was preoccupied when we left. However, by the time we arrived in London, he was able to focus on his work.

The tour was sponsored by a popular television show called *Smash Hits* that was similar to our *American Bandstand*. They produced the tour every year to showcase up-and-coming groups, as well as to help the more established ones. The only requirement was that the bands had to have placed high on the charts to be eligible. That was no problem for our boys, but trouble arose when a few of the more popular groups dropped out of the tour before we even got there. As a result, the tour was put on hold. That left some of the groups, including ours, out on a limb.

The record company helped out by arranging for the boys to go out as an opening act for a popular British group named PJ and Duncan. The tour was relatively short, so we hoped the *Smash Hits* tour would be rescheduled quickly. To no one's surprise, the Backstreet Boys grabbed the hearts of the audience from song one. The girls screamed, cried and sang along with every word. It soon became obvious to the headliners that there were just as many signs for the Backstreet Boys in the audience as for PJ and Duncan. The Backstreet Boys also intruded on PJ and Duncan's merchandise sales and that caused some problems.

The *Smash Hits* tour was rescheduled to begin right after the first leg of the PJ and Duncan tour ended. That worked out well for Backstreet since that allowed them to jump off the PJ and Duncan tour, do *Smash Hits*, then jump back onto the tour. It gave them great coverage in the British market.

ANDRE CSILLAG

On the European tour

The other groups that were signed up for the *Smash Hits* tour made telephone calls to radio stations and record companies in an effort to have the tour postponed once again, but by then it was too late. The damage the boys had done to the other groups was irreversible in the eyes of the fans.

By the time the *Smash Hits* tour began, our boys were the favorite newcomers. Their single was climbing the charts with lightening speed. The only question that remained was whether our group would receive the "Best New Group" award that was presented at the end of each tour.

While the boys attended rehearsals for the awards show, I went shopping to purchase a new wardrobe for them. Rehearsals for the show went well, but the groups that only lip-synced to pre-recorded music did not bother to show up. Once the sound check was completed, the boys piled into the bus for a quick dinner at the local McDonald's. That night Alex was so excited that he could not sleep.

Since there were not enough tickets available for everyone in our group to see the show live, we watched it on television at the hotel. The shopping spree was worth it. The boys looked great in the sexy, black suits I picked out for them, but that was not the way they originally planned to take the stage. They meant to wear black trench coats over their dress suits, but moments before they were scheduled to take the stage, another group walked past them wearing the same coats. They quickly discarded the coats. When they went out on stage, they looked fantastic. To no one's surprise in our group, the Backstreet Boys were given the award for "Best New Group of 1995."

Alex told me later that everyone came up to them and congratulated them on their win. After the show, the boys came by the hotel to get me and we all went to a local nightclub to celebrate. When we realized that the nightclub that we had chosen was filled with transvestites in full garb, we quickly called it a night.

═══════

OUR NEXT STOP WAS AMSTERDAM, Holland. Even though it was very cold, we wanted to walk around the city our first night there so that we could see the sights. That was difficult since the fans had been alerted and were waiting for us at our hotel. Security told me that it was not unusual for record companies to leak information about promotional tours to the radio stations, so that there would be a buzz about the group when they arrived. I am sure that practice didn't hurt record sales either.

We made our way through Brussels, then joined back up with the PJ and Duncan tour. Again, we found ourselves in the middle of a controversy. Out of the blue, the tour management told us that we were no longer allowed to sell merchandise. I was so angry. Selling merchandise was a good way to spread our name and to make a little extra cash for fun stuff on the road. I found a way around that with the help of some locals by cutting a deal with outside vendors to sell Backstreet merchandise outside each venue. Even bootleggers could work those areas without fear of the police.

At around that time, we learned that the single was not climbing the charts in England the way we had expected. Johnny felt that sales had been hurt by Jive's decision to delay the record's release. The only thing that we could figure was that the record company was reluctant to make enemies of the other groups and decided to put our record on a slow track. Of course, we could not prove that. We just had to live with it and let it run its course. In the end, fan support prevailed and the boys came out on top.

That experience did influence how we dealt with Jive's office in England. We decided to make our own decisions about doing interviews and making personal appearances. We scrutinized every request to make sure that it would benefit the boys more than it would Jive. If it was not a high-end magazine, television show or radio program that would help record sales, we would not do it. Since the record company had relationships with writers from the lowest gossip sheets to the highest-end global magazines, our decision did not make them happy.

Our relationship with Jive was strained to say the least. We constantly got the smallest and shabbiest dressing rooms. Poor Johnny was always fighting with someone about something. But the boys persevered. They always did their best to wow the fans and win over the audience.

While on tour, we traveled to Zurich. I must say, there is only one way to describe that beautiful city—expensive! When we arrived at the hotel, we were starved. Since the boys had to change and start interviews almost immediately, there was no time to really sit down and eat or order room service.

That meant Johnny and I had to find a quick way to feed them. The hotel buffet was outrageously expensive, so we decided to make a McDonald's run, if we could find one. The saving grace of every city in the world that we visited was the availability of our very own hometown Mickey D's. Off we went, while the record company rep ran the interview session with the boys.

We hailed a taxi and tried desperately to explain to the driver what we were looking for. Just our luck we found the only taxi driver in Zurich who did not eat fast food. He called his dispatcher and was told, after several minutes of discussion, where the restaurant was located. Finally we were on our way, or so we thought.

After a long ride in the country, which was breathtaking by the way, we finally reached our destination. Once inside, we realized that this had not been the best alternative plan, since the prices seemed to be the same as at the hotel. A so-called "value" meal was almost $10. We had no choice but to purchase the food and head back to the hotel in our $70 taxi. When we reached the hotel, we discovered that Jive had already sent out for food. Johnny and I just looked at each other and laughed. What else could we do?

On December 24 we arrived in Dusseldorf, Germany, at the estate of Mr. Wullenkemper, an old friend of Lou's, who had helped Lou start up his airship business in the United States. Of the several businesses he ran, the airship company was the largest of its kind in Europe. Mr. Wullenkemper had known Lou since he was very young. After Lou's father passed away, he became the father figure in Lou's life. Mr. Wullenkemper taught him about the business and helped him build up financing over the years. He taught us a lot about the European mindset.

One thing we learned was how Europeans have very open minds when it comes to things we Americans have hang-ups about. For example, European magazines actually encourage healthy sexual behavior among teens. From what I learned through conversations with parents, the thinking was that if sex was not kept from children like a big taboo they wouldn't be so inclined to experiment as much. It is not necessarily our way of thinking, but, hey, whatever works.

Mr. Wullenkemper was a superb host who made us all feel very much at home. We were put up in a local hotel that was actually a castle. It was very cool and Alex went exploring right away. After we dressed for dinner, we returned to find a table of goodies waiting for us at Mr. Wullenkemper's house. He had chocolate Santas and cookies everywhere. There were even presents for us.

Mr. Wullenkemper was destined to become a very positive influence on the boys' career. He was the person who ultimately introduced them to the most influential promoter in Germany, a man who pushed the boys' visibility to its highest level. That trip proved the old adage: "It's not what you know, but who you know that counts."

As the tour progressed, I began to see both positive and negative effects on the boys. Their stage performance improved, and they built a large fan base in England and Germany—both major markets. But on the negative side, conflicts began to arise within the group. At the time,

Alex turns on the charm in Germany

I felt that they were headed on a course to self-destruction unless some-one talked some sense into them.

The root of the problem, besides the obvious age differences, was that some of the boys had gained just enough knowledge about the business to be dangerous to the rest. Insecurity played a big factor in that. Lou helped them to achieve some of their goals, but he was also a negative influence. He lived a life full of excess and he taught the boys to become comfortable in that lifestyle.

The impact on Alex was a hard thing for me to deal with. My son deserves all he has and he has worked very hard to get it, but I tried whenever I got the chance to keep him grounded as best as I could. That is very difficult when you have someone pulling your only child into a world of fantasy that every teenager dreams of.

Big Poppa spoiled the boys like a rich uncle who comes to visit and then leaves the parent to cope with the damage. It is not really fair. But what could I do? You should never squash your children's dreams, no matter how fantastic they seem to you.

Journal Entry, December 5, 1996: *Nick has really changed in my opinion over the past years. Unfortunately not always for the better. He started out only 12 years old as opposed to Kevin who was 21. The age difference between the two along with some family pressures and trouble with management has really taken a toll on this child. He is going through his 'spoiled stage' as I call it.*

Howie (aka Sweet D.) is definitely the most timid of the group. He pretty much goes with the flow of any situation. He hates conflict and has said that time and time again. He maintains he is a lover not a fighter. I also see him as the most level-headed of the fellas. He trusts his family's judgment and really listens to them when they give him advice. I believe that Howie has grown up to be a pretty stable young man and hopefully he will hold on to his lovable style.

Kevin—the father figure of the group. But I feel that this role has only been cast upon him due to his age. I don't think that deep inside he wants the responsibility to fall on his shoulders. He is really quite fragile and I hope he can withstand the long-term success of this group. Kevin also tries to learn about the business as much as he can. That is smart.

AJ—he is the hardest for me to write about since he is my only child and I want to be objective in my words. When he says things to me like "I can't stand you!" and lies to my face it hurts me deeply. And what makes it worse is that I know in my heart that some of the things coming out of his mouth are thoughts put into his head by other people who want to control him and separate us. Every time I try to give him some advice he chooses to believe other people above me. I guess he will learn eventually that his family members are really the only ones he can trust forever. Everyone else just comes and goes.

———

CHRISTMAS DAY WE WERE BACK ON THE ROAD. This time we went on tour with a popular group from Holland called Caught In The Act. They were nice guys who did not sing live and the boys showed them up every time. The way Johnny figured it, the boys soon would scare off all the other groups and would then be the headliners. No group would be willing to share their audiences with the boys, for fear of losing them.

We shared a large sleeper bus with one of the opening acts called Just Friends. They were a bit too sugary-pop for my taste, but nice enough to have as bunkmates. The shows continued to go well and merchandise sales picked up quite a bit.

Our biggest problems on the road always seemed to center on the female fans. They were everywhere. We couldn't sleep sometimes for hearing them run up and down the halls all night. My friend Doris and her daughter became big fans of the boys. She told me that our bus drivers and the people who work at the record company had informants among the fans that they pass information to about our schedules.

Originally I guess it was supposed to help the boys with exposure, but it went to extremes. The fans also spent money on all kinds of presents for the boys. Everywhere we went, I had to carry armloads of gifts that I was asked to pass on to the boys. The way I looked at it was that once I gave the fans' gifts to the boys, I upheld my promise to them. What the boys did with the gifts was beyond my control.

Sometimes I felt bad for some of the fans since they seemed to have spent their last Deutchmark on the gifts. I kept most of the ones for Alex. He was flattered that the girls would go to all that trouble to send him gifts. Sometimes the gifts were way over the top—gold chains, earrings, candy, hand-made blankets. It was crazy really. I was always worried that the kids wouldn't have enough money left to buy the album.

Besides the female fans, one of the things that fascinated me about Europe was the way that the music industry differed from its American counterpart. Some of the pop bands there are owned by their management and given salaries. In America, the management just makes a percentage of whatever the group brings in and they can be fired, whereas in Europe it is the other way around.

I befriended a member of a group we traveled with that had some unique problems. Matthias Fuchs and his group were cast members of a well-known German television soap opera that had a loyal teen following. Because of their popularity, a record company signed them and put them out on the road when the soap was not in production.

The only problem was that the television show hired them as actors, not singers. Their sound could be fixed on the television show to insure that they always sounded great, but when they performed live they sometimes had a difficult time on stage. That put a big strain on the members of the group, especially my friend Matthias. He had always dreamed of becoming a pop star. In fact, he had auditioned for his part as a way to get his foot in the door of the music business. Matthias did not get along well with the other members of the group and usually kept to himself when they were not performing.

Because he was under a restrictive contract, he felt trapped by his own career. Staying in the group was his only choice because, if he left, he would have to go into the army for two years. In Germany, once a boy turns eighteen if he is not in a university or working full time he does mandatory army service for two years.

ANDRE CSILLAG

Matthias was not army material, so he stayed with the group until he could find a way out. That opportunity came a short while later, when the group finally broke up and was canceled from the soap. He was relieved.

The Backstreet Boys' final German show took place in a huge warehouse. I stood at the rear of the building, near the doors, where I worked as a merchandise vendor.

Meeting Elton John in Germany

Everything was fine until they opened the doors to let the parents come inside and pick up their kids. It was bitter cold outside and the temperature quickly dropped at my workstation. I was about to freeze my little bum off, when two fathers took pity on me and came to my rescue. They bought me hot coffee and kept the refills coming until they picked up their children.

We finished our European tour on New Year's Eve. After the show, we went to a nightclub, where Alex and Kevin got behind the DJ booth and mixed the music. It was good to see the boys take advantage of some well-deserved downtime before our early morning call to the airport. The promoter gave a party at the same club, but the building had so many levels in it that we were able to have our own floor with just a few fans and record company people.

We all slept well that night as we dreamt of our trip home.

WHEN WE RETURNED TO THE STATES in January 1996, I sought the advice of my psychic, Matthew. I felt that the New Year would somehow be one of both closure and new beginnings for Alex and me. Matthew confirmed my suspicions with a reading. He told me to keep my journals because they would come in handy later on down the road. He also warned me that my trials and tribulations with my son and two women were not yet over. By that, he meant Donna and her daughter.

Boy, was he right on target with that one! Soon after we got back, Donna told me that her daughter had gone back to Boston to live with her father because she was pregnant and distraught over her situation. She tried to blame my son, which would have been the best long-distance trick of all time, since we had both been out of the country for months. Alex and I had a long talk and agreed that it was probably for the best that Marisa went back to her father and continued school there while she got her life on track. The pregnancy scare caused a rift among the boys, but it was quickly squashed when the situation was explained to them.

ON JANUARY 9, Alex's eighteenth birthday, the boys left for South Beach to film their third video. In its infinite wisdom, Jive had decided that the second single that they planned to release was not right. That made it necessary to shoot a different video for another song that would be released first.

The Donna situation was still hovering above the boys since she kept trying to worm her way back into the fold. Lou decided to have a meeting. He told the boys that they didn't have to show up, only Kevin needed

ADOLPH FERNANDEZ

My brother Bill, Alex and me

to be there as a representative on their behalf. I didn't really think that was right. It turned out to be the beginning of a trend that would lead down a bad path with Big Poppa. Since all of us still had an enormous amount of trust in Lou's judgment, we believed that he was just trying to keep peace and move the boys' careers forward.

Once the boys finished the video, there was time to celebrate some birthdays. Nick and Alex were both born in January, so Lou decided to throw them a big party at his house, complete with catered food and a DJ. Lou even invited some members of the press to take pictures of the boys celebrating.

The evening went along fine, until Donna showed up unannounced. Soon after that, Marisa arrived. We all thought she had left town. She informed everyone that she could not get a flight out. How convenient! The boys were very upset about it but did not want to disrupt the festivities.

Alex showed up two hours late with Kevin, who had taken him shopping. Alex should have received his driver's license by then, since the legal age in Florida is sixteen, but he had failed his driver's test twice and still had to be driven around.

There always seemed to be some kind of drama surrounding what should have been happy times for those boys. I guess since they weren't faced with the normal challenges of everyday life, some higher being had decided to put other obstacles in front of them. It was at times like these that I sometimes wished Alex had chosen to be a fireman.

I tried to lighten the mood of the party by getting behind them when they were about to blow out the candles on their cake. As they bent down, I pushed their faces into the icing and ran away. That left poor Howie who was standing behind me to take the blame. After that, all hell broke loose. Cake flew everywhere and my son was first to be thrown into the unheated pool.

Alex had on a sweater and jeans that were too large for him. By the time we pulled him out of the water, his sleeves were dragging the ground. Next, Nick went into the pool, soon to be followed by Alex a second time since he was drenched already. It turned out to be a lot of laughs, despite those who were there to muddy the water.

That week another meeting about Donna was held. What I thought was going to be an end to the madness with Donna soon became a larger nightmare than before. Apparently, Donna had been having conversations with Lou and Johnny behind our backs and somehow had managed to change everyone's mind about firing her.

Out of the blue, Lou stated that we did not have a clear-cut case against Donna. He said that he was going to reinstate her but planned to write up a formal complaint against her by the boys that would be kept in her personnel file.

All of this seemed very odd to me, given that in the last meeting Donna had voluntarily quit. Come to find out, the way the contracts were written, the only way to get rid of her would be for Johnny to buy her out as partner, which meant that Lou would somehow lose money due to his role in the management company.

So the bottom line was that the boys did not have the right to fire just one manager unless the others paid the price. They were not willing to do that, so that meant we were stuck with Donna. It all seemed turned around to me. I thought management worked for the boys, but it was beginning to look like it was the other way around.

It was also brought up at the meeting that since Alex had been dating Donna's daughter he could not voice an opinion. To this day I really don't understand what that had to do with anything. They all seemed afraid of Donna for some reason. The only conclusion I could reach was that Donna either had some incriminating evidence on Johnny or Lou, or she had gone to an attorney and had grounds for a lawsuit. Either way, it was a twisted system. There was some underlying truth that would eventually have to come out. Or so I hoped.

———

WHEN I LEARNED THAT THE BOYS were going to Los Angeles for some television appearances, I planned a bit of downtime for myself. The night before they left, I was out having a nice quiet dinner with a friend, when I received a frantic call on my cell phone. Early on, I knew I would grow to hate those devices! Anyway, I was told that I had to go with the boys on their early-morning flight since a four-hour photo shoot for a major magazine had been added to their schedule at the last minute.

They needed seven changes of clothing for the shoot. I really wasn't upset about it. The truth was I enjoyed the traveling and I found the work interesting. I was up until 2:30 A.M. packing for a 5:30 A.M. flight. The fan-club end of my job had also become more active and I really enjoyed working with people all over the world on the boys' behalf. I certainly could never complain that my job was dull.

In addition, my personal life was heating up. An old boyfriend that I had not seen in months contacted me and told me that he wanted to start our relationship up again. Oh, my God! January was going to be a stressful month. I looked forward to a bit more sanity in the month of February.

In Los Angeles I was constantly referred to as the boys' stylist. How flattering. Just another of my many hats. We were gone for about a week on that little excursion and then returned to Florida to get the boys ready for a charity event in Orlando. At that time, I received good news from Germany. A friend called to tell me that the boys came in at number one on the VIVA Hit List (kind of like MTV Europe). That was great news. Everything went well for the rest of the month, then the boys got back on a plane without me and traveled to Sweden, where they continued recording with Denniz PoP.

For some reason, Jive was still dragging its feet about releasing a second single from the boys' first album. It was frustrating for the boys to be working so hard and then to have their own record company not able to make a decision. Alex told me that he really did not like the business end of the whole thing and wanted me to handle it for him. He had become very confused by it all and no longer wanted to deal with it. All he wanted to do was sing and dance.

Alex asked me to become his personal and business manager. I was thrilled! That would give me the opportunity to remain a close part of his career and protect him from the sharks that had begun to circle the group. We asked an attorney who was also a friend, Judith Segelin, to draw up a formal written agreement. Since he was no longer a minor we both signed it. It basically made me his business manager and gave me power of attorney. I picked up the usual, rescuing-mom role and ran with it.

Since the record company seemed incapable of making a decision, we headed back to Europe, where the boys' popularity had continued to grow. On February 14, 1996, we celebrated the best Valentine's Day ever: the boys' first gold record was presented in Munich at a very nice restaurant BMG had rented out for the evening. Although the location of the party had been kept under raps, the fans somehow found us out. It was an extremely cold evening. It had been snowing on and off all day. The streets were covered in ice, but that was of no consequence to the loyal fans that waited for us to arrive.

When the boys emerged from their limos, the fans went wild. The press and paparazzi were there as well. I was interviewed and had my picture taken with the boys. I had never been comfortable being in the limelight, but I felt I had contributed a lot in helping them to achieve their success, so why not?

BMG's director of promotion made a very nice speech about the boys and everyone involved. Lou was overwhelmed by the occasion. He cried during his speech, as did all the other guys. I was fine until Alex said from across the room, "I love you, Mom." Then I lost it as well. Lots of happy tears were shed.

The rest of that year was filled with amazing events, both in Europe and the United States. March 4, 1996, marked another red-letter day for the Backstreet Boys, when they appeared on VIVA-TV. When we arrived, there were at least four hundred girls waiting outside, so we circled around the back and entered through an electric gate. That became a problem when the bus slowed down to drive though a tight space, giving the girls just enough time to sneak through the gate with the bus.

Security made a path for us and we ran off the bus into the studios. Once inside, we were led down a long hallway to a green room that was about twelve by fifteen feet, with windows along three walls. Although the windows had blinds on them, the fans figured out where we were and began banging relentlessly on the windows.

A few of the girls squeezed their tiny hands in and unlocked the windows so they could throw small stuffed toys and notes at the boys. Finally, extra security was sent outside to move the girls back past the gate.

The show itself went fine, but when the time came to leave, fans had climbed the fences and dropped into the parking lot where the bus was waiting. Security, along with anyone in the building big and strong enough to be effective, ran outside to clear the fans away and make a path for us to get through to the bus. They got most of the fans outside the gates again and we thought we were home free.

After witnessing that scene, the boys felt so badly for the fans that they decided to sign some autographs through the chain link fence. The five boys were giddy with excitement over the whole thing, but Johnny and I were terrified. The only thing that separated us from those hundreds of crazy screaming girls was a fence. And they had climbed that twice already.

With bodyguards close behind, the boys ran back and forth, signing and shaking hands and going just as crazy as the fans. The frenzy reached a feverish pitch. All I wanted to do was get those boys back onto the bus, but they were determined to keep signing autographs.

Suddenly, in between deafening screams, I heard Alex scream out, "Mom, help!" I turned just in time to see my son with a young girl literally wrapped around him and five more getting ready to pounce from the fence. I yelled for security. As they tried to pry the girls off of Alex, he did his best not to freak out. Once freed, he ran full steam ahead to the bus, all the while yelling for the others boys to follow suit.

Howie was the next to be attacked. One by one, the boys realized how totally out of control the situation had become. When that moment of clarity hit, each headed for the safety of our forty-foot refuge. Once we were all on board, we realized that the girls had broken the gate by hanging on it. That made it necessary for security to open it manually in order for us to be able to get out. Six big men pushed open the gates as several others tried to push the girls out of the way of the bus.

As we inched our way out of the parking lot, our hearts were beating so hard and fast that I was certain that they could be heard above the screams. Johnny ran to the back of the bus and grabbed his video camera. He wanted to capture on tape what we thought was a once-in-a-lifetime event. Little did we know it was only the beginning.

The bus, which by then was buried in fans standing ten deep, could barely move. The fans banged on the sides and jumped onto the front, hanging in desperation from the windshield wipers. They were all crying hysterically and screaming the boys' names. It was unbearably nerve-wracking as we inched our way through the sea of teenage girls. Even though we were moving, it felt like we were trapped.

Eventually, the police were called to escort us to safety. Laughably, the first to arrive was an officer on a very small motorbike. He took one look at the situation and turned around to get backup. We could not wait for reinforcements, so we kept going.

As we moved toward the main road, the street narrowed, due to the cars parked along the side. We hoped that would block the girls, but they did not let that stop them. They simply climbed onto the tops of the cars to keep up with us. Hoods were crushed and even convertibles were stomped on. It was amazing to watch those girls push every obstacle out of their way. The people who owned the cars were in for a big surprise.

It took us two hours to reach the end of that small side street, which was about one-third the length of a city block. Fans were everywhere you looked. Randy and the bus driver yelled at the girls to get down off of the mirrors and windows, but they would not stop. They had worked themselves up into such a frenzy that I don't think they even knew what they were doing anymore. Eventually, we turned onto the highway and they were no longer able to follow us. After a few exits, we stopped to see if any damage had been done to the bus. We could not believe our eyes. The girls had written love notes to the boys on every inch of the white bus. It looked like a giant doodle pad covered in marker.

The "snowball" that had started to gather strength the year before was now plowing ahead with greater intensity. It all came to a chaotic climax at the Virgin Megastore in Vienna, Austria, at the Backstreet Boys' last scheduled in-store appearance in Europe. The BMG people in Vienna were very nice, but they were totally unprepared for the upcoming events.

The day we arrived, I had a conversation with the promotional guy and our head of security. Since the experience with the fans at VIVA-TV, Randy and I knew what to expect. We tried to explain this to the BMG representative, but he kept insisting that Austrian teens were not as aggressive as German girls.

The rep believed there would be no problem with the next day's autograph session at the Virgin Megastore. Only 150 fans had come for Haddaway, when he had a number one record. Since the Backstreet Boys' record was only number three for two weeks, he figured that no more than 200 fans would show up for autographs.

Although the boys were scheduled to be at the store at 4:00 P.M., by 1:00 P.M. more than 500 fans had shown up. By 3:00 P.M., they had to close the store. Not long after that, they were forced to shut down the surrounding streets. By 4:00 P.M., there were more than 2,000 fans jammed into both levels of the store. Countless more were waiting outside.

Anyone who was available to help with barricades and security was called in. Once the additional staff were put into place, the boys stepped into the room, causing the entire building to heave with anticipation. It took all the strength of several large heavily-muscled men to hold the

BILL FERNANDEZ

Rushing home for Alex's graduation

fans back. They were put at a second-floor table between the elevator and the exit. I stood behind them and tried to stay calm, all the while videotaping what had turned into an extraordinary event.

Prior to our entrance, Randy, our soundman Jake and I had come up with a plan. If Randy gave us the high sign, we would stop everything and head for the elevator. That was our only way out, safe or not.

From top to bottom, wall-to-wall, fans were everywhere you looked. They hung over the railing and pushed to get to the autograph table. Some fainted as soon as the boys entered. The situation was out of hand long before we arrived. There was absolutely no hope whatsoever of reining it in. The fans were just too far gone.

As the boys signed autographs, the fans got bolder. The ones that managed to get something signed refused to leave since they would have to fight their way through the back half of the crowd just to get out. The signing lasted about twenty minutes. Girls were crying and pleading to either get to the boys or to get out. There was just no place for them to go.

At that point, the crowd began knocking down signs and rushing the boys. Randy gave me the sign. I tapped the boys and off we went, with the boys in the lead. They barely made it onto the elevator. I followed close behind, but the elevator doors closed before I could enter. I began to panic, but once the crowd realized the boys were gone, they backed off. As we rode the next elevator to the main floor, I could not help but raise my head to the ear of the record company rep and whisper, "We told you so, didn't we?"

Once we reached the room where the boys were waiting, phase two of the craziness began. To reach our waiting vans on the street, we had to pass through a narrow crowded exit to the garage and then onto the street. As several fans chased us on foot, we made our escape, thanks to the help of the BMG guys and a few skilled drivers.

———

AS WE TRAIPSED THROUGH EUROPE as an opening act, it became obvious that fans were buying tickets to see the boys instead of the headliners. The boys were now in high demand with the media. Of course, with increased visibility came increased fan frenzy.

Amid all the chaos, Alex tried valiantly to keep up with his tutoring. Graduation was just a few months away and he was determined to receive his diploma with the rest of his class at Osceola High School in Florida. That was the one shred of normalcy he had left. He wanted to maintain it at all costs. Yet, as much as I tried to include time for his

BILL FERNANDEZ

Alex gets his diploma

tutoring, Johnny and Donna fought me at every turn. Thank heaven for people like Susan Horton and Kim, his tutors. Without them encouraging me, I might have caved in, something Alex might never have forgiven me for.

In May 1996, he and I flew home for twenty-four hours so that he could walk down the aisle with his classmates and receive his diploma at the graduation ceremony. The school wasn't entirely sure that he would show up, so he was the very last in his class to walk to the stage. But we didn't care; we just wanted to see him do it.

Mom gave Alex a big party with a cake. She and Dad were so very proud of him. We celebrated what was probably one of the last normal achievements my son would have to hold in his non-celebrity heart. I beamed with pride during the ceremony and felt a great sense of relief. Alex had completed a teenage rite of passage. Against the odds, he had earned his diploma.

The next morning we headed back to Germany. The boys were about to start their first headlining tour and they were biting their nails until they saw Alex come through the wings. Our flight had been delayed, so he barely made it to the stage. But it all worked out. As usual, Alex's angel was watching over him.

Alex's sense of pride at having achieved his goal, in spite of numerous obstacles, was one of the happiest moments of his life. It was one of the last remaining "normal" moments he would have.

CHAPTER EIGHT

The Price Tag of Success

BY THE SUMMER OF 1996, the boys had broken all records for sales and had become a household name across most of Europe. Their faces were on every magazine cover. They were in demand for every major television show and festival. It was quite similar to what happened to the Beatles when they hit the United States.

None of the boys could go out of the hotel without a bodyguard. That made it necessary for each of them to have a bodyguard of his own. Even if they tried to use disguises, it did not seem to matter. Once the fans recognized the bodyguard or girlfriend or whomever was a familiar face next to that particular boy, they followed them. The boys could not hide anywhere.

While they went out on their next tour, I stayed home and tried to salvage the U.S. fan club. Over the course of the year that I had traveled the world with the boys, no effort had been made by anyone in the office or at the record company to raise the numbers in the U.S. database. Jive seemed perfectly happy to have the boys remain on the other side of the ocean indefinitely. Alex voiced his frustrations to me more than once about how he wished they could focus on becoming more visible in their own country.

Adding to their frustration was the fact that they were totally wiped out from the relentless pace they had been keeping. I could see the exhaustion on their faces and hear it in their voices when they sang. They were beginning to taste what it was like to be in the public eye and what that meant in terms of maintaining one's privacy. Sadly, they learned all too soon that it meant that you gave up your right to have any.

We still lived in our original, three-bedroom apartment in Kissim-mee, Florida. The only difference was that it seemed as though the entire world knew our address and phone number. When we traveled, I spoke to my parents periodically and they told me stories about getting phone calls in the middle of the night.

The European fans who traveled to America were bold enough to come to the door to try and get a glimpse of Alex's room or to see if he was there. For a while Mom and Dad were really good sports and tolerated all that crazy behavior. They even stood at the door and talked to the people and answered their questions.

After a while, the phone calls got crazy and they became concerned. We changed the phone number and made sure the front office knew not to tell anyone what apartment we lived in. Although we lived in a gated community, that did little to dissuade the fans. They lay in wait for someone to drive in and then they rushed in behind them.

I was baffled as to how the fans knew our address and apartment number. Then I learned that the information was printed in a magazine article that had been published some months before. I was furious when I found about it and asked some of my friends in Europe to locate the magazine. I was amazed when I finally saw it. Pictures of our building and our exact address were in the magazine.

The accompanying article was based on an interview that we had given to journalists who had come to our home with the explicit understanding that our address would not be printed and they could only print the pictures of the apartment that we approved. They were so nice while they were interviewing us that we were surprised to learn that the story had become some sort of exposé by the time they returned to Europe.

When I saw the article I immediately got in touch with the journalist and told him not to expect a lot of cooperation from me in the future. Of course, he was apologetic, but the damage had already been done. That particular journalist eventually went to work for a higher-end magazine that was more credible and we did work together again. But I did ban him for a long time.

The article resulted in numerous incidents with fans. Once, I was in the apartment taking an early morning shower as my niece, Kelly Cline, stuffed envelopes in the back bedroom. As I walked out of the bathroom to go across the hall into my bedroom, Kelly's voice stopped me in my tracks.

"Stay where you are," she said breathlessly. "There's someone in the window."

"What?" I blurted out, running into the bedroom and peeking back out towards her.

"I just opened the blinds to let in some light and there was someone standing at the window with a video camera."

"Are they still there?" I asked.

She banged on the window and yelled at them to leave—and they did!

At that point, we were both beside ourselves. I was mortified. That window faced the basketball court and a path that led to the back of the building. After that day, I made sure that the blinds in the back room were always closed.

How terrible it was to have to think about something so trivial. It got to the point where I could not answer the door myself or fans would start screaming and crying just because I was at home. They automatically thought that if I was there, so was Alex—and they would have an absolute fit.

Another problem we faced during that time was the constant battle between Jive and the boys' management. Jive was ecstatic over the boys' sudden rise to international fame, but they seemed unconcerned about the boys' health and mental state.

Young celebrities are like children caught between two battling parents. But in this situation the prize is not custody of the child but, rather, who ends up with the most dollars. They book appearances, interviews, promotional tours, events, autograph sessions, whatever they can. No one ever considers the welfare of their "meal ticket." They just keep working them until they drop. Then they move on to their next cash cow.

Johnny and Donna were the first ones in our group to buy homes, cars and expensive jewelry. They were quick to take credit for the band's success and rarely thanked anyone working for either of them. I was, of course, just a thorn in their side. I would have been tossed out early on, if it were not for my persistence and the love between my son and me.

Management screw-ups invariably were blamed on Jive or someone else. It was a constant tug-of-war between management and the record company, and also between Donna and Johnny as a couple. They never seemed to be in agreement anymore. And Big Poppa added a third wheel to the operation by strolling in and out of the scene whenever it was convenient for him. He opened a new restaurant and he signed more acts to his Trans Continental record label, which he kept telling us was created just for the Backstreet Boys. One of the new acts was *NSYNC, a five-member group that looked and sounded like a Backstreet Boys clone.

By then, the boys were tired and frustrated because they had worked their butts off for so long and still saw no real reward for it in a monetary sense. When they toured, the boys each drew a few-hundred-dollars-a-week advance, but when they returned home, the salary draw was cut off and they received nothing.

———

FINALLY, THE ALBUM WAS RELEASED in Germany, where it immediately soared to number one. Soon the boys had their first gold album. When the second single from the album was released in England, it, too, did well. The group was now ready for its first real tour as headliners. It would include a band and dancers, the whole nine yards.

But, by then, fame had taken a toll. For every rung of success they climbed, there was an accompanying sacrifice. Sadly, Kevin and his long-time girlfriend, Kristen, broke up. According to Alex, it was due to the insane schedules the boys were keeping. It seemed to be a mutual decision. Kristen was a beautiful young woman who had been acting and dancing for years. She wanted a career of her own and deserved a shot at finding her own place in the business. Even though Kevin understood, I still remember the hurt-puppy look on his face when we talked about it. He has a soft heart inside a rough shell. That shell is sometimes easily cracked.

Backstreet fever had spread to Canada, and it was impossible for the boys to go anywhere without a bodyguard. They weren't even safe in the hotel. The press laid in wait in the lobby, right alongside the fans, and pounced the moment any one of the boys walked by. The boys did not want to appear mean, so they usually stopped for a few minutes to sign autographs or take pictures. When they wanted it to end, they gave a sign to their bodyguard, who then whisked them away. I always tried to be nice to the press and answer questions about the boys so that they did not have to. Naturally, that was not always good enough for some journalists.

Mingled in with the fans and music journalists were an unsavory lot that obtained autographs from the boys to resell for ridiculous amounts. Those guys sometimes returned to the hotel later that night with posters, pictures and CDs supposedly signed by the boys. The bodyguards and I took great pleasure in cutting the boys off from them. Once the boys understood what was going on, they stopped signing autographs for them altogether.

When it was time to hit the road again, I traveled with the production crew as makeup and wardrobe mistress. For most of the tour, local women were hired city to city to help with my day-to-day tasks. I was in charge of setting up the boys' dressing rooms with wardrobe and coordinating with catering about food. I also had to set up a changing area each night for the boys to do their quick changes during the show.

The final task was to wash clothes from the previous night or take them out to be cleaned. With five boys dancing every night, there was also a lot of mending to be done. When something could not be mended, I went out and bought a replacement. I think they ate underwear and socks for dinner, the way that they disappeared.

Life on the road could be very tiresome and lonely. I will never forget the first night that I watched the boys drive off after the show. I stayed behind to clean up their dressing room and to pack. The crew did not sleep in hotels every night like the artists or the musicians. Most of the people that work behind the scenes just pack up and move on to the next city every night. Our bus was our hotel.

I was just one of the crew. I slept on the crew bus with a bunch of guys and two other women. I became pretty good pals with a sweet, hard-working woman from Croatia named Dvorka. She had very dark eyes and black hair. She spoke good English and was fluent in German, Italian and French. She had a good heart, and we had some healthy laughs together during that time.

Unlike most of the boys, I rarely slept on these flights, even on the occasional private jet.

ANDRE CSILLAG

The guys that we rode with were usually loud leathery two-packs-a-day Germans. The first thing they did when they got onto the bus was light up and crack open a brew. They worked hard and played harder. All in all, they were nice, good-natured people. They had only the deepest respect for me as Alex's mom. I never wanted to be treated special. They soon found out I could be one of the guys. It did not take long before we were spending our days off together, hanging out or going to a nice restaurant. They knew all the best places to go.

Since most of the crew spoke English well, there was no language barrier. After spending the better part of two years in Germany, I was beginning to understand a lot of words. To the dismay of some, I understood more than they knew. Sometimes I repeated stuff to the boys or Johnny that the crew members were saying among themselves. It got pretty funny at times to see the looks on their faces when they thought they were being sneaky. I would come back with a remark that made them aware that I knew what they were saying. Other times, I had German-speaking friends stand within earshot and explain to me what was really going on. Either way, I was adept at keeping up with the slicker players.

Still, there were times that I felt out of place. Not because I felt better than they were as people, but simply because I missed being with Alex and the boys. My job had become very basic and routine. I enjoyed what I was doing, but I missed having daily interaction with my son.

My new job with the Backstreet Boys gave me a chance to see how things ran on the other side of the curtain. I saw how a show was put together from the inside out. It was amazing to see those people pull together to meet deadlines. I really must give the crew a lot of credit for what they did. After all, once their job was done for the day, they only had a short time before the artists showed up, expecting everything to proceed without a hitch. Sometimes it even does.

Tradition dictated that the crew play jokes on the artists during the last show—and did we ever! One time we attacked the boys with water cannons during their closing number. Another time we dropped a hundred stuffed toys right onto their heads while they were all center stage singing. We stuck props to the stage so that they could not be moved and that was always good for a laugh.

Luckily, the boys all had a good sense of humor about it. We got pretty creative after a while. It was a challenge that we looked forward to during every tour. The boys even came up with their own bag of tricks for their band mates and the crew.

At this point in their careers, the boys had the crews' admiration, as well as the adoration of fans everywhere they performed. I remember hearing from several crewmembers during that first tour that they had not been this excited to work with an act in years. The energy and talent on stage was amazing.

Sometimes I was overwhelmed with pride, especially when the crew told me how Alex seemed to be one of the most natural performers that they have ever seen. He just looked like that was where he belonged. They would go on to say how much of a pleasure he was to work with off stage as well. Never once did Alex act as if he were better than they. Alex could always be counted on to be polite and thoughtful.

Oftentimes, he hung out with the crew on days off and backstage. They genuinely liked Alex as a person and a performer. It was an amazing time for me as his mom to hear those wonderful words. I know that all of the boys are talented, but since I did not raise all the boys, I could not help but feel proudest of Alex.

Even the media loved Alex, and they had a special affinity for Howie as well. They were the two who never turned down an interview. Whenever any of the other boys had a conflict in their schedules, we knew we could count on Howie or Alex to come to the rescue with the media. And they did it with style and grace.

By the end of that tour, it was the norm for the show to be sold out and for hundreds of fans to be left without tickets. Sometimes Johnny or I would try to find extra tickets right before the show and go outside to give them away to the neediest family that we could find. Like a single mom who could not afford the tickets for her children or a dad with a crying daughter by his side. What a great feeling it was seeing those little girls' faces light up when we handed over those tickets. I always liked that part.

The meet-and-greets were the other fan-related job that I got to deal with on a daily basis. At every show, usually before the boys hit the stage, we lined girls up in narrow hallways or in extra rooms. Once the boys were dressed and ready to go onstage, they came out to meet the girls, take pictures and sign autographs for them.

Many times there would also be terminally ill children or children in wheelchairs for the boys to meet. That was very difficult for them to handle. Sometimes they cried when they saw the children. Naturally, that was not the best mood generator that the boys could have before going on stage. To alleviate the pressure on the boys, we were forced to qualify the degree of sickness with which a child could get into the meet-and-greets.

That may sound like a cruel thing to do, but we really had no choice. If the boys became too emotional before a performance, it could set a mood that would last for a long while into the show. That was not fair to the rest of the audience. We would compensate the fans who did not get in to see the boys by sending them something personally autographed by the boys and usually that sufficed.

Occasionally, Jive or some of the magazines ran contests and very sick children would be given the chance to meet the boys. We finally had to put the kibosh on that. We gave them autographed shirts or albums instead. Part of my job was to somehow make nice with everyone. I usually found a way to please. After all, the boys' reputations were always on the line.

Another fun thing I got to do with regards to the meet-and-greet schedule was that at every show I would choose some fans to come backstage and help me out with translation, among other things. They helped collect the hundreds of stuffed toys the audience threw on stage during every performance. The stuffed toys and gifts were a new phenomenon. We always arranged for the stuffed animals to be donated to an orphanage or children's hospital. Otherwise the promoters would just throw them away.

Most of the stuffed toys were either brand new or keepsakes that really meant something to the fans. There was just no way we could take them all with us. In good conscience, I could never bring myself to just throw them away. Each one also had a note or letter attached that I kept for our fan database. The boys enjoyed reading them.

The toys that the girls threw on stage eventually became a hazard for the boys because they would trip on them during their choreography. More than once, they fell and almost twisted an ankle or sprained a knee. We asked the fan club volunteers to go onstage after the opening acts were done to ask the audience, in their own language, to throw all of the toys on stage at that time, so that we could make sure we collected them properly and gave them to each boy.

Those poor volunteers were bombarded. They took big brooms and pushed the toys to the sides of the stage, where they could then be bagged and taken to the boys' dressing room. It was a noble effort that sometimes worked and sometimes didn't. There were still those diehard girls who saved their toys to throw at their favorite boy while he was performing. But at least the major threat for broken ankles was eliminated.

For quite a long time, the boys wrote response letters to each fan as part of their weekly schedules. Eventually the number grew so large that it became impossible for them to answer each and every one, so we responded from the fan club. I still divided the gifts among the boys. We shipped lots of boxes filled with toys, cards and gifts home during those tours. The luggage bins under our buses filled up pretty quickly, so keeping the toys on the road with us was never a option.

The other thing we found strange was the way the fans responded to the magazine articles that were written about the boys. For example, if a boy was asked what their favorite gift was and, say, Alex responded "jewelry," well forget it! That would be enough for fans to start throwing bananas onto the stage with rings or bracelets wrapped around them. More than once, my son was pelted in the face or body by a flying piece of jewelry tied to some fruit. He learned how to duck and be very alert while on stage. This was especially true if he got near the edge, where they could better target him. I remember several welts on his forehead from rings and chains.

One time the boys were asked what their favorite foods were. At the very next concert, right after the article came out, they were inundated with boxes of Mac and Cheese for Brian, gummy bears for Howie, and so on for the rest of the boys. The gummy bears are soft, but when you throw them hard, they hurt.

What a trip! It got to the point where things were confiscated at the door before the kids were let into the venue. After all, someone could really get hurt by some of those things. I was always grateful that they couldn't bring cheeseburgers into the venues. Alex would have been covered in them every night. Not pretty.

We also had to make sure that when the boys did interviews they made it quite clear that they did not want the fans to bring that stuff to the show. Eventually, it died down, but for a while it was pretty crazy.

Another part of my job was to escort the photographers into the pit area as the lights went down and the boys hit the stage. Those areas were usually around forty feet long and maybe five feet wide at best— not much space in which to move around in the dark. After the first three songs, security and I escorted them out. Sometimes it would be quite a circus act as we tried to maneuver both television crews and still photographers in and out of those small areas. They were never happy when it was time to leave.

Inevitably, there was always that one photographer who would try and pull a fast one. They would say that they had permission to take more photos or that was not three songs or whatever they could come up with. But when the bodyguards stuck their hands in front of their lenses and told them in a firm but nice way to pack up, they usually did.

After a while, I developed such a good relationship with the media that I started getting phone calls directly from them. They would ask me for a special type of interview or some other request. That was how I learned the media game and got to know the most influential journalists who wrote for the top magazines. I always tried to fit them into the boys' schedules as best as I could. It paid off well for the boys when they got rave reviews and the best spots on magazine covers.

Donna was supposed to be involved in the media coverage, but, given the fact that she was thousands of miles away and not aware of what was happening on the road, I began to make some of the calls myself with direct approval from the boys. It worked out better that way. The only problem was the record company. They sent requests to the office in Orlando and Donna gave them her blessing without ever talking to the boys or anyone else about changes in the schedule.

That brought about conflicts because it left the boys no free time. Donna sometimes scheduled interviews on their few days off. That was when things came to a head. A meeting was called to set things right.

After a couple of meetings with the boys, Johnny agreed to allow them to see all interview requests before they were approved. My job description began to change at that point. I became the go-between. For a while, Johnny helped out by going over the requests with the boys after the show, but he wasn't always around and someone had to take on the role so things would run smoothly. The options were to either have Donna come out on the road and do it, or give it to me. The boys were dead set against Donna and chose me.

For a while, I was able to juggle my various responsibilities. Eventually, as the shows and media events became larger and more frequent, it became necessary for me to have some help. The pressure was intense and at times I felt as though I was on the verge of a nervous breakdown.

Finally, I told Johnny that I was feeling overwhelmed. He sympathized with my situation and talked to the boys. They agreed to hire a couple of extra people to help with the wardrobe and makeup responsibilities so that I could focus more on public relations and the fan club. At that time, the drummer in our band had a girlfriend, Angie Lehman, who was a hair stylist and makeup artist. She was hired to take on those responsibilities. With that, I was able to breathe a bit easier.

Many strange things happened during the shows that I, as a parent, really did not understand. Fans often fainted, which meant they had to be pulled over the barricades. Sometimes, as they were being carried off by security, they would miraculously recover long enough to grab for a boy or to jump onto the stage and run after their favorite.

More than a few times, security had to run onstage and detach girls from the boys during a performance. The boys liked that so much that they egged the fans on. Alex and Brian sometimes jumped into the pit between the stage and the audience and ran back and forth, touching the girls' hands as they went.

Alex also liked to jump on the larger bodyguards' shoulders and ask them to walk across the pit area so he could reach further into

Me, Nina and Angie

the crowd. Pretty soon all of the boys started doing that and the security teams had to learn to guess when the boys were ready to jump. They kept an eye on each other and doubled up on that side as soon as one of the boys made their move.

At one of the summer-festival venues, the stage had a long runway that extended about sixty feet into the audience. At one point during the show, the boys all went to the end of the runway to sing a nice slow song. Suddenly, Nick stood up and accidentally knocked Howie right off the end of the stage. When that happened, everything went into slow motion. We watched in fear as he fell toward the screaming girls. Security managed to grab him at the last minute and push him back up onto the stage. Howie suffered no ill effects from the fall, but it was a close call that could have had disastrous results.

All the boys had accidents and mishaps of one kind or another. There were so many times during the shows that they had to run off and do a quick change, or get from point A to point B, that it was inevitable that things would go wrong. The larger the shows got, the greater the opportunity for things to go wrong.

As the tour progressed, the fans seemed to become more aggressive in every country. Mobs of girls blocked us from getting into hotels. Sometimes they rushed the elevators when the boys tried to get on with security. The situation became so unmanageable that neither the boys nor I could enter a hotel through the front doors anymore. We had to go in through a service entrance or kitchen.

Alex and I have seen the best and worst of many hotels all over the world. Once you walk through the kitchen of a hotel, you know whether you want to eat there or not. Sometimes we did. Other times we didn't.

The fan frenzy over the boys became so great that year that every time the boys performed with local acts, the girls screamed only for them. Naturally, that caused some bad blood between the boys and some of the European groups, despite the fact that it happened through no fault of their own.

Once, the boys and I went to watch another group perform. A group of girls caught sight of them in the back of the venue and audience members turned their backs on the group that was performing. They waved and screamed toward our guys. It was embarrassing for everyone since the boys had not meant to cause a commotion. We tried to leave quietly, but the fans would have none of that. In the end, they piled us all into vans and drove us back to our hotel.

The Backstreet Boys concert went very well in Vienna, where about 50,000 people turned out. The audience yelled for the Backstreet Boys while all the other groups were on stage. The local television station taped the show, so we were able to watch it when we got back to the hotel. We saw how aggressive the girls in the audience became. The promoter almost stopped the show because of it.

The police and medics thought a girl had been injured, so they just stopped the music in the middle of one of the boys' songs. The boys were stunned, but then just kept on singing a cappella. Then the MC took the microphone from Brian and told everyone what had happened. It was a mistake and no one was hurt.

They say that imitation is the sincerest form of flattery. We witnessed that in Switzerland toward the end of the tour. During one of the shows, a small group of children who called themselves the Mini-Backstreet Boys asked if they could perform for the boys. Oh my gosh—it was the best! Those five little boys, ranging in age from six to eight, ran out onto the stage and lip-synced to one of the boys' songs.

If that weren't cute enough, each one of them was dressed as their favorite Backstreet Boy and sang his part. We roared with delight as we watched those little Swiss tikes mimic every nuance. The best part came at the end of their performance. Our guys ran out onto the stage and grabbed their mini-look-a-like and gave him a big hug. Of course, the crowd went nuts and loved every minute of it.

As the boys' popularity increased, we had problems with unlicensed vendors who came out in force at the venues. They were followed closely by ticket scalpers. In Europe they didn't have very stiff laws that governed that sort of thing, so we had to contend with it ourselves. I went on a few runs with security to see how they chased away the unlicensed vendors.

It was rather fun finding them stationed just around the corner from the venue, especially when we approached them and they hawked us to purchase a knock-off shirt or poster. As we would get closer, they would see the backstage passes around our necks and begin to pack up. Suddenly, they would lose the ability to speak any English. We usually had some local security with us to get over that little hurdle.

It was hard to keep those guys down for long, though. As soon as we left the venue, they would come back out to sell their fake merchandise. I even heard that there were a few times when the local security or crew would try to run them off and they would have the audacity to put up a fight. They wanted that money too badly to let anyone stop them. During one altercation, I heard that one of our crew lost an eye from being hit by something. It was pretty terrible. I think the boys helped him out in some way, but I really don't remember how. Money can do terrible things to people.

Those types of things happened more and more often. Between dealing with the fans and the unlicensed vendors—and all of the unexpected crises—it got to a point where it was difficult for any of us to have downtime. With the help of the promoters in some cities and our security, we managed to find a few fun places to hide for a while. All of the boys really liked go-carting. That was something we searched for the moment we hit town, so that we could shut down for a few hours and play.

Usually it was not a problem. I was surprised at how popular the sport was in Germany. They had some very cool tracks there. Many of the carts were much better than the rinky-dink ones we were used to in the States. Alex and I really enjoyed spending time on the track with some of the other boys and security.

Nick, it turned out, was a very aggressive driver. One time he ran over one of our bodyguards who barely fit into the cart. His name was Todd and he was well over seven feet tall. His knees were up into his chest as he drove. It was quite a sight to see. As Todd rounded the corner, he wiped out.

Nick came up behind him and just kept on going. As he proceeded to run right over him, our poor bodyguard was stunned. He was not hurt in any way because the large frame of the cart kind of sheltered the blow. Afterward, the boys gave Nick a good talking to and told him he needed to take his anger out some other way. Nick took it in stride. He had not meant to hurt anyone.

The boys were right about Nick's anger. He seemed to be getting an attitude and we really did not know why. His parents were out on the road pretty regularly, so it was not that he missed them. It appeared as though someone had convinced him that he was the favorite among the fans and therefore the best Backstreet Boy. That was a dangerous game to play. Understandably, it began to cause problems within the group.

It was true that for a while the boys' producers used Brian and Nick to sing lead vocals, but, like everything else, that too changed. As the boys became more polished, the leads were given out to everyone. For Nick to be under the impression that he was better than the rest was not a good thing.

At rehearsals, the atmosphere became tense if one of the boys messed up, especially if it were Nick or Kevin. Kevin was a perfectionist. There were times that he would come down too hard on Nick for a simple error. He had the group's best interests at heart, but he did not really know how to communicate that to them.

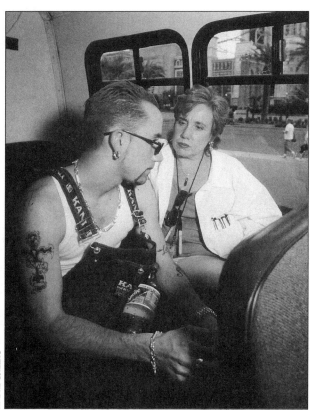

After being on the road for so long, it was inevitable that the boys' relationships would come under a strain. Arguments erupted on a daily basis. I remember a few good ones in which the boys almost came to blows. They were about silly things, like who messed up at rehearsals or who was off with their harmony. Had it not been for Johnny or security cutting in, things could have gotten out of hand very quickly.

The boys did not realize it at the time, but they were acting just like siblings. For Alex

Intense discussion on tour

ANDRE CSILLAG

130

this was both good and bad. He loved having the other fellows around when things were going well, but when the fights broke out he was the first to walk away.

Alex has always hated confrontation. From childhood on, he did everything he could to avoid conflict. He especially hated arguments with me—and, believe me, we had our share. They usually resulted in the two of us not speaking for a while. Eventually, we would get over it and talk it through.

———

AFTER SEVEN WEEKS ON TOUR throughout Europe, we finally headed home. All of us were exhausted and ready for a break. The tour was a raging success and everyone was pleased about it. Every show sold out and the merchandise sales went well over expectations. Our rest would be brief, as Jive was already putting a new video shoot together as we flew home. At least this one would be filmed in Orlando, so we would not have to travel very far.

For the video, they used a local middle school that Howie had attended as a child. It was pretty cool for him. Some magazines from Germany came to see the shoot and get pictures for the fans overseas. Jive sent a representative to make sure the shoot ran smoothly. Thank God it was Nina. She had had some run-ins with Donna and there was no love lost there, so when Donna showed up at the shoot and saw Nina, she left pretty quickly. I was unsure why, but at the time I was too busy to care.

That was a particularly tough shoot for the boys. It was done at night and they simulated a rainstorm, using very tall sprinklers on the set. The water was cold and I was very afraid they would get sick. We kept running up to them in between segments and padding them down with dry towels. Alex sneezed his way through most of the night. I was convinced he was coming down with a cold. He appeared to be really stressed out that night and I didn't know why. Later, I understood.

Marisa was briefly back in the picture and apparently had some sort of fight with Alex over a comment he had made jokingly. She did not think it was funny and just stood around pouting until she finally left with her mother. It was just one more thing to drag Alex down, but there was no convincing him of that. In an odd way I felt that he liked the stress of their relationship, or rather that he thought that was how it was supposed to be.

I didn't understand that because none of my relationships had ever played out in that way. Even during the worst of times with his father, we did not yell and scream in front of him. I could not imagine where he was getting his warped opinions.

Then it hit me. Johnny and Donna had engaged in constant fights over the past two years. Threats were always being thrown back and forth. They never really seemed to enjoy each other very much. It was like those love-hate things you hear about. It dawned on me that perhaps that was what Alex was basing his relationship rules on.

When he did ask for my input, I tried to make him understand that when you truly love someone you want to be with them and have fun. The object was not to fight just so you could make up. I hoped it would sink in. He had started down a bad road that would lead him into some bad relationships with unhappy endings. No parent ever wants to see his or her child suffer. I certainly wanted to steer him in the right direction, but at the age of almost nineteen, he was not about to listen to me. I could only stand by and be there when he reached out to me.

Around that time, I found myself in desperate need of a break. In July, I decided to accept a long-standing invitation from my newfound friends in Zurich, Marco and Evelyn Duschletta, to pay them a visit. Marco worked for BMG and Evelyn helped me run the fan club from her home. They had a daughter, Jasmine, who was as beautiful as her mother. She spoke no English, but we had fun just the same. Both Marco and Evelyn had been extremely helpful to the boys and very generous as friends to me.

What a blessing it was to get away for a while. I had a wonderful time and I got to see parts of the countryside I would never have been able to see during a tour. Marco took me on a train ride up into the mountains and it was spectacular. I stayed with them in a spare upstairs room and got to meet some of the other young fans who helped Evelyn with her fan club duties.

Everyone was kind and sweet. One day we had a great

Randy Jones and Evelyn Duschletta

132

outing in celebration of Swiss Independence. It was just like our Fourth of July. We went to a park, had a cookout and sat on a blanket on the grass. The weather was sunny and warm. All around us, people enjoyed the day with their families. Later that evening, we watched fireworks and had lots of laughs.

———

BACK HOME, WITH THE TOUR finally finished and the money collected, it was time to sit down and discuss finances. It was of great concern to all of us, considering that it had always been a battle getting Lou to give us any kind of accounting figures.

Lou hired an entire accounting department to deal with the tour and payroll. I was not very happy to hear that the people Lou hired had never had any experience in the music or touring business, but, once again, trust was on the line. That line, however, was beginning to wear a bit thin. It was becoming painfully obvious that while everyone around the group seemed to be reaping the benefits of the boys' hard work— new homes, fancy cars, expensive jewelry—the boys themselves were hardly rolling in dough.

I was not the only parent with that concern. All of the parents had voiced their concerns at one time or another. We were all in agreement that something had to be done, but what? It was a tricky situation. None of us wanted to broach the whole "trust" issue, as that always seemed to result in unpleasantness. Ultimately, we had no choice.

Brian's mother, Jackie, was the first to act. She had a lawyer in Lexington, Kentucky, send a registered letter to Lou's office demanding an accounting record. That got Lou's attention.

After weeks of excuses about uncollected funds from the tour, we finally were able to see some figures. When that happened, Alex and I were horrified. Not only were we not rolling in dough, we were rolling in debt. For those first couple of years, the boys had been living on advances against future earnings. That meant that until all of the accrued expenses—food, travel, lodging, publicity, clothes, equipment, etc.—were paid back, the boys would not see a dime. None of this had ever been explained to us. We never had any say in how the money was spent or who got what.

Alex and I were devastated. I tried to explain to him that despite the fact that he had finally passed his driver's test, it would not be possible for him to buy a car. We were broke. He had a hard time understanding that. Both of us were furious and felt really betrayed. At that point, we decided that a meeting should take place involving only the parents and the boys. We had to decide how to handle the bomb that had just been so unceremoniously dropped into our laps.

On top of that, tension began to develop between Alex and me. He was at that age where he wanted to rebel against my influence. I knew that other people were in his ear about how he should be an adult and take control of his life. That would have been fine if he had had a clue as to how he was supposed to do that. In addition to that, he had been asking a lot of questions about his estranged father recently.

One day, with the help of Marisa, he found out his father's address and went out to find him. Over the years, questions about his father had come and gone during different stages of my son's life. I always tried to tell him the truth as I remembered it. It was Alex's choice to go and find him. I suppose I knew in my heart that someday he would want to do that. It saddened me that this was the time he chose, since it made me feel a bit betrayed. It was like he was running to anyone but me for advice.

Mom found the situation especially disturbing. She had not only helped to raise Alex from the time he was a toddler, she had lived through my stressful divorce and Alex's ultimate abandonment by his father. After finding him and spending several hours with his father, Alex returned home to tell me what he had done. He told me he needed to ask

AJ with Grandmother and Grandfather

him some things about why he left and why he had never tried to communicate with him for all those years.

His father told him that he had lost track of us (of course, if he had been paying child support all those years, that would not have happened). He was also convinced that I had bad-mouthed him so much to Alex that he was sure Alex hated him. My son's response was pretty amazing. He told my ex-husband that he had never heard me say a bad word about him. I had just answered the questions that he had asked me with honesty. I was elated to hear that. I hugged my son and told him it was okay to spend time with his father if that is what he really wanted to do.

Over the next few years, Alex tried to reunite with his father several times. Soon it became painfully clear to him that his father's newfound interest in him had something to do with the fact that he now had a pop star for a child. Alex was very disappointed with the way his relationship with his father progressed, but he managed to get over it, or at least to hide his feelings for a while longer.

I felt bad for Alex and consoled him the best I could. Then we moved on. What I did not realize at the time was how all of those feelings of confusion, distrust in Lou and once again disappointment by his father had started to churn up in my son. He was holding a lot inside that he had never talked about. The signs at that point were so small that no one in the family really saw what was happening to Alex's personality.

I truly believe that with everything happening at once—the pressures of stardom, the tension between us, the financial problems—his mind was tugged in two different directions. It was AJ, the happy-go-lucky performer who was adored by millions, versus Alex, the troubled young man trying to escape his pain.

Alex threw himself into his work. He also spent a lot time trying to salvage his relationship with Marisa. As time wore on, I began to feel less a part of his life. He was drifting away and I felt powerless to stop it. I had hoped that the incident with his father would bring us closer together, but it really did not. If it was possible, we seemed more distant from one another than ever before. Alex also moved further away from the rest of his family.

Alex's apparent lack of interest in my mom, my dad and the family in general caused my mom to feel distraught. Since Alex was home so rarely, no one wanted to confront him with that because they wanted to make the best of the time they had together. But it was obvious in Mom's face that she was deeply hurt by the way Alex treated her. I doubt that she ever really recovered from that.

By that time, he was calling home infrequently. It was only when he had a problem that he bothered to call. Mom loved him so much that even for that nugget she was grateful. She was always there to lend an ear and to try to help him when he asked, but his questions dwindled with each passing month.

The gap between my son and me widened over the next several months. He started surrounding himself with some unsavory types. It all began in Germany, when he and Brian slipped away without telling anyone and got their first tattoos. He knew how upset I would be, so he hid it from me as long as he could. When I found out, I was so upset that I did not speak to him for several days. He has since gotten many more tattoos, up and down each arm, as well as on his shoulder and stomach.

For a while, he seemed closer to Donna. I felt at that point that my son listened to everyone around him except the people who really cared about him—his family. The keen sixth sense he once possessed was no longer intact. He had lost the ability to surround himself with good people. The onset of "glommers" began.

——————

By 1997, THE BOYS' POPULARITY in Canada was so great that they out-charted that country's reigning pop queen, Celine Dion. Each boy had his own personal bodyguard 24/7, but that was not enough to alleviate the fears I had about Alex's health and safety. I could hear the strain in his voice and see the exhaustion in his body.

The boys got sick a lot. I tried to keep them full of good food and vitamins, but there is only so much the human body can take. Alex and Nick both got strep throat several times. When one boy got something, it inevitably spread to the others, given the close quarters on the tour buses and in the dressing rooms.

Alex started taking a lot of nighttime cold medicine to help him sleep. That worried me. He complained about stuffiness and seemed to get an inordinate amount of headaches. He was tired all the time. I tried to talk to Johnny about their schedules, but with the increasing number of things on his plate this was an issue that was constantly overlooked.

CHAPTER NINE

Who Do You Trust?

At THE END OF 1996, the Backstreet Boys were sent on a promotional tour of Asia and Australia. Our first stop was Taipei, Taiwan. Record company reps from AVEX (Jive's Asian counterpart) had seen the boys perform in Poland and Germany and requested an Asian tour since that market is always into the latest American craze.

It was difficult to reconcile our vision of the reserved Asian culture with that of the boy-crazed fans who jumped up and down, screaming for the Backstreet Boys. I soon learned that when it came to pop stars, teenage girls were the same the world over. Their reactions ran the gamut from crying and fainting to just going nuts in general.

The boys did hours of press interviews in Taiwan. They then moved on to the Hard Rock Cafe in Jakarta, where they had their first actual performance. The fan reaction was the same: girls throwing toys and notes, screaming and crying. The boys only performed a few songs with music behind them and ended a cappella.

That was what really caught everyone's attention. These guys could actually sing. That was a rare occurrence in Europe and Asia, where the fans were used to hearing track music with vocals. When a group sang live, it amazed them. No studio magic was necessary with the Backstreet Boys, just nice harmonies that sent the fans into la-la land.

The Asian tour was intense. There was a large area to cover and Jive gave us limited time, so we jumped from country to country. From Jakarta we went to Seoul, Korea, where a television show got completely messed up by a production assistant who took the boys to the wrong side of the stage, making them miss their cue. They were very upset, but nothing could be done since the show was live.

The language barrier was a real problem. Nina and our soundman repeated over and over what the boys needed in the way of equipment, but they always wound up using whatever they were given. Even so, they tried desperately to win over that market.

We moved on to Bangkok, Thailand. As we traveled through Asia, the one common factor we noticed was the intense traffic that clogged the roads. Between the bicycles, carriages, cars, buses and people, it was pretty scary to even be on the sidewalk at times.

The boys accomplished their goals no matter what obstacles were put in front of them. Since this was a new market, the "big head" syndrome seemed to subside. They were forced to start from square one.

ANDRE CSILLAG

The boys in Japan

138

That meant pulling together and doing what they had to do in order to make the impact they wanted. It was good to see that they still had some hunger left inside of them to draw on when it was needed. The trip put things into perspective. Going to the U.S. market with big ideas in their heads would not have gone over too well with American fans. That little trip down humility lane served them well.

Food became a bit of an issue on that tour, since not all of the boys were really into Asian cuisine. Alex was always on the lookout for a Mickey D's and Nick was right behind him. Brian was also pretty picky when it came to his eating, especially if it was green. Stir-fry was not high on his list. Kevin and Howie, on the other hand, were in their glory. They both loved Asian cuisine and ordered up whatever was new and different. I enjoyed eating out with the two of them since I, too, was always up for trying new things.

A few of the groups from England and Germany had tried to get a foothold in that market, but they had had no success. It stood to reason that everyone probably thought that our boys would meet the same fate. The main difference was the boys' talent and their ability to sing live. In every country that the boys' album had been released, it had entered the charts at the second-highest possible level. In some smaller countries, it did not take many sales to achieve that, but it was still impressive and better than all of the other pop bands at the time.

As we continued on our travels, we went to Malaysia, then to the Philippines. The fans gave us a great reception wherever we went. Word spread fast. It was an amazing phenomenon to be a part of. Fortunately, it was one of those times when Alex and I seemed to be able to put our mom-and-son differences aside for a while. We focused on our surroundings and tried to have some fun.

My job, which at this point only focused on wardrobe and makeup, was not as stressful, since the boys only needed to dress in wardrobe for performances and photo shoots. They wore their own clothes for everything else, so that limited the amount of baggage I had to haul around. When they did press interviews, they would just bring me what they wanted to wear that day. They had gotten to the point where, even if they were just going from one room in the hotel to another for interviews, it was still necessary for them to maintain a sense of Backstreet style.

By then, they had each developed their own style. That was something I had to be acutely aware of when I helped them dress for the shows. Since I had been traveling with those five young men for so long I could dress them in my sleep. The only difficult one, of course, was my own son, who changed his style from day to day right along with his hair color, accessories and facial hair. I left him on his own and just made sure that he was clean and pressed.

Dressing the boys, organizing the media interviews with Nina and setting up the meet-and-greets meant my schedule was full. Nina was great to work with. She was really organized and handled any rough spots with a great deal of professionalism. We also got along great as friends and had many things in common.

Our spiritual beliefs and family values were right on target with each other. Nina came from a typical Italian household of loving parents and siblings. Her sister, Polsia, was a long-time veteran of the music industry. The two of them were very close, both on a professional and personal level.

We were all excited about our next stop on the tour, Australia. Nina was especially thrilled since she had spent most of her childhood there. She had dreamed of returning someday to live. We all soon discovered why she was so fond of that vast continent. It was amazingly beautiful and exotic. The locals were some of the kindest and warmest people we had ever met. The record company there welcomed us like family and made us all feel as though we were on holiday.

All the shows went well, except for one night in Sydney. The venue was a youth center and it was in a part of town that was not too cool and there were too many guys in the audience. Some of the guys near the stage threw water bottles at the boys and Kevin got really mad. He walked up very close to the group of guys and got in their faces as he was singing. Then he flicked off one of the guys' baseball caps.

I could see in Kevin's face that he really wanted to get into a fight, but the performance was cut short when a small riot broke out in the parking lot. Apparently, this was a very nasty part of town and the kids outside beat up one of the security guards and that was when the trouble began. When they broke down the glass doors at the entrance, that was our cue to leave. Our bodyguards gathered us up and hustled us out the back in an instant. It was a little scary, but it all ended well.

All of the remaining in-store sessions and shows in Sydney went fine. I think the incident in the youth club was just a bad booking on the part of the record company. The people who turned out were not our target audience. We sadly bid farewell to Australia and moved on to Tokyo. It was the end of October and we were all beginning to show signs of exhaustion.

═══════

WHEN WE RETURNED HOME, we found out that another group that Johnny and Lou had been working with, *NSYNC, had released their first single in England. It did not do very well and I cannot lie and say I was unhappy. I had seen the look of grave disappointment in the boys' eyes when they talked about the other boy band. It was very hard for all of us to understand why it was necessary for them to have another boy band.

Did Lou and Johnny think that the Backstreet Boys had gone as far as they could go? Were they ready to move on to the next project? Alex confided to me on several occasions how angry he was with Johnny for managing the other group. He and Johnny and Brian used to go golfing together quite often. Now that would undoubtedly change. The closeness they once shared seemed at risk.

The only explanation I could see was that Lou and Johnny wanted to duplicate the success of the Backstreet Boys. Why else would they want that group when they already had our five boys? The five boys in *NSYNC were very similar. Alex was afraid that his group was going to be cast aside.

When confronted with that, Lou and Johnny insisted that they were moving ahead very slowly with the other group and that it would not affect the Backstreet Boys. I knew that could not be true. Both men would have to split their time between the two groups, and Johnny had

Alex and me fooling around in Japan

ANDRE CSILLAG

already become less of a presence for the Backstreet Boys. All of this was bound to have an impact on the boys' feelings.

As 1997 wore on, we forged ahead. Another single was released in England and it did very well in the charts. At the last minute, a trip was put together so that the boys could do a television show there. Johnny could not make it, so Donna went to oversee things. What a mistake that was! She seemed to have a chip on her shoulder.

On a personal level, Donna and Johnny were on the outs. Most of her time was spent on the phone with him, embroiled in nasty screaming matches. She flew off the handle into a jealous rage over some girl from Germany who had spread rumors that she had slept with Johnny. It resulted in an ugly scene in the lobby bar of our hotel. Everyone just left her standing there alone and went to their rooms.

Shortly after that incident, there was a welcome new addition to our team, Nina. She quit her job at Jive and took a position as the boys' tour manager. I was very happy about that since she shared everyone's opinion of Donna and did everything she could to keep her off the road. It felt like our group was complete.

ANDRE CSILLAG

As time went by, I became more involved with press and fan club events than with clothing issues. That made me happy. I was not really cut out for the wardrobe slot after all. I enjoyed being out there on the front lines, where I was able to keep an eye on Alex. Having Nina there eased my stress, since she watched over all of the boys and really grew to love them as I did. Even the crew looked out for them.

It had become standard procedure that someone always

Me backstage with Steven Tyler

142

needed to "speak" to the boys for one reason or another right before they went on stage. They had made it very clear that they wanted to become more involved in every aspect of their careers. In a way that was a good thing, but when it came to scheduling it was a nightmare. The boys wanted approval over merchandise and touring, but it quickly became clear that they really did not have the business sense to deal with it. Lou and Johnny had always made the business decisions for them.

When those impromptu business meetings came up, the shows invariably ran late. The promoters would get angry and the boys would get fined. Arguments

Me with John Norris, MTV News

over fines would ensue. None of the boys were willing to give up their personal time for those business meetings. When we tried to schedule a lunch or breakfast meeting, at least one or more of the boys would not show up. That would cause arguments between those boys who had attended and subsequently made decisions and those who had failed to show up. Spending almost every waking moment of our lives together was taking its toll on us all.

THERE WERE A FEW TIMES that I felt comfortable enough with the group of people who were watching over the boys that I stayed off the road. That enabled me to concentrate on developing press releases for the boys when they returned to the States. Donna did not realize it, but since she made enemies at every turn, people were beginning to depend on Nina or me for all of the boys' press and promotional scheduling.

Nina and I rarely spoke to Donna about press issues. Everything worked a lot more smoothly when she was not involved. We came to the same conclusion early on about Donna. Every time she had a tantrum it was to get a reaction of some sort. When you stopped reacting to her insults and manipulations, she usually moved on. When we had to deal with Donna, we kept it short and sweet.

While we were in England, a female fan that had come to the meet-and-greet began crying when it was time for her to leave. She said a gift that she had brought Kevin had been stolen. She claimed she had brought an expensive diamond for Kevin and had set the box down to take a picture with him. When she picked the box up it had been ripped open and the diamond was missing.

Kevin had the bodyguards ask the other fans if they had noticed anyone around the box and everyone said no. Kevin felt sorry for the girl and told her that she could come backstage after the show and he would see her again.

During the show, the record company rep investigated the incident and took a business card from the girl that had information about the gem. By the end of the show, they had found out that everything she had told us was a lie. The business did not exist and there probably never was a real diamond. She was escorted out and that was the last we ever saw of her.

Later that year, it became apparent that the boys could no longer walk through airports like normal passengers. There were so many fans at each one that it was dangerous for them. From that point on, we were picked up either on the tarmac or outside the gate in private cars with dark-tinted windows and driven directly to our hotel or wherever. If passports had to be shown, security collected them from us, displayed them to the proper authorities and then returned them to us back at the hotel. Not going through the checkpoints made things a bit less scary, but we still had to contend with the enormous number of fans at each hotel and outside each venue.

We added local security in every country. That made it easier to cut through the red tape during our comings and goings. Even getting out of parking garages had become a scary feat. The fans would move from the front of the building to the street entrance outside the garage before we had a chance to get into our vehicles. Everywhere we went, we had to run in order to stay one step ahead of the fans. The girls had gotten so aggressive that the boys actually feared for their safety at times.

The girls grabbed onto clothing, jewelry, hair or whatever they could get. Alex lost a ring that way while onstage. A girl grabbed him so tightly, that it came off. That was the last he saw of it. He learned quickly not to wear things that could be pulled off or at least not to let the girls grab him like that.

Howie got more than a few pieces of clothing ripped when he tried to be nice and got too close to the fans. It was a nerve-wracking situation to watch. If any of the boys stopped, even just to sign autographs, girls would jump the barricades and try to grab them. They were constantly being warned by security to keep moving, but sometimes they just could not resist giving a crying girl a hug. They all learned the hard way to listen to security or get grabbed.

Slowly, the level of success they had achieved began to dawn on each of the boys. Brian commented to me before a show that when he entered the catering room, all heads turned. He felt like he was being treated with a new level of respect. Each boy began to get the same impression in his own individual way.

For his part, Alex seemed to enjoy it. It was at that point that he asked me to start calling him AJ. I had a hard time with that because that had always been his stage name. To me, that name did not represent who he was to me but who he was to his fans. He had taken quite a liking to the AJ persona and used it to his advantage. He liked the way it gained him new friends and how it made him feel like a big shot. With all of that, he still seemed to have an air of insecurity about him. Alex remained the people-pleaser who hated confrontation.

I started to see some subtle changes in my son that I did not care for. He hung out a lot with the musicians and was always the big spender. Each week he went through his per diem of hundreds of dollars too quickly. That forced him to ask me for money. When I didn't oblige, he went to the tour accountant and got an advance against his next check. I did not like his new lack of respect for money.

Journal Entry, April 17, 1996: *On more than one occasion, I have tried to talk to Alex about those things. Each time, he blows me off. He said that they are making plenty of money, so why not spread it around. Those words sounded like Lou talking, not Alex. As far as the money goes, yes, he is right, some is being made, but by the time Lou takes out what Alex and I owe, there is not much left. It is enough for bills and to help Mom and Dad a bit.*

My son's attitude has begun to change. I feel powerless and at a loss as to how to make him see what is happening. I tried talking to the band and asked that they watch out for him. While I believe that sometimes they do, most of the time they just want to party. It is of little concern to them who pays the bill.

As the tour moved back across the Atlantic to Canada, we saw the same levels of fan and media reaction to the boys. I made a couple of great friends in Canada. To this day, we are still in touch. It was a good group of people to work with. Our record company rep was named Stephan Drolet. He was a great guy who, in addition to not being too hard on the eyes, also had a big heart. He always did everything he could to make us feel at home. Even after the workday was over, he was always around to ensure that we had a good time.

Chantal Blanchard, the publicist for our Canadian promoter, was a spunky French Canadian with a great professional, yet fun, personality. Her organizational skills helped the boys get through the interviews and meet-and-greets as quickly as possible. We worked well together and had fun all the time. She worked with another great person named Leesa Lee. We made a great team and were able to keep the boys on schedule.

As we moved across Canada, fans followed in caravans of cars. On several occasions, we had to stop so that the bus driver could get out and tell them to stay farther away because they were making him nervous on the long night drives. It was insane.

Toronto became Alex's nightmare beginning with that tour. During one of the promotional events, we took the boys to a television studio of a network much like our own MTV, where they were scheduled to sing to a small audience, sign autographs and take some pictures. It all seemed routine until we drove up to the studio.

There were more than five thousand girls surrounding the building. We could not even get inside. If that were not bad enough, we had more

BILL FERNANDEZ

than our usual number of people. Some of the boys' family members had decided to join us for that part of the tour. Our usual two vans grew to three. I had been put in charge of the family members, so it was my job to make sure that they got inside and seated for the show. Kevin's mom and Brian's parents were there, along with some members of Howie's family. We pulled

Leesa Lee, me
and Chantal Blanchard

into the parking lot around back, where we waited until the boys got inside.

Once we all got into the studio—and the boys cranked up their performance—the other family members looked on in awe as the fans screamed their approval. That was a new experience for most of the other boys' families. They had only heard about the craziness from their sons.

During the set, Randy watched over the audience, as another member of his team set up barricades outside so that a path back to the vans could be formed. That same bodyguard was asked to develop a plan to get the boys and us away safely since the numbers of fans outside were growing by the minute.

That done, we waited for the boys to finish their performance.

Once the show was over, we followed the same procedure to exit the building—the boys first, we second. I awaited our cue to leave on my walkie-talkie, but all I could hear were girls screaming and men screaming back. Then, through the garbled noises, I heard a heart-wrenching voice that nearly took my breath away.

"He's hurt bad, we need to get him to the hospital."

Who was hurt? One of the boys? A fan? What just happened? Questions raced through my mind. I could not interrupt the radio communications since they obviously needed to talk to each other. Finally, after what seemed like an eternity, one of our bodyguards came back to get us. He just looked at me with this kind of odd, scared expression on his face and grabbed me by the arm.

I instinctively knew Alex had been hurt and said, "Okay, so now we know who got hurt. The question is, how bad?"

The bodyguard said he did not know any details. I rushed the family members into the van and tried to hold myself together until we got back to the hotel. By the time we arrived and unloaded our van, Alex had already been taken to the hospital. Randy was with him. Todd was ready to take me there straight away.

As we drove the short distance to the hospital, Todd filled me in on what had happened. There were supposed to be barricades outside the studio where they boarded the vans, but someone had mistakenly erected the barricades in the front of the studio instead of at the back door where the boys exited. Once the boys entered the unprotected no-man's land between the studio and the vans, fans surrounded them.

Alex ran for the van and got crushed by the swarming crowd. Todd tried to get him free. The girls were screaming so loudly that the van driver could not hear Alex writhing in pain. His foot had slipped off the brake and the van had run over my son's foot. When the driver realized

ANDRE CSILLAG

Alex brandishes his cane
after the accident

that his foot had slipped, he stopped the van. Unfortunately, the van stopped while the tire was on top of Alex's foot. Finally, Todd got him loose and threw him inside the van. He was screaming in pain and they rushed him to the hospital. Well, I am here to tell you that Alex's guardian angel was definitely watching over him that day. His foot was not broken and he just had a bad ankle sprain. The x-rays were clear.

We were all befuddled by the events of the afternoon. Thankfully, no one else had been injured, but there was one bit of unpleasantness that still had to be attended to. The bodyguard who had botched the barricade placement had to be held accountable. It was not the first time he had gotten into trouble, so he was terminated. Alex and I felt bad for him and told him that we did not hold it against him.

BY THE TIME THE BOYS RETURNED HOME, it appeared that word of their fame had finally spread to the States. With the release of their video, "Everybody (Backstreet's Back)" in the fall of 1997, the boys began to receive media attention in America. I was happy for them because I knew how much they craved the respect of their peers. They wanted the respect of other American artists, record producers and writers.

They also wanted a greater say in their career. Most pop groups are told what to do by their record company from the time they wake up until they go to sleep. They have little or no say when it comes to writing music or having any creative input in their videos. The boys wanted to be true musical artists in every sense.

One result of their newfound confidence was that they were less eager to follow suggestions made by Johnny or Jive Records. Since they were quickly becoming the largest pop group in the world, no one wanted to start a war with them. Instead, they backed away and tried to make the boys happy, at least for the time being.

Accompanying the boys' desire for greater creative independence was the sobering realization that they were now more financially dependent on management than when they first started out. As Alex and I learned more about our financial situation, we became very angry. From day one, the five boys had been charged for every dime that had been spent. Every dinner with Lou, every golf game with Johnny, every hospitality suite that Donna used, everything. That realization overwhelmed all of the boys and their families. Then we learned that we were building up a bill with Jive as well. All of the promotional expenses in the United States, along with recording fees and transportation costs, were taken out of the record sales.

The thing that angered us the most was the fact that no one had ever bothered to explain any of that to us, not even when we asked. Finally, we met with some attorneys in New York whom we asked to go over the contracts. We were amazed to learn just how unfair the contracts were. Lou got a piece from all sides—management, merchandise, record sales, touring profits, everything.

We were all in agreement that management deserved its fair share—we even agreed that Lou deserved a bit more, given the fact that he was the one who had backed the group financially from the beginning—but the numbers we were shown were absolutely outrageous. The other parents and I were so angry with Lou at that point that it was a good thing that he was not in reach. Each of us felt as though our children had been horribly taken advantage of. I felt particularly awful, considering that I had added to the expenses by taking a small salary.

The other parents and I decided to make Lou, Johnny and Jive Records account for every penny that thus far had been earned and spent. Thinking back on it now, the betrayal that Alex and I felt then was not unlike what we had felt when his father left the first time and then again more recently when he showed his true colors.

I believe that Alex felt doubly betrayed. He had formed a tight bond with Johnny. The two of them genuinely enjoyed each other's company, whether it was in the studio or on the golf course. When the reality of what had gone on hit Alex, it only added to his inner turmoil. I understand why my son may have developed a deep mistrust of men. All of the men that he trusted, with the exception of my dad and his uncle, had their own agenda—and it usually didn't include his best interests.

During that time, Alex confided in me that performing had become less fun. All of the meetings with attorneys, along with the business affairs that had to be attended to constantly, weighed heavy on his mind. The business of the business was getting to him. Alex was only nineteen, but he felt the same pressures as the CEO of a major corporation.

As his free time dwindled, Alex frenetically tried to cram as many pleasures as possible into his life, including the spontaneous impulsive shopping sprees that he had become famous for. He seemed intent on spending every cent of what little money was coming in. We began to argue a lot about money.

Alex bought his first car, a really nice BMW 325i. It was not the car he originally wanted, but he took the advice of his uncle and purchased a used one instead. With the help of my brother, Alex managed to get a pretty good deal. No sooner did he buy the car than he decided to change it. He painted it bright yellow and re-covered the entire interior in white leather. It caused the break up of a friendship, since the guy who did the work never consulted me and charged Alex an exorbitant amount of money.

Then Alex felt the need to change the wheels and tires for no good reason. He spent an absolute fortune on that. Thus began another trend that involved wasteful spending in an effort to hide from his problems.

What worried me the most was the uncertainty of Alex's financial future. I had no way of knowing how long the income stream was going to last. I tried desperately to get him to invest his money and save it. His response was always, "It's my money and I can do with it what I want."

On top of that, I saw AJ's stage persona begin to dominate Alex. The two had melded into one. AJ from the Backstreet Boys now lived in my house. I kept waiting for Alex to reappear. It was to be a long and tortured wait.

Friends from his past popped out of the woodwork like termites. I tried to tell him that they were nothing more than fair-weather friends. It was blatantly obvious to everyone but Alex. They did not like him for himself but rather for being a Backstreet Boy. Every time Alex came home, his entourage of hangers-on increased. His group now included people who a few years earlier would not have given him the time of day. With each passing visit, he pulled further away from me. I felt totally helpless and there was no doubt in my mind that he was on a dangerous course.

Alex's quest for independence peaked when he leased an apartment with one of the other boys. Once he moved out of my apartment, all lines of communication disintegrated. He avoided his family and continually sought the advice of strangers.

On more than one occasion, he upset my mother by telling her that he was coming to see her, then failed to show up for hours, if at all. It was so painful for us as a family that we confronted him with an ultimatum: either straighten out your attitude or don't bother coming to see the family at all, because the pain is too great.

Alex claimed that he didn't realize he had hurt us. He blamed much of his behavior on his schedule, as well as the pressure he was constantly under. When he promised that he would work at making things better, I felt a glimmer of hope.

At that point, turmoil raged both inside and outside of the group. The boys no longer knew whom they could trust. Lou and Johnny seemed to be more interested in the new groups they had signed, including *NSYNC. Once we had hired attorneys to start looking into the financial end of things, Lou got very defensive and stopped coming around. When he did show up, Brian usually refused to look at him.

Adding to the stress, Alex expressed his rebellious nature with body art. He got tattoo after tattoo. That caused more problems with his family and me, not just because of the tattoos, but because it was representative of other excessive behavior, including his willingness to live up to the bad-boy image that had been given to him by the magazines. He reveled in the attention that image brought, especially among his female fans. With Marisa out of the picture, he was free to play the field—and he did, big time.

Legally, he could not go to bars unless we were out of the country. When we traveled, he took advantage of the lower drinking ages to party. Soon the partying became as excessive as his lifestyle. AJ seemed intent on drowning out Alex.

———

WE SCHEDULED THE MEETING for a Sunday. The boys had to decide whether or not they wanted to remain with Jive. Not only had the attorneys found discrepancies in the financial statements from management, they uncovered the same problems with the statements from Jive. Our attorneys felt that it was grounds to make Jive pay up or let the boys go. Since the boys were so popular, we all felt Jive would probably settle.

Another consideration was the fact that Jive did not seem to know what to do with the boys in the States. After discussing that issue at length, the boys concluded that it was BMG, not Jive, that had worked their butts off to break the boys in Europe and Asia. Now it was Jive's turn to step up and show what they could do. So far, they had stumbled around like complete amateurs.

The Backstreet Boys had worked too hard and too long to let their shot at success slip away just because their record company did not want to take a chance on them in their own country. They had yet to help the boys top the charts and something needed to be done to rectify that. All we kept hearing was how there was no money in the budget for this or that. Every one of us knew that the boys had made the people around them, including the record company, millions of dollars. In our eyes, that was criminal.

CHAPTER TEN

Attack of the Glommers

THE BACKSTREET BOYS HAD SPECTACULAR YEARS in 1997 and 1998, achieving a mind-numbing level of success both internationally and at home. They appeared to be unstoppable. When we traveled to the MTV Europe Music Awards in November 1997, I realized just how far they had come. The respect they had gained within the industry became obvious when they were asked to perform two songs and close the show.

The boys started off with a ballad and then came backstage for a quick change. They then turned right around and did a full-out version of "Backstreet's Back" with dancers. It was an amazing performance!

As I watched with Nina from the greenroom backstage, I was filled with pride. All of the boys' vocals were perfect and the choreography was tight. And the reaction from the audience was as enthusiastic as the performances.

Nearly a year had passed since Alex moved out of my house. It had been an eventful year in a number of ways, both good and bad. Many of the lawsuits that had been filed against management were negotiated. We all had to go through the enormous amount of accounting that finally came to us once the attorneys got involved.

It took many meetings with the attorneys and accountants before we discovered just how badly the boys had been mistreated. Lou had always taken the stand that he had put up millions of dollars to get the boys where they were. We came to find out that was not entirely true. He had used investors' money to pay the bills; he just happened to be one of the major shareholders. Big Poppa always needed to look like the big shot to the boys and everyone around him. As time went on, we realized that many people other than Lou were involved in the boys' career.

One by one, Lou's investors went out on the road with us. Each one called himself a manager and talked like he had been in the record business for years. They all had a piece of the Backstreet pie and made everyone aware of it once the boys were successful. Of course none of these shareholders ever had any background in the music business. It was just another venture that their buddy Lou needed money for, and they bit.

The web of lies kept growing larger and larger.

Another disheartening fact was that Johnny never really tried to warn the boys or explain to them what was happening. In some ways I imagine he must have had regrets about knowing what the boys had really gotten into with his recommendation. Yet he was indifferent to how much he had hurt the boys. If he cared, I saw no signs of it.

When asked about why he never told the boys the truth, he said that he had a bad experience of being ripped off by groups before. It became his practice after that not to get too close. That really did not make sense, since he had gotten extremely close to both Brian and Alex, probably the two boys most hurt by his actions.

I had several conversations with Johnny over the years. He always seemed to just be on the edge of telling me what was going on, but he never crossed the line. Knowing that he is a good and kind-hearted person, I can only surmise that maybe he was too wrapped up in the almighty dollar.

Eventually, the boys too turned against him, especially since he was the one who helped Lou start up *NSYNC. It looked to us as if he was preparing to move on and manage another band. It was one more disappointment for my son.

Brian made the first move when he filed a lawsuit on behalf of the boys. It really came as a shock to everyone. No one had been aware that Brian and his family had taken steps to hire their own attorney. His mom and dad had had enough of the runaround and decided to take matters into their own hands. Even though it came as a big surprise to the rest of the boys, they got behind it.

One good thing that came out of the attorneys' negotiations was that we were able to settle up with Lou on Alex's debt. That meant that any more money that came in would be Alex's to keep. Lou made sure everyone received a statement of the accounting. Once that was done we were also given a day to go in and discuss it with him.

Alex and Nick had incurred the highest bills due to the fact that they had been tutored for so long. Alex also had some of my debt included in his. However, I had been diligently chipping away at that once I started getting an actual salary from Lou. I had the accounting department take a portion from each paycheck and apply it to that debt. I felt guilty that I had played a small part in the amount of money that Alex owed, but truly it could not have been helped. There was simply no way I could have been out on the road with him as a guardian and held down a full-time job at the same time.

At the time, I thought that what I did was right and to this day I still feel that way. The most important thing at the time was that I was there to look after my son. If nothing else, at least my presence was felt. Everyone knew that for a while they had to deal with me. Alex trusted me and knew that I would never do anything to hurt him.

Even though Alex moved out of the apartment, I tried to be as open-minded as possible and let him do his thing. I always tried to be there for him if he needed me. At one point, we had a talk about his relationship with Marisa and how Donna had affected them both. It turned out that Alex had some real issues with Donna that he had never been able to talk about before.

As he opened up to me, I felt a sense of relief. It was good to be allies again. He told me that he had tried pot for the first time with Marisa. He also said that Donna had tried to influence him with regards to me controlling his life. That was why she had encouraged him to move out. He admitted that for a while he had thought she was right.

Once, after a particularly heated argument with her mother, Marisa decided, once and for all, to go back up North to live with her father. Alex was devastated, but he understood that his family would be there for him no matter what. After that I felt much better about things. Alex and I also came to an understanding about our current relationship. There was no denying that he was growing up. I needed to come to terms with that as much as he did.

It was during that year that my mom reconciled with the fact that Alex was reaching his manhood. She was there for him when he needed to talk and continued to be there for me. For everyone's sake, I kept the lines of communication open as best I could.

When I look back on those years now, I see the beginning of a pattern that Alex would continue to follow for years to come. Unknown to everyone around Alex, there was an insecurity that raged inside of him. I never understood where that came from. The odd part about it was that it never appeared on stage. AJ always took control of the audience and the stage. AJ never had a doubt when it came to his movements or his voice. But when Alex stepped out of the lights that insecurity was right there. It was usually expressed in the form of self-criticism or hidden emotions. My hope was that once he began to reap the rewards of the group's efforts, he would realize that his talents and his life were really coming together. I hoped that there would be no room in his life at that point for the insecurities that sometimes paralyzed him.

I tried to make him attend all of the meetings with the attorneys, since it was his future that was at stake. He humored me, but it was obvious that he wasn't listening. He never asked any questions and never really voiced an opinion that was contrary to the group. I just hoped that some of it would sink in. It was important that he understood how the music business worked. Alex needed to know that there were times when he had to be confrontational and stand up for his rights.

My son had always hated confrontation, even as a child. To discipline him all I ever had to do was not speak to him. He always folded under that pressure. We never had many arguments when he was small. In fact, I felt he had more confidence in himself as a child than as a man. That was very odd considering that he had always known what he wanted to do and he was in fact fulfilling his dreams. Why would that not instill confidence as an adult? How many adults ever see their dreams come true in a lifetime, never mind by the time they are twenty?

At the request of our accountant, I convinced Alex to form a company. It would help him escape some tax consequences and put him in a position to eventually go somewhere with his future as a solo artist. The thought of pursuing a solo career had not entered my son's mind at that point, but I knew that someday the ride would end and he would need something to fall back on. Some day he would have to come to terms with the fact that Backstreet Boys would not last forever. It was nice to think that those five boys might end up like the icons that had come before them. The chance that they would still be playing to packed houses when they were well into their fifties was a slim one. In the music business, you just never knew.

Alex decided to call his company AJ Shadz Inc. It would be classified as a production company in case he ever wanted to do shows on his own. I also registered the company as a publishing company. That way, if Alex kept up with his songwriting, there would be a time when he would no longer have to split the profits with anyone. He liked those ideas and I made them happen.

After I persuaded Alex to put some money away for his future, I was able to breathe a bit easier. He was trying very hard to develop his own sense of self. After having been a part of the group for such a long period of time, I could see that he needed his own identity back. Since there was more money coming in, we both decided it might be a good idea to invest in some real estate. Alex said he wanted to buy his own home. I hoped that would help him settle down and enable him to sort some things through.

One day, during a short stay at home, Alex was out running around when he called me. He said he had been looking at houses and found one he really liked. He wanted me to see it. I drove to the house and we walked around with the real estate agent.

"So how do you like your son's new home?" the real estate agent asked.

I was floored. As I stood there in shock with my mouth hanging open, Alex just smiled and gave me a big hug. While he thought it was a great surprise, I did not know what to think. The practical side of me was crunching numbers in my head to see if he could afford it. The mom side of me was happy for him. It was, after all, his very first home and a good investment for his future.

When the real estate agent saw the look on my face, she knew it was time to take her leave and let us talk. We did. But even if I had been dead-set against the idea, it was too late. The papers were signed and he had the key in his hand,

Later that day, I went home and tried to explain all of it to my parents. They reacted in much the same way as I had. What none of us could understand was why he had been in such a rush to buy a house when he was about to leave on a major tour that would keep him on the road for the next several months.

A pattern was taking shape right before my eyes, but I failed to see it. It was that instant gratification, the compulsive pattern of "I want it now," that would continue to dominate his life for years to come.

Over the next few months, whenever Alex was home for a day or two, we went shopping for furniture and other necessities. Those times when I was not out on the road, I would buy things at the store so that he would have them when he got home. I must admit, it was fun not having to care so much about the cost of things, even though I still checked price tags and looked over every receipt.

For a while, I fell into the same trap as Alex when it came to spending money. I was having so much fun helping him decorate his new house that I went a little wild. The truth was, I wanted him to be happy and that seemed to be doing the trick. He had somewhere to call his own. As a mother, I was proud that at his age he could afford to have those kinds of things. My child had worked all of his life for what he had. I did not want to be the one who deprived him of what was rightfully his.

For a while, things rolled along without incident. We went back on tour with another album ready to hit the shelves. It seemed as if things were falling back into place for Alex and me, that is, until the ants started emerging from the floorboards again under the guise of being his long-lost friends.

While on the road in Europe, Alex informed me that he had hired a friend to be his housesitter. She was a woman in her late twenties who had a son who did not live with her. She and Alex had somehow become friends over the past couple of years. He told me that he really enjoyed her son, who was around six years old.

Alex assured me that there was nothing romantic between them. He said she just needed some extra money to supplement her income from her job at Universal Studios. I was not at all happy to hear that my son had opened his home to a virtual stranger. Just to be on the safe side, I had a friend, who happened to be a cop, patrol the house a few nights a week. That was when the true story came out.

On more than one occasion, my friend told me that there were several cars parked at the house during the evenings and on the weekends. The woman appeared to be having guests over at my son's home. I took the information to Alex and told him to call her and confront her about it. He did. They had a falling out and she left shortly after that. I was just relieved to have her off the premises.

———

OUT ON THE ROAD, the boys' entourage had gotten bigger. It became necessary to lease more buses to carry everyone, as family and girlfriends spent more time traveling with the boys. That added to the ever-growing expenses. Sometimes it even led to problems among the five boys when they had meetings or tried to discuss legal matters. In my opinion, having so many outsiders sitting in on those meetings with attorneys made the situation much too public.

Then disaster struck. Somewhere on tour, Howie lost his backpack. In it were all of the legal documents concerning the lawsuit against Lou. It did not take long for what had started out as a secret negotiation to turn into a public circus. The press got wind of the situation and reported on their difficulties in newspapers and on television.

Questions arose about the lawsuit and about Lou and management. In a way, I suppose it was not a bad thing. It certainly prompted all the concerned parties to more quickly reach a settlement. New contracts between the boys, management and Lou were drawn up, following our attorneys' guidelines.

By Thanksgiving, the boys and I left for New York to be in the Macy's parade. While there, we had two meetings to formulate a plan for the new contracts. One of the main topics of conversation was over management. Johnny's name was the only one mentioned. In addition, the attorneys gave more details of just how badly the boys had been raped at the original contract signing. We felt misled and betrayed by all of the people we had trusted.

I felt as if I had gotten Alex into the biggest mess of his life. Every instinct we as parents had felt during that original signing should have been dealt with. There was only one thing that kept ringing in my head: maybe I should have done this or that. Maybe if I had hired an attorney to look over the deal, it would have been okay. Maybe if we had made the record company wait, this never would have happened. If I learned nothing else during those negotiations, I learned that no one could be trusted. If something appears too good to be true, then it is.

I became increasingly cynical after that and even more suspicious of everyone around Alex who claimed to be his "friend." I hoped that he had learned some of the same lessons. Sadly, that was not the case. Again, Alex depended on me to handle everything—and as usual I did. It did not occur to me that I should see to it that he absorbed some of the unpleasantness for future reference. It would have served him well in the years to come.

One of the strange things that happened during the negotiations was that Jive Records suddenly became our best friend. It was as if they were happy to have management out of the way, so that they could come in and take over the reins. At that point, the main players who dealt with requests for the boys were Nina and me and, on a rare occasion, Johnny. But by then, he was spending most of his time with *NSYNC and on his impending divorce from Donna.

The boys grew increasingly unhappy about all the time Johnny spent away from them. Their feelings were really hurt by his lack of interest in them, both personally and professionally. There was a definite void in their lives. It made them sad to know that they would never have his undivided attention (and in some cases his friendship) again.

They compensated for their disappointment by burying themselves in the ever-growing amount of work that lay ahead of them. The upside of that year was that the boys made many strides in the U.S. They were honored by their peers with music awards and they were embraced by the media, especially television. They performed on all the major shows like *Regis & Kathy Lee*, *The Tonight Show with Jay Leno*, *Saturday Night Live* and more.

The hangers-on also came out in force. Whether people showered the boys with gifts with the hope of receiving something in return, or whether they did it in an effort to get the boys to sign endorsements, inevitably each time a gift was given a price was attached. Maybe not right away, but at some point someone had a niece, sister, cousin or whomever who wanted passes to a show, or entrance to a meet-and-greet. People who had not shown their faces for years asked for free tickets and backstage access.

The backstage area quickly became a three-ring circus made up of what we affectionately called the "glommers." They were the people who really had no business being there but had somehow managed to weasel their way in. Howie suddenly had family in every city we visited. It became a bit of a joke just how many relatives Howie seemed to have hidden away. But, I must admit, most of them were usually very nice.

I suppose stardom affects everyone in different ways. Family members that we hadn't seen in years came to see Alex. It became part of my job to make sure that during every show there was a VIP room set up for family and friends. That enabled the boys to visit with them before they went onstage. If we had those people corralled in a room, they were not roaming the backstage hallways getting into trouble.

From the moment we arrived at our hotel, I would be on the phone talking to the promoters, Nina, security, the record company, press or whomever else I needed to deal with before we left for the venue that afternoon. Usually, I arrived at the venue several hours ahead of the boys to ensure that everything was in place. It was my job to find rooms and set up passes for the meet-and-greets and VIPs, and make sure all the boys' guests found their way backstage.

Once the boys entered the building, the chaos that ensued was my daily nightmare. On very rare occasions I actually got to eat dinner with Alex before a show. But he usually waited until after the performance to get something back at the hotel. I would just try and grab a bite with my photographer buddy, Andre, who had been with our little group for a number of years. We had come to be great friends. He was so familiar with the business that nothing much fazed him.

Andre was there to capture on film every event that appeared worthy of a magazine story or cover. He worked independently and at his own expense. That meant that, unlike the salaried crew, he answered to no one but the boys. Andre had become my mentor in a way. There were many times when I felt as if I was on my last thread of nerves. I could always talk to him. In his wise way, he helped me work things out. We shared some great times.

After the boys arrived at the venue, they played pool or basketball, or ran a sound check, or had a meeting with the crew to go over mistakes or changes from the previous night's show. Once the boys were done with what we liked to call "the grip and grins," they were off to get dressed and ready for the show.

After joining the boys for prayer, hugs and kisses before they ran to the stage, I accompanied security out into the pit with the press. I made sure that everyone got the shots that they needed during the first three songs, then I led them out of the building. The record company rep made sure that they disposed of their cameras if they returned to watch the rest of the performance.

The crew had such a large amount of equipment to pack up and move out that they had to start tearing it down as soon as the boys were on stage. At the end of every show, the boys ran off and we wrapped them in robes and towels as they scurried to their bus. The boys always did one encore. After that, the band continued to play to make it seem as if they were coming back. It was not until the house lights went on that the audience realized the show was over. By that time, we were halfway back to our hotel or on to the next city.

As the years wore on, I continued to refine the meet-and-greet process. Media access was limited to high-end magazines. Of course, I had my issues with the media during those years, but generally our relationship was pretty stable. If a bad article came out, I found out who the culprit was and they were dealt with accordingly. That usually meant the boys would not grant them another interview for a very long time, if ever. That did not happen with many magazines.

Everyone understood each other's place. The magazines needed the boys on the cover and the boys needed the limelight. That being the case, they trod lightly. During the interviews, I was always the heavy. It was up to me to pull the boys out when they wanted to end the interview. All in all, I could probably count on one hand the times that I fought with journalists or photographers or record company people over the boys. I am very proud of the years when I was known as the tour publicist for the Backstreet Boys.

THAT YEAR, THERE WAS AN INCIDENT that put a real scare into all of us—
Brian underwent open-heart surgery. As a child he had been diagnosed
with a heart problem. Luckily, it had not acted up for several years, but it
was something that he knew would have to be addressed sometime. That
time arrived when we least expected it. The boys were devastated when
they heard the news. Alex and I prayed on several occasions with the other
boys for his safe recovery. The media had a field day with rumors while he
was in the hospital and then later when he went home to recover.

The first rumor was that Brian was not returning to the group. That
escalated to a rumor that both he and Nick were quitting the band. No
one took much notice until some phony legal documents hit the news.
Then the record company started getting suicide threats from distraught
fans. At that point, the boys had no choice but to go on record and
squelch the rumors.

Around that time, my dad started having some medical problems and
that added greatly to my stress level. I called home every day, just to
make sure that he was doing okay. First, he had to have prostate surgery.
Because of his age and the fact that he had diabetes, his recovery time
was longer than normal. In addition, we were told that he had had a
couple of incidents that they called mild strokes.

Mom was extremely upset. I was thankful that she had my brother
and other family around her for support. I felt very bad that I could not
be there to help her. Dad's medical problems finally subsided, which
helped to ease my stress a bit. But the tension on the road was quickly
reaching crisis levels.

The boys were hurt by Johnny's apparent lack of interest in them. That
hurt was expressed as anger. There were countless fights between Johnny
and Brian when he went back out on the road. I was not sure how it
would all turn out. At the time, I recall thinking that Johnny was acting
very immaturely. Those boys had played a pivotal role in getting him
where he was. Actually, it was the six of them together (the five boys,
plus Johnny) who had worked so hard for the success they'd achieved.

Now that was over. The boys felt that they had been cast aside for a
newer version. Johnny didn't see the hurt underneath their anger. It was
as if he were not the adult in the scenario. Instead of sticking around to
work it out, Johnny spent more time with his new group and less with
the boys. There were rumblings of firing him.

Finally, the boys got fed up and gave Johnny an ultimatum: it's either
them or us. With that, Johnny chose *NSYNC and left. Abandoned yet

again, Alex felt betrayed and confused. It had become painfully clear that all the talk of our being "one big family" was merely lip service when compared to the almighty dollar. It was a hard lesson for both of us to learn. Again I felt that there were only a handful of people I could trust. Most of them I was related to. The fact that Alex was slipping further away from me made the hurt that much more difficult to overcome.

During the time that Brian recovered from his surgery, Alex moved into his new house. He was able to relax and enjoy some downtime with his new girlfriend, Amanda. She slightly resembled a younger version of Elizabeth Hurley. Apparently, she had aspirations of being a singer. I assumed that was what the two of them had in common.

I did not really know Amanda that well, so it was hard for me to determine anything about the relationship. At first, she did not live with Alex, since he made it very clear that he wanted to be on his own for a while. They dated and spent a lot of time together, but in my eyes he did not seem to have a real commitment to her. I was relieved, given the fact that it had not been that long since the whole Marisa and Donna affair had become a closed chapter. However, new problems lay in wait.

Alex spent more time with the glommers. That left less time for his grandparents or me. Family functions became glorified meet-and-greets to Alex. He would show up to make an appearance and then quickly dash away to meet a "friend" for dinner or a movie. I tried to pin him down about his new group of friends, but he never wanted to say very much.

One friend that he did tell me about was someone that Alex had gone to high school with (although Alex only went to that school for six months). This young man had lost his mother not too long before running into Alex. He became Alex's golfing buddy, party buddy and eventual roommate. That was fine, except that this kid never shelled out one single dime to pay for anything.

A few more glommers started using Alex's new home as a partying palace. They swarmed in, trashed the place, crashed overnight and then left the next day. Sometimes, when I visited Alex, I found bodies lying in sleeping bags or wrapped in quilts throughout the house. After a while, Alex began to feel taken advantage of. Unfortunately, he had way too big of a heart. That, coupled with his phobic fear of confrontation, limited his ability to throw the glommers out.

I saw an opportunity to solve two problems. First and foremost, I wanted to get those people away from my son or at least out of his house. Secondly, I was tired of living with my mom and dad and I welcomed the

ANDRE CSILLAG

Alex and Howie in South America

idea of some space of my own. With those two thoughts in mind, I sat Alex down and we discussed our options. He agreed that things had gotten out of hand. He admitted that he wanted the glommers to leave.

We both agreed it was best for me to move in before the next tour. A new tour of the U.S. and Canada loomed on the horizon. That would be followed by a trip to South America. I went furniture shopping and found a nice bed to start off my new room at Alex's house. After that, I took a few trips to St. Augustine to the antique shops for some nice accessories. I had a great time.

The summer ended much too quickly and we were off again.

CHAPTER ELEVEN

A Farewell & a Confession

W ITH BRIAN BACK ON TRACK, we set out for a few dates across the country and into Canada. Shortly before the tour ended, the boys took a break to attend the MTV Awards. This go round, the boys were up for several awards. On our way to the awards, Howie learned that his sister had been admitted to a hospital for treatment of complications associated with lupus, a disease that she had battled for a long time.

Devastated, Howie left for home immediately, but by the time he arrived at her bedside she was gone. She was only thirty-five. He was only able to spend a short time with his family and really had no time to grieve. This business is ruthless. Each of the boys, except for Nick, lost loved ones over the course of his career. None of them had the proper time to adjust to the loss. Their schedules were always so packed that they were lucky if they had time to fly home and attend the funeral.

Howie dealt with the loss as best as he could and we continued on the tour. He did not want to disappoint his family, but he had an obligation to his band mates. I think his family understood.

Once the American and Canadian tours ended, we returned home for a few days to regroup and prepare for our first South American tour.

Since the album was blowing out the charts there, Jive wanted the boys to hit all the major markets.

Ordinarily, that would have been an exciting prospect, but with Johnny's departure, the boys were in management limbo. They had no management and were in more demand worldwide than ever. The one thing they had not thought through before giving Johnny an ultimatum was who would take over his duties.

None of the boys had a clue as to what went on behind the scenes. They knew nothing about what it took just to get them through one of their busy days. I tried to keep things afloat as best as I could. I had cultivated a good rapport with both Jive and the media. Feeling that the boys were comfortable with my way of doing things, I stepped in to handle the day-to-day scheduling. I truly felt that if I didn't do something to help them stay on track, the Backstreet Boys would cease to exist.

At that point in their career, the boys were in huge demand by every major television show, high-end magazine and radio program worldwide. The other person in all of this mess who was left in limbo was Nicole. Her years as an assistant to Johnny and Donna had taught her an immense amount about the music business. Nicole was the glue that held things together while we were out on the road. She even kept in touch with my mom and dad to let them know how Alex and I were holding up under the intense schedule.

Mom always appreciated how much Nicole loved the boys and how hard she worked for them. Nicole was one of the most organized people I had ever met. Wherever we happened to be in the world, Nicole always made sure all of the memos and communications managed to reach us.

Me, Nina and Nicole hanging out

DOUG GOTLIN

Nina and I both knew we could count on Nicole to be there for us and get us whatever we needed. She was our anchor. As the situation with management grew messy, Nicole desperately wanted to quit, but she needed the paycheck as much as we all did. That consideration, coupled with the reality that she had come to love the five boys, was somehow always enough to make her stick it out.

When the boys finally ended their relationship with Lou, Johnny and Donna, Nicole had a rough couple of weeks trying to figure out where she would end up. Nina and I kept telling her to hang in there. We would make sure the boys kept her employed. After all, we needed someone on the home front to keep us going.

Over the course of the next few weeks, Nina and I met with the boys and they decided to keep Nicole on to operate the home office, while Nina and I remained on the road with them. The only problem was that since the boys had broken all ties with Lou, there was no actual office left to run things from. I offered the spare bedroom in my mom and dad's apartment.

In between tours, Nicole and I set things up in the office and got the schedule for the next tour rolling. Nina was based in New York, so she went back and met with Jive to move the tour along at that end. Turmoil swirled all around us, yet the boys never missed a beat. Somehow we were able to affect a smooth transition.

Unfortunately, we may have done our jobs too well. Nina and I had a couple of run-ins with some of the boys' girlfriends out on the road and that caused some problems. As a result, the boys began to act resentful toward us. All we were trying to do was hold it together for them, but they didn't always see it that way. There was always a problem with something or someone that caused delays and caused tempers to flare. It was a never-ending battle.

––––––––

THE FIRST DAY OF THE SOUTH AMERICAN TOUR (which happened to fall on Friday the 13th), got off to a shaky start when the boys walked into a press conference more than an hour late. As a result, the initial response from the press and the fans was not good. They were booed. The boys turned the situation around by charming them with their usual antics and frankness. Once they got past that first day, the response in South America was overwhelming, considering that the Backstreet Boys had never been there before.

In Argentina, the boys were booked on a very strange television show that was filmed in an amusement park. The only way to get there was by helicopter or boat. The boys opted for the boat. By that time, our hotel had been surrounded by thousands of fans, so we had to sneak out of the back, while decoy vans drove out the front.

We drove for forty minutes in a very cramped mini-bus without air-conditioning from the hotel to the producer's home. From there we boarded an amazing cabin cruiser, complete with full bar and food. Our security surrounded us in two speedboats. It was like a scene out of that old television show, *Miami Vice*.

The ride to the park was like a floating party. A couple of the boys sat on the bow of the boat and watched the sunset as we sped along the beautiful waterway. Howie, of course, had his video camera with him and filmed scenery as it whizzed by.

Alex appeared uneasy about the boat ride. I took him aside and asked him why. He told me that he felt like he was on a drug runner's boat and that made him feel very uncomfortable. While it did appear to be a bit strange, we had traveled so much and in so many different ways over the years, I told him not to worry about it, that he should just add this one to his list. My little pep talk didn't do much good. He seemed exceptionally relieved when we finally reached our destination.

As we approached the venue, we saw fans lining the banks. At some spots they were even jumping into the water as they tried to take pictures of the boys while screaming their names. Once we arrived backstage, everyone breathed a bit easier. The show was wild! The stage was covered, but the 20,000-member audience was seated outdoors.

The show went fine until Kevin had a slight mishap. Apparently, when he adjusted his battery pack for his microphone, he cut his hand without realizing it. He was in the middle of a song and reached out to a fan. Suddenly, she jumped back as she saw his bloody hand approach. Realizing that something was wrong, Kevin looked at his hand in horror and ran to the side of the stage, where Nina grabbed a towel and wrapped it around the wound. He finished the show and we ran his cut under some water to see the damage. It was actually just a small nick, so with some quick bandaging we were off.

We headed straight for the airport to make our flight. Most of the people at the show had not realized that we were leaving right away. They had gathered around to wait for the boys to come out, sign autographs and take pictures. The boys actually did stop for a minute to do that, but we had to rush them along in order to meet our departure time. Since we had finished on schedule, we were able to spend two extra days in Buenos Aires before we flew home. We all needed the short break.

It was during that time that Nina came to my room and informed me that she was leaving the boys once we got back to the States. I was shocked by the news and begged her to stay. She said that the boys had become too big-headed for her. She felt she could no longer be an effective tour manager for them. I was devastated.

I called Alex and pleaded with him to get the boys together and try to come to some understanding with Nina. He made a valiant effort, but some of the other boys did not agree, so Nina left in September 1998.

FOR THE NEXT FIVE MONTHS, it took every waking moment of every day for Nicole and I to maintain the boys' monumental schedule. There were still two major trips to plan for overseas, as well as several promotional

Grammys after-party, with Chevy Chase, his daughter and Ann, Kevin's mom

NICOLE GOTLIN

events in the States. We were barely able to keep things going, even with the support now of my family and Nicole. I was beginning to feel the stress with anxiety attacks and many sleepless nights. I began having headaches. Fearing that I would have a breakdown, Nicole constantly urged me to relax.

Alex and I were still living in his house. During that time a number of strange events had occurred in our home that I was not very happy about, not the least of which was the gradual infringement of Amanda's family into our lives.

Amanda had slowly moved her belongings into the house. She seemed to stay overnight for longer periods of time. Somehow that indicated to her family that they had the right to come and go as they pleased. That really upset me. Alex spent more time with Amanda and her family than with his own.

They told me on more than one occasion that they did not care that their daughter was dating a Backstreet Boy. As the relationship between Alex and Amanda grew, so did the gap between Alex and me. It appeared that my son had again aligned himself with a family whose matriarch was only interested in advising him how to live, especially if it benefited her daughter's singing career and her family.

I became less and less tolerant of Amanda and her mother. That was especially true during the several weeks I spent recovering from unexpected surgery. I got no help from any of them, including my son. Had it not been for Nicole, my family and friends, my recovery would have been a lot longer.

During that time of extreme craziness, Alex's behavior began to worry me. He became more withdrawn. Most of his time was spent out at night until the early hours with Amanda and her brother. Alex claimed he was playing pool or visiting with friends. But I did not like the way he looked or acted. His face had taken on a tired drawn look. It seemed that all Alex was interested in was sleeping all day and partying all night. That caused quite a few arguments between the two of us.

We spent the rest of that year promoting the band at home. The boys went back into the studio to record their next album. Many of the photo shoots and interviews that were scheduled were done with one thought in mind: it was important to position the boys in a way calculated to push them over the top in the U.S. market.

Even though the boys had conquered most of the world, they still felt that they needed to win over the American audience in order to make their success complete. To this day, I am amused by the fact that one of the most successful years in the boys' history was set up and marketed from the spare bedroom office in my house. I am quite certain that no-body ever knew that. Everyone looked at the Jive office in New York as the headquarters. In reality, it was our tiny makeshift office.

In some ways, the first five months after Nina left were the worst and the best in my memory. I felt closer to all of the boys during that time since they had no one else, besides family, to talk to. Sadly though, Alex's attitude toward me vacillated. He went from worrying about my health, due to all of the stress, to resenting me for trying to act as a manager for his group. The fact was, I never wanted to be their manager.

There was a very weird vibe hanging in the air. I noticed that none of the boys ever approached me and asked about my salary or asked if Nicole should get a raise for her efforts. I knew that the current situation could not go on indefinitely. Finally, the boys and I had a meeting, during which I told them that I would help them find new management by setting up appointments for them with prospective candidates.

Over the next few months, Nicole and I, with the help of David Zedeck, our booking agent in New York, screened managers for the boys. Once word got out that the Backstreet Boys were looking for new management, we were inundated with inquiries. David had been the boys' booking agent from the very beginning, so there was a time when some

Clive Calder, Kevin and David Zedeck

of the boys wanted him to become their manager. Oddly, they were never able to come to terms.

As the year wore on, several meetings were held with prospective managers. One management group in particular rose from the heap, The Firm. They were a duo that had split from a well-known agency in Los Angeles to form their own company. Their client list included Korn, Limp Bizkit, Ice Cube and television's *Party of Five* actress Lacey Chabert. That was an odd mix of clients, but The Firm seemed to have all the right answers and they were obviously eager to work with boys. Of course, who would not want to represent a group that was as successful as the Backstreet Boys?

By the end of the year, my cellular phone would not stop ringing and my nerves were completely shot. During that time, Nicole was about to become engaged to her future husband, Dr. Douglas Gotlin. We were all thrilled for her.

I had no life of my own any more. Alex and I spent more time not speaking than we did speaking. My parents were concerned about me having a nervous breakdown. I prodded the boys endlessly to make a decision about management.

As time passed, it got more difficult to get them together in one room to discuss anything. There was always a reason someone could not attend. They had become strangely ambivalent about their careers.

Finally, I had enough. In a last-ditch attempt at keeping them together, I called David and asked him to come down from New York and meet with the boys to try and talk some sense into them about their future. They were on the brink of superstardom and couldn't seem to get their heads out of the clouds long enough to focus on their careers. Luckily, David got through to them and things appeared to get back on track.

Our schedule at the end of that year was horrific. The boys were booked for a huge New Year's Eve concert and Showtime special in the largest auditorium in Orlando. Since the boys would not be able to celebrate the New Year, given the fact that the concert would end too late for them to go anywhere, they decided to have a party at the arena after the show.

On top of all that, Doug asked me if I would arrange for the boys to sing a song to Nicole at the after-show party so that he could propose marriage to her. At that point, I was ready to be taken away in a padded wagon. I had television producers, concert promoters, our booking agent, media and event planners and Nicole's future husband all breathing down my neck. I wondered how I would possibly make it through the night.

It was always a challenge to put on a concert in Orlando, since it is the boys' hometown. We had to put up with entourages the size of a small country and guest lists from hell. I recruited the help of my niece, Kelly Cline, to work with the party people and Nicole, as well as to handle the guests and VIPs for the night. I had to focus on being sure that the boys met their deadlines with the producers from Showtime. It was very scary to have a packed house of screaming frenzied fans surrounded by camera teams on all sides. I was positive that someone was going to get hurt.

The Showtime feature had to be shot with two endings since the producers did not want the television audience to know it was a New Year's Eve concert. The boys ended the show with a chorus from the Prince hit "1999" and then re-ended the show with the usual encore for the cameras. Of course, the audience did not care since that meant they got to spend extra time with their favorite five.

Before the boys went on stage that night, the management team that they had pretty much decided on came backstage to talk with us. I still remember the wave of relief that swept over me as I heard the boys say that they were definitely hiring them. They wanted them to start in January. I broke down and cried tears of joy. Kevin came and gave me a big hug. One or two of the other boys thanked me for my efforts over the past months. A kind word goes a long way, especially in the music business.

Looking back, the show was, without a doubt, one of the most energetic concerts the boys ever did. My son was in rare form as he bounced from one end of the stage to the other and the crowd screamed for more. They played to all of the cameras and made sure the home audience would get as much out of the show as the people in front of them. It was a great performance.

Me, Nicole and Kelly at the New Year's Eve concert

DOUG GOTLIN

As we neared the end of the show, more people gathered outside the entrance, where the party patrons were supposed to gather. Poor Nicole and Kelly had the time of their lives trying to make people understand that if they were not on the guest list they would not get in. It was a nightmare.

Fortunately most of the family and friends that we had invited were in the audience watching the show. That made it easy to corral them after the show and get them backstage for the party. Everyone at the door had a reason to get in, or so they said. Finally, after an hour or more of fighting with so-called guests, Nicole and Kelly had had enough. They closed the doors and joined the party.

All the while, I had Doug as my constant shadow. He wanted to be sure that I had not forgotten about the big surprise he had planned for that night. Doug has long since become one of my favorite people. I have told him on more than one occasion that he was lucky, given my state of mind, to have lived through that night.

To Doug's delight, I rounded up the boys, they sang, he proposed, Nicole accepted and everyone was happy. The best part was that Nicole had absolutely no clue about what was going to happen. She and I had been so caught up in our work that she did not have time to watch Doug act weird. It finished off the year nicely and I was done with my role as pseudo-manager. I had survived.

ANDRE CSILLAG

Alex with Nicole at her wedding

Alex told me during the party that he was relieved that they had made the decision on management. He was worried about my health. The last few months had been some of the most stressful of my life. I had anxiety attacks along with a lot of stomach problems. That night, I lost my cool with one of the girlfriends about backstage pass issues. I just walked away because I simply didn't have time for her nonsense.

I hoped at the time that Alex's concern about my health was a sign that our relationship was on the mend. That was not the case.

Journal Entry, January 3, 2000: *The last few months have been some of the most stressful of my life and definitely of the boys' career. If it had not been for a few saviors in my life like Andre, David, Nicole and Kelly, I don't think I could have survived it mentally. The anxiety attacks I have not had for years have started up again. Anyway, the trouble hopefully is now going to subside a bit because of the new management team the boys hired on New Year's Eve. It was a very emotional night for us all. The stress of once again doing a hometown show coupled with the final management decision coming down from the boys. The evening actually started out pretty calm but soon got out of hand with the boys going into endless meetings and some fights with girlfriends. At least the show went well!*

The Backstreet Boys' new album, *Millennium*, was released in May 1999. It broke all sales records and entered the charts at number one. That made all the lunacy and my near-nervous breakdown in those five months in 1998 almost worthwhile.

We soon discovered that one of the prices of success that Alex had to pay was the loss of his privacy, even in his own home. One night we were awakened and startled by flashes from a camera in the backyard. I went out onto the porch and yelled that I was calling the police and the culprits quickly scattered.

After that, Alex and I decided that I would buy his home, which was in a non-gated community, and he would move into a new home in a gated community. He found a beautiful new home but for some reason was hesitant to move out.

That seemed really odd to me considering his recent bout of independence. His relationship with Amanda was rapidly approaching the traditional doom-point of three years. He had gone three years with Marisa on and off. Now Amanda seemed set to become the next casualty.

I was not really upset by that since I had never developed a real fondness for her or her family. Finally, after a couple of months of prodding, I convinced Alex that he needed to be on his own. The new house was only a few minutes away and he could come to visit anytime he wanted.

I truly hoped that my son would now find some peace of mind and happiness. At least with the gated community there would no longer be the threat of fans knocking at his door. However, even with the protection of the gates, the two-legged predators still managed to get to him.

Glommers of a more threatening caliber latched onto him and led him down a dangerous path. By that time, his keen sixth sense had completely taken leave of him. The people close to him tried to get through but to no avail. Even his beloved grandmother, who made excuses for him time and time again, was disgusted by his behavior. He retreated daily into his cave-like bedroom, not emerging until well after dark.

The stress level became so high when Alex was at home that I actually felt relieved when he left to go out on tour. When the Millennium tour began, Alex returned to his normal hard-working routine. I traveled to Los Angeles a few times to meet with the new management team. I tried to give them some insight into the dynamics of the group, both from a personal and professional perspective.

At first they seemed to really want my input. However, as time passed and they felt more comfortable with the boys, the mood changed. They fired most of the people who had been with the boys for years—crew

members, accountants and band members. I realized that what I initially mistook for hunger during their early interviews with the boys was really nothing more than pure greed.

All the boys ever heard from them was how they were going to make them more money than they ever had made before. Of course, that meant more for management as well. The same destructive spiral was beginning all over again. Unfortunately, the boys saw

At the Grammys in 2000

ANDRE CSILLAG

through none of it. They just continued to agree with whatever those guys said. Ironically, nothing was really better. It was amazing how ruthless they were. I don't know why I was surprised. I had seen this scenario before. Same game, different players.

They replaced me with a very pricey publicity firm named the Mitch Schneider Organization, MSO for short. I was never really told much when it happened. All of a sudden, people who I had never met showed up and announced that they were the new public relations team for the boys, which did not really surprise me. That left me running the fan club and meet-and-greets. I was not angry since

ANDRE CSILLAG

Alex looking glamorous at the Grammys

it meant more time for myself. What disturbed me was the way that those guys carried out their plans. They were totally heartless and without class.

I reorganized the meet-and-greets for the boys for the new tour and renamed them "fan conferences." How that differed from the normal meet-and-greets was kind of neat. Instead of having the fans sit in a room where the media controlled the show, I reversed it so that the fans were in charge. That meant that the media took a back seat and literally sat in the back of the room. After answering questions from the fans, the boys posed for pictures and signed autographs and then left.

That worked out great. It enabled us to fit more fans into every conference than had been the case before. As soon as the new management realized what a good idea it was, they took all of the credit for it. That was the final straw for me. I was so tired of being pushed around by those arrogant people. I told Alex on several occasions how I was being treated and, to my disappointment, he never spoke up in my defense. Nor did any of the other boys. It was like all of the work I had done for them was just washed away. No one remembered or cared.

I felt discarded and used. I had given it my all, but no one, including my son, ever really seemed to appreciate it. It occurred to me that he had never really come to my defense with Donna either. He told me things in confidence, but when it came to being out in the open about his real opinion, he could not face the confrontation. That behavior was beginning to scare me. I needed to just move on.

I resigned from my position with the Backstreet Boys and started my own consulting company, Timing is Everything. With my experience, I felt that maybe I could do some good with other young artists in the area. I still had the old fan-club office, so I just changed gears. Nicole stayed on to help. Technically, she still worked for the boys, but she did not know how long that would last.

I was still very active in Alex's financial affairs. As his portfolio grew, I learned more about how to invest for his future. During that time, I also

KELLY CLINE

Me with the very sweet Alice Cooper

became involved with a former boyfriend. The time had come for me to work on my personal life as well. My mom and dad were another large factor in my decision to leave the Backstreet Boys. They were getting older and health issues were beginning to surface. I needed to be there for them. I wanted to make certain they had everything they needed.

I felt that I had a lot of loose ends with my family and wanted to be sure to tie them all up. I had spent so much time out on the road in recent years that I did not really feel like a part of the family anymore. I needed to get my life back on track in so many ways. Also, Nicole had begun planning her wedding and I wanted to be a part of that.

To help manage Alex's assets, I enlisted the help of my niece, Kelly, and her husband. I figured that we needed to surround ourselves with people who could be trusted. In my mind, that meant family. It was not so much the money staying within our little group as it was the trust factor. Everyone outside of my family seemed to have their own agendas when it came to Alex and his money. There is an old saying that more money brings more problems. Whoever said that was right.

Kelly helped with accounting and paying bills and my nephew Bill Cline, who was a plumber by trade, helped keep our houses in running condition. He was very good at fixing most everything and my son had acquired a lot of stuff: cars that needed to be serviced, a house that needed yard work and more. I also needed his help since I was living alone.

During one of Alex's infrequent visits to Orlando, we had a brief conversation in my bedroom that, looking back, I should have paid closer attention to. Communicating at length was foreign to us at that point in our relationship. Our conversations usually ended with frustration, anger and exasperation.

On that particular day, I was trying to reach out and convey to him how important it was to maintain the lines of communication with his grandparents. I told him that they were beginning to experience some health problems that had me concerned.

Out of the blue, Alex confessed that he felt he had a problem. He said he partied too much and drank too much. Alex always had a flair for the dramatic. His comment was so unexpected that my first instinct was to brush it aside as nothing more than an attempt to change the subject. I see now that I was in denial. Certainly, I did not realize that I was making it possible for him to continue his self-destructive behavior.

CHAPTER TWELVE

AJ–1 / Alex–0

THE 2000 GRAMMY AWARDS, which took place in February, should have been a high point for the Backstreet Boys. The boys were nominated in four categories, including "Record of the Year," which put them up against Cher, Santana, Ricky Martin and TLC, and "Album of the Year," a category that also included the Dixie Chicks, Diana Krall, Santana and TLC. They had sold more than ten million copies of their most recent album, *Millennium*—and they were arguably the hottest male group in the world.

When I arrived in Los Angeles, I expected to find everyone overjoyed, but I sensed an enormous amount of tension between Alex and the other boys. Nobody was talking, so I didn't know what the problem was.

To the boys' disappointment, they lost in all four categories, with the top awards—"Best Record of the Year" and "Best Album of the Year"—going to music veteran Carlos Santana.

I planned to leave immediately after the awards, but Alex said that he wanted to spend some quality time with me and insisted that I extend my stay. Once again, Alex's excessive nightlife took precedence over any good intentions that he might have had. He never showed up for our visit. As I sat alone in my hotel room, I grew angrier by the minute and was left to wonder what had happened to my son.

I did not track Alex down until the following day. When I finally reached him on the telephone, he said, "Gee, Mom, I have been in the studio writing—heading back there now. Why don't you come with me?"

"What about the quality time we planned to spend together?"

"As soon as I am done there today, which should only be a couple of hours," Alex said. "We will go out—just the two of us."

"Okay," I said, "but I really don't want to hang around there all night with you."

"No, Mom," he said. "Really, it won't take long and I need your help to talk to someone."

"Who?" I asked, not eager to get involved in more work.

"The guys we are working with have a manager who wants to show us a contract for some songs we are writing and I want you to look it over."

It turned out that the guys that Alex had been spending his time with in the studio were some mutual friends, members of a band named EYC that had opened for the boys years before and had since split up. Alex wanted to help them write some new material in the hopes that they might get back together and land a new record deal.

I went to the studio with Alex, but after hanging out there for several hours, I realized that he was not going to leave anytime soon, so I took a cab back to the hotel. On the way, I called Alex's bodyguard, Marcus Johnson, a very large black man with close-cropped hair and a dazzling white smile. I asked him to change my flight back to Orlando. I wanted to leave first thing the next day.

As I was leaving my room the following day, Alex called.

"Mom, Marcus told me that you changed your flight. What's up?"

By then, I was not in the best of moods. "I am sick of the

Alex plays with puppy Panda on the tour bus

ANDRE CSILLAG

same routine with you, Alex," I said. "You say one thing and do another. I don't need to be here, spending money on a hotel room when I can be home resting up from the last tour."

"But I thought we were going to do some things together?"

"Alex, be real—I am not going to sit around until you find the time to spare for me. I am done."

With that, I went down to my cab and left. Nothing more was said and Alex did not return to Orlando right away. Instead, he

Alex with Panda on Halloween

DENISE MCLEAN

went to New York with one of his unsavory friends. It was then that I realized that there was more to his personality change than met the eye. I was worried at that point, but I was unable to put my finger on exactly why.

━━━━━━

ALEX LEFT ON TOUR a short time later. About a month into the tour, he called me and said that he and the musicians from the band had decided they wanted to do something different together. Since the tour had been split into several sections, with breaks in between, they had ample time off to do other things.

Alex asked me to put together a charity show, the proceeds of which could be used to benefit some worthy cause. Since the boys already had an ongoing relationship with the head of marketing for VH1's Save the Music Foundation, I suggested that the profits go to them. Their staff would be able to put up a banner, organize meet-and-greets and help us put the show together.

At first, Alex wanted to do an entire tour, but he really didn't have enough time off from the Backstreet Boys tour to do that, so I convinced him to try one show in Orlando. That would allow us to gauge fan reaction before we committed to the expense of an entire tour. After all, the object was to try and make some money for charity. That was fine with Alex, so I got to work on it right away. It really seemed like something I could sink my teeth into. It would give me a break from all of the fan club stuff that I had done over the past several months. That had started to get a bit tiresome.

At the time, the decision seemed an easy one for me. I was more than ready to get back to work. I had Kelly and Nicole on my side. The three of us shared the same work ethic, so we made the perfect team. At first I was really excited. There was a lot of stress in my life and the show was a welcome distraction.

The biggest issues in my life at that time were my parents and their health problems. Mom had to have a pacemaker installed after she was diagnosed with congestive heart failure. That happened not too long after Alex left on tour. Dad was so upset over Mom that his health was affected. His blood sugar level became unstable.

We had to hire daytime nursing care to deal with laundry and cooking, in addition to overseeing Mom and Dad's medications. Going through the interview process took a while. Finally, we found a wonderful husband-and-wife team, Marion and Abel Rodriquez, who lived nearby.

With that, my focus turned to my relationship with Alex. The solo show would give me the opportunity to see if Alex and I could find common ground for a relationship, one that did not include the pressures of the other boys, their management and the various Backstreet business affairs that invariably got in our way. I really hoped that we would be able to reconnect.

We decided to do the show on Alex's upcoming birthday.

Things came together very quickly. We were able to get the brand-new Hard Rock Cafe Universal Studios CityWalk complex for the show. All the radio stations in town played up the event. It was something different for the media, since the only other Backstreet Boy who did any charity work was Howie. He had formed a foundation benefiting lupus after his sister died and he did fundraisers every chance he got.

Everyone was curious to see what Alex could do on his own. Even the record company was excited for him. They allowed him to perform some Backstreet songs without any legal hassle. It all seemed to happen rather effortlessly. In a way, I felt as though I were back where I belonged. In addition to helping my son with his career, I was also helping to give back to the community that had been there to support him and the other boys for the past several years.

To my surprise, Alex decided to take on a new persona for the show. He called himself Johnny Suede, a name that he had gotten from a clothing line. Johnny dressed in suits and had matching fedoras and shoes for every outfit. Alex then decided to take his alter ego one step further: he gave Johnny a British accent. He said that way he could really become someone other than Alex or AJ.

That sounded a bit scary to me, but I let it go. Everything went along fine until we unexpectedly received a letter from Tom DiCillo, a screenwriter/producer who had produced a 1991 film titled *Johnny Suede*. The film starred Brad Pitt and was about a musician who had a Ricky Nelson fixation. Alex never saw the movie.

In his letter, Mr. DiCillo said that we would have to pay him in order to use the name. We were finally able to come to terms with him for the one show. Due to the fact that we had already done the advertising and printed the tickets, we had no choice. He graciously agreed to let us use the name, just that one time.

The show was a big success. All of the major teen magazines were there and did full spreads on the event. They even gave the show good reviews.

"AJ McLean celebrated his twenty-second birthday last month in typically flamboyant style by dressing up as his alter ego Johnny Suede and laying on a solo concert in Orlando for fans," cheered the British magazine *Top of the Pops*. "He began the show hand-cuffed to a chair, carried on to the stage by a tough-looking cop. But don't worry, AJ hadn't done anything wrong—quite the opposite in fact—the show raised $25,000 for charity. What a generous soul!"

We were able to give Save the Music a big check at the end of the show. Something that I took notice of that evening was that when Alex discarded his alter ego at the end of the show and hit the stage as AJ from the Backstreet Boys, he could not do it without downing several shots of Jack Daniels. I

Johnny Suede raised $27,000 for Save the Music

ANDRE CSILLAG

185

even joined in for one round, but as I watched him, I grew concerned about his drinking. The band, of course, did not discourage him. Looking back, I should have discussed it with him.

In the days immediately following the show, I remember feeling connected to and needed by Alex in a way that I had not experienced since the early days of the group. The show seemed to give Alex a new wave of confidence as a solo artist. I cannot tell you how many times people in the industry had prodded me to have him try and do more on his own. His range was so big and his talent so electrifying that he didn't need any one else. He was a one-man dynamo. Yet it was not in Alex's nature, and betraying the other boys would have been out of the question. Since the "Johnny Suede" performance had been done for charity, no one could really fault him.

By that time, a few of the other boys had formed foundations and were doing things to promote them. Alex was entitled to do the same. Watching him perform alone was an amazing thing for me. It was as if he were little all over again. He took control of that stage and that audience with such polish and panache.

The songs that he sang were a deliberate departure from the usual Backstreet fare. Each song showcased his voice in a different way. It was

DENISE MCLEAN

a real treat for the fans. It was proof that they loved him for him, whether he was Alex or AJ or Johnny. In their eyes, he had transcended being just another Backstreet Boy.

Since he did the show on his birthday, I felt it only fitting that I pull a joke on him. I had the nightclub make up a huge cake. I then enlisted the help of my niece, Kathy. The night of the show, she dressed in a white halter dress as Marilyn Monroe, complete with a blonde wig and beauty mark.

In the middle of the show, she rolled the cake out onto the stage. Alex froze as she made her way

Alex at a surprise party for his birthday in L.A.

closer to him. To his surprise, she started singing "Happy Birthday," like Marilyn did for President John F. Kennedy. At first, Alex did not recognize his cousin, but as she got closer, he opened his eyes real wide and his mouth dropped open. It was hysterical! In an instant, Alex knew I had been behind the entire thing and he let the audience in on the joke. Everyone loved it.

―――

THE BACKSTREET BOYS TOUR resumed a few days after the concert in Orlando. By that time, Mom's health had started to deteriorate. I was torn between my mother's needs and my son's problems. On the one hand, there were the phone calls with doctors, hospitals and other family members; on the other hand, were the never-ending, often disturbing phone calls from the road regarding the fact that Alex had fallen into the hands of the glommers and was spinning out of control.

Usually the glommers tried to hide behind titles like "record producer" or "record label president." In reality, they were all just con men and sometimes drug dealers. My son was getting in with a very bad element. They used his name to get into the hottest nightclubs and they made certain that everyone knew whom they were with.

Everyone around Alex, including the other boys, tried to warn him about the sleazy characters he was befriending, but he would not listen.

I spoke with some of the other boys. They told me stories of his partying and not showing up for press events the next day or causing problems in the hotels. I then turned to Marcus for help. Marcus had been Alex's bodyguard for three years, and I trusted him implicitly. He appeared ominous but was a pussycat at heart; Alex even referred to him as "Uncle Marshmallow." I knew he cared about Alex, and I pleaded with him to talk some sense into my son. He tried, but his words only fell on deaf ears. All he could do was try to watch Alex's back as much as possible. He pulled some of the glommers aside and asked them to leave, but they turned to Alex for protection.

I was caught in the middle of an emotional tug-of-war and I felt completely helpless about both situations. I could not be with my son twenty-four hours a day to keep him out of harm's way. Alex had surrounded himself with dangerous people, each of whom had his or her own agenda. He mistook sharks for friends and continued to feed them.

Making matters worse, Amanda was still in the picture. I was none too happy about that. Some strange things had happened with her and her family that led me to believe that she was not right for my son. I just kept hoping that Alex would grow tired of her and end their almost three-year relationship.

In my opinion, Amanda did not try to discourage Alex's wild behavior. She just stood by and enjoyed the benefits of dating a Backstreet Boy. According to Marcus, they fought constantly, often in public. From all accounts, she had also become quite spoiled and demanding, like she was the pop star. Often, when they were going to events, she made Alex wait for her to get ready, which meant they were always late.

As usual, Alex avoided confrontation. That was something that he would have to resolve if he wanted to become a man. His knee-jerk reaction to confrontation was to run and hide. It was when he finally realized the seriousness of his situation that he began to hide himself away in a cocoon of drugs, drinking and partying.

My mother's illness grew worse and, according to her doctors, the prognosis was not good. They believed that she had a year to live, at most. She had begun to retain fluids and her heart was no longer able to pump them out of her system fast enough. She had to be constantly monitored by doctors so that she would not get pneumonia.

To help her enlarged heart, doctors put her on medication that had liver damage as a possible side effect. It was one thing on top of another.

ANDRE CSILLAG

Marcus taking care of Alex, as usual

Dad was a mess and we had to keep a close eye on him as well. Mom was so weakened by the disease that she could no longer walk and was confined to a wheelchair.

Dad was still battling his diabetes but he got around pretty well. While he still drove on occasion, that, too, was becoming less frequent. He underwent cataract surgery to improve his failing vision, but his diabetes impeded the recovery. We soon had to stop Dad from driving at all since, in addition to his vision problems, his reflexes had gotten slow. It was really hard convincing Dad not to drive anymore. After quite a bit of coaxing, though, he finally agreed. At that point, I think he realized just how unsafe it was for him to be behind the wheel.

I closed down the Backstreet Boys fan club once it became clear that neither the boys nor their new management had any intentions of ever cooperating with me. It's rather difficult to run a fan club for a group when you are given zero information regarding the group and their activities. We did the best we could with what we had to work with, but I felt that I was no longer giving the fans what they deserved. I could no longer in good conscience take their money. I had to fire the staff and start all over.

I began work on a new project with an old friend, Ken West. We decided to market a video anthology of the Backstreet Boys in their early years. He still had all of the original videotapes from every tour, plus he had shot footage for me of the Johnny Suede show. I purchased a high-end computer system for editing so that we could put together a nice package, but given Mom and Dad's situation, I was not able to devote much time to the project.

Since my schedule, at the time, was more flexible than my brother's, I drove my parents to their appointments. I also checked in on them frequently to make sure they had everything they needed. We had a friend of the family named Aunt Marquess (aka Aunt Sue),

Ken West and me on Halloween

ALEX MCLEAN

who stayed with them overnight. She had been my sister-in-law's friend since childhood. Aunt Sue was an older woman with a wealth of experience in home healthcare. We trusted her implicitly. It certainly comforted me to know that Mom and Dad were in good hands.

My stress levels were enormous. My brother was a wreck. He and my sister-in-law, Darlene, tried to help out as much as they could with meals and doctors appointments, but it was a lot for anyone to handle. We stayed at the house in shifts. Soon we realized that the situation was taking an enormous toll on all of us, both emotionally and physically. The stress of watching Mom go downhill so fast was too much at times.

Matching the anguish I felt over my parents' condition was the concern that I had for Alex's health and well-being. I was torn between going on tour with Alex or just waiting it out until he returned home so that we could deal with his problems. All I really wanted was for Alex to ride in on his white horse and be the pillar of strength that I so desperately needed at that time. That was not meant to be.

It was not until that time that I realized just how weak he really was. He did not have the proper coping mechanisms to come to terms with the fact that his grandmother was gravely ill. It was an issue that we all

DENISE MCLEAN COLLECTION

Nicole, Bill Cline and Aunt Sue

had to come to grips with, yet Alex chose to continue digging himself a bigger hole in which to hide.

Alex could have focused on making his grandmother's last days on earth pleasant ones, but he hurt her terribly by choosing to ignore her. Our family had always been the sort that would come together in a crisis. We were small in number but big in love and support when something hit anyone of us. I had felt bad about the years I had not been around to help them through their rough patches. Everyone understood.

They stood behind Alex and me every step of the way. They never asked him or me for a thing. No one in the family ever took advantage of Alex or his fame. When he came home, they treated him the same way they had during his childhood years. Nothing changed for them. He was still the same Alex he had been all those years ago. If he saw it as something else, he was wrong. The only thing that his family ever tried to do was protect him from the sharks—and sometimes from himself.

———

LATER THAT YEAR, Alex phoned me from the road and said that the tour was coming up on a break. He wanted to put a charity tour together once again using his alter ego. He had spoken to the musicians and they were all for it. This time he wanted to add some singers and juice up the production a bit. I told him I would make some calls and put a budget together to see if it could be done in that short period of time.

I also did a bit of soul searching. Could I in good conscience leave my mom for a number of weeks? I spoke with my brother. He thought it would be good for me since he saw firsthand the strain that I was under. I decided to give it a shot.

In a matter of weeks, I put together a nine-day tour. We had buses, a band, venues and promotion in place. All that remained was a rehearsal space and some hotel rooms for a few of the band members. Nicole helped put the Orlando rehearsals together. Once again, with the help of our "team," we made it happen.

When Alex came home, he had about six days to rehearse the show and buy wardrobes for himself and the band. We decided to give the proceeds to the VH1 Save The Music Foundation, as they were a pleasure to work with and made very few demands of Alex. All that they really asked for were a few meet-and-greets and a press conference. They gave us a ton of support on the promotional end of things and helped us get in touch with some major networks to cover the shows. Since we only played in small venues that held from 1,500 to 4,000 patrons, that meant we could charge a minimal amount and still make some money by selling out the shows.

By the time the tickets went on sale, there was a real buzz about the concert. Most of the shows sold out quickly. We probably could have held the concerts in larger halls, but we needed to keep our costs down. Some of the venues we played in were ones that the Backstreet Boys had performed in on their first tour. Our friend and booking agent from New York, David Zedeck, got us great deals from the promoters. He helped us cut expenses so that we could make a profit.

The promoters were easy to deal with. The fact that they had known the booking agent and me for so many years helped us get some very sweet deals. David had been the natural choice for booking the tour. He was a dear and trusted friend. He also helped me find a good tour accountant. Alex promised some of the staff from the Backstreet tour that they would have a place with him on his tour, so I had to make good on those offers as well.

I was less than thrilled with that, since The Firm had hired them and I did not know them very well. Most of them turned out to be independent contractors who were reasonably loyal to whomever was signing their paychecks. I negotiated reduced rates with everyone since our goal was to raise as much money as possible for the charity.

BILL FERNANDEZ

At Christinis Restaurant in Orlando for my forty-eighth birthday

We named the tour the Nine City Swang. I tried my best to keep an eye on Alex during the tour and he tried to stay healthy by eating right and getting enough sleep, but it was hard for him to resist partying with the band. A few times I really had to get on his case so that he did not get into trouble.

Looking back, I think that Alex was nervous about performing solo. As the tour progressed, he improvised more in an attempt to make the show more entertaining for the fans. He got great reviews. The only hitch we came across was with his name. The writer who allowed us to use it for the first show asked for a lot of money to use it again. We refused and subsequently dropped the name. Alex and the band tried to come up with a new name, but they couldn't think of anything appropriate, so he became Johnny No-Name.

As we moved from city to city, the press became more intrigued by his new persona. Alex invented an entire background biography for his character. It was a little bizarre, but it caught the magazines' attention and they loved it. The more he talked about Johnny, the more stories he was able to invent.

The main question everyone kept asking was, "How come Johnny and AJ from the Backstreet Boys are never seen anywhere at the same time?" Alex's answer to that was that Johnny was always in jail when AJ was out in public. AJ usually appeared at the end of the show, when he performed the final number and the encore.

We hit all the major cities, including New York, Chicago, Las Vegas and Los Angeles. As the tour went along, Alex's confidence in his abilities as a solo artist grew. Paralleling that growth was an improvement in our communication with each other. I felt better about that, but Alex still had a difficult time dealing with his grandmother's illness. Unless I called her and personally handed him the phone, he avoided the issue. I tried to talk to him about the inevitable outcome of her disease, but he did not want any part of that conversation.

I also talked to him about his drinking. He said he knew that there was a problem, but that he was getting it under control. That was not the case. After each show, he was so fired up by the excitement of it all that he went out with the band to blow off steam. Once he returned to his hotel room, he took some over-the-counter sedatives in an effort to get some sleep. I warned him that was a dangerous combination and tried to get him to stop, but he insisted that he understood the dangers and

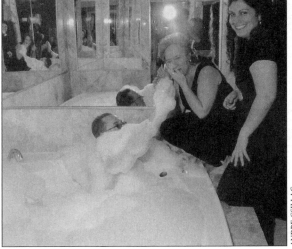

Alex, Nina and me in Las Vegas

ANDRE CSILLAG

knew what he was doing. Almost every night, he went out until dawn and then slept all day. He said that was the only way he could get some rest.

I felt helpless and frustrated. Since he clearly was not ready to admit the severity of his problem, or ask for help, all I could do was stand by and watch him slowly destroy himself. My hope was that he would seek professional help once the tour ended. I enlisted the help of other people on the tour to talk to him and our combined efforts seemed to make a difference. Finally, Alex said that he realized that we were trying to help him and he agreed to see a professional once we returned to Florida.

I called my brother and asked for his help. I knew that the core of the problem was with his grandmother's illness, so I focused on trying to find Alex a therapist who would be able to tackle that as well as the rest of his problems.

When we completed the tour for Johnny No-Name, we were able to hand the Save the Music Foundation a check for around $50,000, after expenses were deducted. The show had been very popular among AJ's fans. We started getting numerous e-mails, letters and phone calls asking

ANDRE CSILLAG

Fooling around with an expensive prop during a video shoot in Las Vegas when Johnny would perform again and how his fans could help with donations for the charity. That prompted an idea.

Alex and I decided to form a foundation to support his future Johnny No-Name shows. He discussed it with the other boys and no one seemed to object, so I went to work setting it up. We called it the JNN Foundation and with it we could raise money for various charities. I felt that would be a way to showcase Alex's philanthropic efforts. He even seeded the foundation from his own pocket.

———

BY THE END OF 2000, the Backstreet Boys tour was complete and everyone took a break for the holidays. That gave us time to tie up some loose ends with the foundation. It was during that time that we planned one more Johnny No-Name show that would take place at the end of the year. Once again, we called on our friends at the Hard Rock Cafe.

We were able to schedule a year-end bash at which Johnny No-Name could fill the house with a fan party. We used that occasion to let everyone know about the newly formed JNN Foundation that would go into full swing the following year. We sold out the place and raised more money for several local charities of our choice.

When Alex finally came home, he was visibly shocked at how frail his grandmother had become. The sight of her affected him more than we realized. He started making excuses to travel out of town for so-called Backstreet business. He befriended a local glommer, who claimed to own a record label in Orlando, and he started writing and producing for some of the artists on that label. Eventually, I found out this friend was a bartender that worked for a local poolroom.

Alex stopped coming to family functions unless it was absolutely necessary. He obviously was having a very difficult time dealing with his grandmother's illness. He later admitted that when he was out on the road he sat in his room and drank in an effort to forget about his grandmother. That led him into a crushing depression. I suppose at that time I was also in denial about him and my mom.

I had a very hard time coping with all of the problems. Dealing with drug use and excessive drinking was foreign territory to me. Most people told me there was really nothing I could do anyway. Alex had to hit bottom and ask for help. That probably just fed my denial. I adopted a "wait and hope for the best" attitude.

Only later did I realize that no one, not even his manager, had done anything to help him, for fear of rattling one-fifth of the money machine. Instead of helping him, they just labeled him a lazy loser and let it go at that. They never bothered to ask why Alex was engaging in that type of behavior. It never ceased to amaze me that, invariably, everyone around Alex fixated on the all-important "bottom line." The fear that they might lose out on some precious commission was what drove each and every decision.

I did receive a number of phone calls from the boys voicing their concern. They said they thought Alex needed help, but they did not really know what to do about it. With his behavior becoming more erratic, I again searched for a therapist who could treat him while he was at home. I found one named Vicki O'Grady. She had a very enthusiastic attitude and was always positive, plus she was recommended by a mutual friend.

To no one's surprise, Alex blew off his first appointment with the therapist. My brother gave him a good talking to and he agreed to show up for the next appointment. To make certain that he kept it, I drove him there. Alex and I did part of the session together, so that I could better understand what he was going through. I was desperate to bring him back into the real world before his AJ persona swallowed him whole. I did not want to lose him.

Vicki was helpful and Alex liked her, so he agreed to continue his sessions while he was in town. It was my hope that working with the therapist, focusing on the holidays and concentrating on his upcoming show would keep Alex too occupied to have much time to associate with the scumbags in town. Unfortunately, he made the time.

It was around that time that Mom had to be taken to the hospital again because her body was retaining fluids. They treated her with strong diuretics and sent her home. Once that crisis passed, she seemed to improve during the Christmas holidays. She even felt well enough to attend the Johnny show at the Hard Rock Cafe. We put her and my dad up in the front row of the balcony, surrounded by family. She had binoculars and watched every minute of the show with a big smile on her face. That made me very happy.

Sadly, she took a turn for the worse not long after the first of the year, when the pacemaker stopped working effectively. She took to her bed and refused to eat for long periods of time. When she was no longer able to walk to the bathroom it became necessary for them to insert a catheter. None of us felt that she could last much longer under those conditions. We took it day by day.

Early in 2001, Alex went to Los Angeles for a press event. While there, he walked into a karaoke bar one night and was struck by a beautiful girl named Sarah Jo Martin. She had the body of a model with long legs and curvy hips. Her face was heart shaped with a beautifully bright smile and sparkling eyes. Even though Alex was impressed with her looks, when he heard them introduce what song she was going to sing, he just laughed and walked out. Apparently, she planned to sing a heavy-duty R&B song.

As Alex stepped outside for a smoke, he heard her begin her song. It was the voice of an angel with attitude. He rushed back

Alex, always the performer, gives his annual Christmas speech

into the bar. As soon as she finished her set, he introduced himself. She did not seem impressed. Not in the least discouraged, he laid the old AJ charm on her and asked her out on a date.

She said she was too busy to go out with him. Undeterred, Alex pursed her even harder. Finally, she gave in and agreed to go out with him. It turned out that they had quite a bit in common. Sarah had recently experienced the sudden loss of her sister and she understood Alex's anxiety over his grandmother.

Alex remained in Los Angeles for a long time, both because of Sarah and because Backstreet was shooting a music video. While he was away, it became clear that my mother did not have much longer to live. She had refused to get out of bed or eat for a number of days. My dad was beside himself. Over the past few months, we had taken Mom to the hospital several times when she got that way. This time was different. She was tired of being sick and wanted it to be done with it.

On Easter Day, the nurse who had taken care of Mom and Dad helped us make a decision to call in a hospice nursing team. We knew that meant we were down to days with Mom. I wanted to alert Alex to the grave circumstances he would be coming home to, so I called him and explained what was happening. He was devastated. He said he would hurry home just as soon as he could. He spoke to the other boys and they cleared a few days in the schedule for him to return to Florida.

The boys were aware of the situation and did not give him any problems about leaving. They all had met Mom at one time or another. In the early days, she even cooked dinners for them when they were rehearsing. They never forgot that.

Alex flew home on a Saturday, but we did not see or hear from him until late Monday. We tried to contact him several times to let him know what was going on. Our efforts were in vain since his cellular phone had been turned off and he did not pick up his house phone. I knew that my son was hurting terribly and would not let anyone help him. Instead he turned to the glommers for support. That tore me apart.

Not only was I worried about Mom and Dad, but also I was in a constant state of panic over my son's whereabouts. I knew instinctively that he would run for a drink to try and escape what was happening. I was upset with him, but at the same time I felt the need to help him. My stomach was in knots and my nerves were a mess. I did not sleep or eat for most of that week.

Finally, Alex called and told us that he was coming over. He made it clear that he did not want to be questioned about where he had been, so we avoided the subject. His grandmother was our main concern at that point. Alex visited intermittently during that week, but then he disappeared for hours at a time without saying where he was going.

My brother and I, along with family and friends, stayed at Mom's bedside during those final days. We wanted her to know that we were there and tried to make her feel as comfortable as possible. In her delirium, Mom had been getting angry with Dad and it was stressing him out terribly. She would wake him up constantly, yelling about one thing or another. Most of it was due to the hallucinations she experienced as a result of her medication. There was not too much of that Dad could take, but he wanted to be by her side as much as possible.

Nicole came to stay with me at the apartment and helped me through that terrible time. She had always been there for me. She is very much like a daughter to me. She loved Mom in her own way and since she had lost her dad many years before, she knew all too well what I was going through. Nicole helped me keep my sanity probably more than she knows during that week. For that I love her.

On Wednesday, the Hospice nurse told us that Mom could pass at any moment. For that reason, we tried to keep Alex around for as long as he would stay. He was acting very weird. He kept coming up with one reason after another to leave. Having him around had become more tiresome than helpful, as I kept asking the same questions over and over again. Why did he have to go? What was so important that he needed to leave us at that moment?

At the time, I did not realize that he was leaving to drink or take drugs in an effort to ease his pain. I could not see through my own suffering. His need for me was great, but I was so involved in that situation that I was unable to give any more of myself. I was splintering apart from the stress.

In a way, denial had become a viable alternative for me. I know now that using Mom as an excuse for blinding myself to my son's condition was probably wrong, but, on the other hand, what could I have done to stop him? Alex had the time, money and connections to obtain whatever he wanted. I was not about to get in my car, follow him around town and try to get in the middle of the mess he had made of his life. He would only be able to get help when he was ready.

I had heard numerous horror stories of overdoses and arrests. There were so many bad things that happened to kids when drugs and alcohol were involved. I felt an urgent need to protect him like I had always done. Alex was still my fragile, little boy who needed his mother to take care of him. Or so I thought.

Mom hung on for longer than expected. Everyone was able to take a turn sitting with her alone to say what he or she needed to say and be at peace. Alex used his time with her wisely, I think. My brother had an exceptionally hard time saying goodbye to Mom. The nurse and I talked to him and we explained how Mom's time had come and he needed to let go. It was so very difficult for all of us. As we sat with Mom, Alex suddenly informed us that he had to leave to get something for her. He said he would be right back. I think he just could not face what was about to happen.

Mom slipped away quietly shortly after he left on a Thursday night, at home with all of her loved ones around her except for Alex. She passed while he was out getting a doll in his likeness and a heart-shaped crystal to give to her. Alex returned just as the funeral home arrived to take away her remains. He gently placed the doll and crystal under the sheets so that she could take them with her.

Everything had been pre-planned. My brother and I had chosen a funeral home a month earlier, which meant we did not have to face those decisions during our greatest time of grief. It was the best thing we could have done. Dad needed us so desperately, and we needed each other. I could not imagine sitting in a strange place trying to make those kinds of decisions while in a state of mourning.

It was a long night. We all crashed from exhaustion and cried ourselves to sleep. Alex brought blankets and pillows with him and stayed the night. Even though her passing had been totally expected, it was still a shock to know that she was gone forever. I would never be able to speak to her again or hug her or listen to her laugh. It was a devastating time for me. I tried my best to be strong for my son and my family. The death of a loved one is something that you never get over. It is made that much more horrific if you are a close-knit family. I still miss her.

The next day, Alex was due to fly to Los Angeles to finish the video shoot, but he didn't want to leave, so we sat down and talked. After a lengthy discussion that often got very emotional, we decided that it was best for him to honor his obligations to the group. He left for L.A. the next morning and returned a few days later to attend his grandmother's funeral. He gave a loving and tearful eulogy at the service. Seeing the love that my son had for his grandmother warmed my heart. Little did I realize that I was seeing the last of Alex for a long time. The AJ persona was gaining strength by the day.

I felt terrible for him since he had to turn right around and fly back out of town the very next day. Alex had no real time to grieve. That fact alone would be reason enough for him to fill the huge hole in his heart with self-pity, drugs and alcohol.

———

WITH A NEW BACKSTREET BOYS TOUR about to begin, Alex reluctantly boarded a flight the next afternoon to begin rehearsals in Los Angeles. Work had always been a solace for him, so we felt that was the best decision. What I failed to realize was that I was putting him right back into the hands of the enemy. His downward spiral had begun in earnest.

Rehearsals for the tour went fine. Alex seemed to be coping with the loss of his grandmother very well. I kept in touch with him as much as possible. I found a bit of comfort in the fact that he had a new girlfriend to focus on. My hope was that she would bring him some much needed peace and happiness.

Sarah had opted not to come to the funeral with Alex since she really did not know our family yet. She thought it only right that he spend that time with us alone. That sentiment impressed me right away. Here was a person who actually thought about someone else's feelings for a change. It was a concept that none of his former flames had ever embraced. At least things seemed to be looking up on that front.

Alex told me that he was going to take it slow with Sarah. She had gotten out of a relationship not too long before the two of them met and she was not interested in anything long-term. That was fine with me, as he was at a very vulnerable point in his life. Perhaps getting too involved too quickly would not be the best thing for him.

I focused on helping Dad and my brother cope with their grief. I also devoted time to getting the JNN Foundation started. Kelly and Nicole were on board and there was a lot to learn about running a charity organization. I felt it would be a welcome diversion. It kept me from dwelling too heavily on the death of my mom.

I kept in touch with Marcus on a regular basis just to be sure that Alex was not getting into trouble. Sometimes he indicated there were certain individuals hanging around with Alex who were having a negative effect on him, but when I questioned Alex about them, he said they were friends, people he played pool with or partied with at the occasional club. I later found out that he had grossly minimized the situation and was hitting the party circuit hard, staying out into the wee hours of the morning with the creeps that he called his friends.

When Sarah was not around, they sometimes stayed with Alex in his hotel room. I suspected that some of them made money from him by supplying him with drugs. It had become obvious to the boys that the situation was growing grimmer by the day, but they did not know how to cope with it.

The tension between the five boys had escalated while they were in Los Angeles shooting the video. Alex had been drunk on the set and had been seen taking drugs. Things were getting totally out of control. I got a phone call late one night from Alex, during which he admitted to trying cocaine. He claimed that he had only done it one time and he promised never to do it again.

Alex used the excuse that he was tired and sick and needed something to keep going during the all-night shooting schedule. As he cried to me on the phone, it was clear that he was upset with himself. I desperately wanted to believe him.

Then he began to cry.

He seemed to be under a lot of pressure—and he was clearly cracking. I could sense he was depressed about the death of his grandmother and had been unable to grieve because of his work schedule. I made him something to eat and kept him awake long enough to eat it. When he fell asleep, I went home to gather some blankets and pillows in order to stay the night with him.

Over the next few weeks, Alex's behavior became more and more suspect. We barely saw him or heard from him. When we tried to contact him during the day, he was always sleeping and would not answer the telephone.

One day, he got up late in the afternoon and left to have dinner and meet friends. He spent a lot of time at his favorite pool hall and at a local topless club. The creep he brought back with him, along with his new-found "friends" from the pool hall, saw much more of my son than any family member. Dad was very disappointed in him for not coming around to see how he was doing. My brother was quickly losing patience with Alex. His disregard for our feelings cut through the family like a sharp knife.

I felt I was losing Alex to the gaping black hole of drugs, alcohol and depression. He was self-medicating to dull the pain that he felt. That meant that he had to hide from his family so that we would not discover the truth. Kelly's husband, Bill, who was the caretaker at Alex' house, had been instructed by Alex to cover his bedroom windows with black plastic so that no light would come into the room while he was sleeping during the day. For that reason, we named his room The Cave. That was exactly the impression you got when you stepped into the room.

Alex had spent a fortune furnishing his new 6,000-square-foot home, but those new friends of his helped him ruin it every chance they got. There were cigarette burns on the counter-tops and on the furniture. Drinks were spilled onto the carpet and just left to dry. It was a pigsty, but no one seemed to care, including my son.

I hired a cleaning lady to visit Alex's house once a week. That was a losing battle with the way he kept letting people run rampant in his home. What they did was a sin. I did not know who those people were, but if they showed up while I was there, they were unceremoniously booted out the door.

Alex's total disregard for what was going on in his own home was beyond my comprehension. He did not seem to care about what he had worked so long to obtain. Once, he loaned his Mercedes to one of those lowlifes and they told me that he gave it to them to keep. My question to them was, "Did he give you the payment book as well?"

Since I did not consider my son to be Elvis, who was known for giving cars away, sometimes to complete strangers, I asked a large, male friend to get the car back. That seemed to work. It was just another example of Alex's lack of willingness to face anyone and do what was right for himself.

Alex fell into the lifestyle of the predators who surrounded him. He took comfort in the false security that drugs and alcohol gave him. Over those weeks, the few times that I spoke to him, he sounded terrible. He always had the same excuse for the way he sounded. He was very tired and sick and was taking cold medicine that made him groggy. He had an answer for every question.

Everything came to a head when the other boys came to town to attend a press conference before leaving on tour. I received a phone call from Kevin later that week. He told me that Alex had not shown up for the press conference and was nowhere to be found. He had tried every phone number and had looked in every place that he could think of, with no luck. Kevin had always been like an older brother to Alex. It was not unusual for him to be the first one to react if Alex was hurting or in trouble.

Kevin told me that they had to postpone the press conference. That was especially bad since most of the journalists had flown in from overseas. The boys were desperate and frustrated, and that only fed my own frantic worry. Kevin just wanted to know if I had heard from him and, if so, had he said anything about the schedule?

"I haven't talked to Alex in several days," I said.

"Okay, we'll take care of it," Kevin answered, unable to hide his anger. "We're going over to Alex's house."

Hearing that made me a bit concerned. As much as Kevin loved Alex, he was known for his temper. But I knew in my heart that the boys had to come to terms with Alex's behavior. Maybe if they confronted him, he would listen. He had stopped listening to his family or to his therapist a long time ago.

A few hours later, I got a call from Alex begging me to come to his house. He said he was very sick and was too weak to get out of bed. He told me that he had taken some pills the night before and thought he might have taken too many. He sounded horrible and was coughing as he spoke.

"Should I call 911?" I asked, uncertain of what to do.

"No, don't do that," he said.

That seemed odd. I realized that he was again in trouble with the boys and wanted me to bail him out. Apparently, he had been home the whole time the boys were looking for him but refused to answer the telephone because he knew they were angry.

When I arrived at the house, it was dark and smelled of alcohol and garbage. There were beer bottles everywhere and cigarette butts all over the floor. The place was a mess and my son was nowhere in sight. I called out for him and he yelled back to me from his bedroom. As I reached the door, I noticed that the knob had been torn off and the door was hanging from the hinges.

"What happened?" I asked, looking at the busted door.

"Kevin and Brian came over to see me," he said. "When I didn't go to the door, they busted in and lit into me for not showing up at the press thing. They were pissed. They said they didn't believe that I was sick."

"Well, are you sick?" I asked.

"I took some sleeping pills that made me feel really weird."

Then he began to cry.

I knew what was really wrong with him. He was depressed about the death of his grandmother and had been unable to grieve because of his work schedule. He was under a lot of pressure—and he was clearly cracking. I made him something to eat and kept him awake long enough to eat it. When he fell asleep, I went home to gather some blankets and pillows in order to stay the night with him.

When I returned, he was still asleep. I made up the couch in the living room and settled in for a restless night. At dawn, I was awakened by the sound of the front door opening and closing. In walked an obviously drunk Alex.

I could not believe my eyes.

"Where have you been?" I asked.

"I was hungry when I woke up, so I went to McDonald's to get something to eat," he said, trying to hide the fact that he had been drinking.

I felt hurt, angry and foolish all at once. My stomach turned to knots and I started to cry. He continued with his fabrication, but I just asked him to leave me alone and I left.

Later that morning, I got a call from Kevin. "We're all over at Alex's house," he said. "We need to talk."

The boys felt that Alex did better with someone from home out on the road with him. They thought it would be a good idea if I joined him on the first leg of the tour and if the therapist could come out once or twice a week to work with him on his drinking and depression. That was fine with Alex, who assured everyone that he would stop his drug use. In my ignorance, I truly believed I could stop my son from drinking and doing drugs by just being present. I would later find out that is not how the "sickness" works. Over the next several weeks, I learned quite a lot about my son and myself.

CHAPTER THIRTEEN

Road to Recovery

THE BACKSTREET BOYS set out on their next tour in a bus that departed from Alex's house (no one wanted to risk Alex not showing up at another location). I went along to ride shotgun. For the first couple of days, things went fine. It appeared as though Alex was making a real effort to kick his habits and get back on track.

I finally got the chance to spend some time with Sarah. I liked her a lot, though I must admit I had my suspicions, given her aspirations to be a singer. However, once we had a chance to hang out together, my apprehensions fell away. She was a stunning woman, with a beautiful smile, kind eyes and a charming personality. She had the kind of looks that turned heads whenever she walked into a room. Alex thrived on that.

Sarah also seemed to have a pretty stable head on her shoulders, a definite departure from the other women that Alex had dated. She was a bit taller than he, especially in heels, but that didn't matter to him. He wanted to please her all the time. Given that was how he had acted with all of his girlfriends, I just watched and waited.

After the first week, I scheduled the therapist to fly in and meet us at the next city. She was to stay for a couple of days. The goal was for her to get in as much time with Alex as was possible. It was a costly expense, so I wanted him to get the most out of it that he could. The boys spent a lot of money on the road for frivolous stuff. I felt that this was something worthwhile. The expense was Alex's alone, so no one could complain.

The tour staff understood the situation. They helped to arrange her travel and hotel bookings. That assured me she would arrive without incident. Vicki was also a recovering alcoholic and drug addict herself. She could speak from the heart when it came to her patients. I liked that about her.

She showed great concern for me and we had a few conversations about how I should handle Alex's situation. I was still hesitant to call it an addiction. Vicki helped me understand that what my brother had told me was absolutely right. Alex would not be forced into recovery until he was ready. That meant he had to reach his bottom. In other words, he had to reach that point at which he had nowhere else to go. That was a really difficult concept for me to accept. I think it is for any parent.

Imagine having to purposely step outside the protective bubble you have formed for your child. In our case, I think my instincts were even stronger than normal in that area. It had been just the two of us for so long and Alex had chosen a field where the sharks circled continuously. I had grown so used to keeping the predators at bay that it was difficult for me to reconcile with the idea of leaving him to fight them off on his own. And he was still suffering from the loss of a woman who had been like a mother to him. In a way, we had both lost a parent.

Actually, I was still having problems coping with my mother's death. With all of the other pressures on Alex, I was certain that he was having even greater difficulty. I did not make excuses for his actions, but I tried to get into his head so that I might understand just what he was thinking. There was not one reason that I could find that warranted the beginning of his drinking at such a young age. I was never one to consider drinking a solution to life's problems, nor were my parents. We were all social drinkers.

In the beginning, when I first went out on the road with the band, I tried to keep up with them. It was a way to feel like I was part of the group. But I quickly realized that I was not going to be able to do my job if I was up every night drinking with them until all hours. They had no responsibilities before 5:00 P.M. the next day, whereas I had to be up early to work a normal office day. Going out with the boys became an isolated event for me, something that I did on occasion if the next day was free.

The question, of course, was why Alex chose the path that he did. He had everything he could ever wish for: fame, fortune and a family who loved him no matter what. I really could not understand what was going through his mind.

I do know that when Donna was around, certain situations arose that involved pressure to partake of alcohol and marijuana. He told me then that he had experimented, but in the early days it was easier for me to keep a close eye on him. That was not the case anymore.

Unfortunately Alex always wanted to please people and fit in. I believe that led him to the mindset that experimenting was okay. It made him feel like he belonged to something, especially when he had adults doing it with him.

Back then, Alex told me that he tried drugs a couple of times and gave it up. It made him sleepy and he did not really like it. Had he lied? My son had developed a manipulative nature over the years and he was definitely prone to exaggeration. Maybe all of his shenanigans were a way to keep me off his back. I was getting myself more confused by the minute. I decided to take Vicki's advice and step back to watch him and see where he was headed.

When Vicki was around, he tried several times to manipulate situations and use her sessions as an excuse to drink. For example, one night we went to a very fun place. It was a restaurant, bowling alley and arcade, all in one. While we played video games everything was fine. Then we had a nice meal and did a bit of bowling. All of a sudden Alex left and returned with a beer.

Sarah and I looked at one another and asked him why he had done that.

"Vicki told me that I should try to cut down on my drinking instead of stopping altogether," he said. "She said that if I could make it through an evening without alcohol, that was fine, but if I couldn't, it was okay to do so in moderation."

"That doesn't sound right to me," I said. "I want to talk to Vicki about this."

Alex got very defensive. Then he started pacing around the place.

"You're just using blackmail to get me to stop drinking!" he said angrily.

Finally, I said, "Look! Just do what you want. I'm leaving!"

Then I left.

When I spoke to Vicki the next day and told her what happened, she said that Alex had twisted her words and used them to his own benefit. She also told me that he had all the symptoms of an addict and that I needed to treat him like one. Since I didn't quite understand what she meant by that, we discussed it further.

Finally, I asked her straight out, "Is my son an addict?"

"Yes," she said.

I was shocked and scared at the same time. Visions of him dead in a gutter from an overdose flashed into my mind. What was I supposed to do? She explained to me again that there was nothing that I could do.

My heart sank as I left her hotel room. Tears filled my eyes. What had I done wrong? Had I protected him too much? His whole life played through my head. All I saw was happiness. We had nothing but love in our house after his father left. My parents had done everything, sometimes too much, to make him feel loved and special. He had never wanted for anything. I had worked two and three jobs to see to that. I could not understand what was happening.

My head was swimming when I returned to my room. I called my brother and he told me that there was a predisposition to alcohol abuse in our family. He had his own bouts with it over the years. Some of what he said came rushing back to me. I remembered how many years before, he would go on drinking binges and had to be found and brought home. But where did this come from?

I tried talking to different members of my family to see if anyone else had that type of problem. The only one I came up with was Dad's father. He was a big partier and womanizer. The man spent money like water and never gave his son a second thought. He would hand him money and tell him to get lost. That was the extent of their interaction. Could that have been where the problems in the gene pool began?

I asked Vicki what she thought. She told me not to kill myself trying to figure out where it came from, but rather to deal with the problem at hand. So that was what I tried to do.

═══════

LESS THAN A MONTH AFTER the tour began, I realized that I had to leave Alex to attend a previously scheduled VH1 Save the Music Foundation fundraiser in New York with my nephew, Billy. Before deciding for certain about making the trip, I waited to see how things went with Alex. If that situation took a bad turn, my nephew would have to go without me. First things first.

As it turned out, Alex seemed to be doing fine. Sarah agreed to stay with him until I got back from New York. I felt fairly comfortable leaving, since I knew in my heart that things were going to run their course, with or without me there.

The night before I left, there was a knock on my door at a very late hour. It was Sarah. She was frightened, almost hysterical. I told her to calm down and tell me what had happened. She said that Alex had gone back out after they returned from the arcade. He was gone for several hours and she was sure that he was out looking for drugs.

Finally, upon his return, she said, he became frantic and terribly angry. He had a tantrum, during which he punched a few walls and trashed the hotel room. Sarah was afraid for both him and herself.

I sent Sarah back to Alex and asked Marcus to meet me at my son's room. By the time I dressed and got there, Alex was on the couch, crying and holding his hand. He said he thought he might have broken it. I took a moment to look around the room. There was furniture and clothing tossed all over the place. He had broken a glass from the bar and Sarah was trying to pick up the pieces. She was visibly shaken and avoided looking at me.

I asked Alex what had happened. He told me that he was angry with himself because he had fallen off the wagon and had tried to score some drugs. He had wound up drinking for most of the night. I was a bit confused by that because when I had taken leave of him, he was calm and seemed to be looking forward to relaxing in bed and falling asleep while watching television.

Apparently, he had fallen asleep for a while. A craving that he could not get rid of awakened him. In an effort to find someone who would go

Alex and me on the *Today Show* with Ann Curry and Matt Lauer

MARCUS JOHNSON

out with him, he went out into the hallway and knocked on a bunch of doors. When that didn't work, he went downstairs to drink in the bar. By the time he got back up to the room, he was angry and acting crazy. Sarah did not know what to do, so she came to me.

I held him and tried to calm him down. I felt better knowing that Vicki was due to arrive the next day. He would be able talk to her and work through what was ailing him. When Marcus got to the room, he helped us clean up the mess.

Sarah pulled me aside and told me that she had had enough. She planned to catch the next plane to Los Angeles. I convinced her to stay, at least until I got back from New York. She agreed and we all got back to a normal night's rest.

The incident made me realize just how desperately Alex needed help. I was torn over whether to go to New York. After a conversation with Vicki the next morning, I decided to go and leave Alex in her capable hands.

At the end of my stay in New York, I received a call from home. My brother was concerned about my dad and was at his wit's end. He sounded terrible. I was forced to make yet another tough decision. I called Vicki. She said she had made some significant breakthroughs with Alex and that he had been quite cooperative.

In an attempt to help him with his anxiety and cravings, they had tried hypnosis. It sometimes worked well with addicts since there were triggers she could use. In other words, if she knew Alex got anxious when he saw a beer commercial on television, then that was a trigger that she could program through hypnosis for him to ignore the commercial or replace it with something not harmful to him like a soda or candy. He had used it a couple of times and it seemed to help.

With that bit of good news, plus the fact that my nephew agreed to go out on the road for a couple of weeks with Alex, I decided to go home and see about Dad. I know now that alcoholics are great liars and manipulators. Alex had become a master at both. Those few events made it very clear to me that I had to make every effort to learn all I could about my son's addiction.

I was not prepared for any of it. Alex had always been a relatively easy child to raise. He was always focused and knew what he wanted. Now he was fixated on his addiction and trying to control it, but without the proper tools that was not going to be possible. I prayed that Vicki would be able to give him the tools that he needed.

The last time I had been this worried about Alex was when he was only a few months old. He had been diagnosed with a double hernia and had to spend one night in the hospital for surgery. Well, you would have thought they had told me that he was on his deathbed. I went nuts. Up until that point, he had been a happy and healthy baby.

It turned out to be very minor and I brought him home the very next day. While I was a bit afraid to touch him at first, the nurse explained that the teensy-tiny butterfly bandage was all that remained from the surgery. This time around was very different and infinitely scarier for me. There was no doctor who could make it go away with a simple operation or a one-night stay in the hospital. This was a major, life threatening physical and mental issue that had to be dealt with by professionals. My task was to make Alex understand that.

Less than a week after I returned to Orlando, I was getting ready to go visit my dad, when the telephone rang. It was midday on Sunday. A chill went through me, as I instinctively knew it was Alex before I even picked up the receiver.

"Mom," Alex said.

In that one word, I heard everything. He was scared, terribly scared, more so than I had ever heard him before in his life. He began the conversation by frantically begging me to allow him to come home. After getting my emotions under control, I willed myself to be strong for my son. I tried to speak as calmly as I could when I asked him what had happened. He said he had been sleeping in his room when Kevin came to his door to get him for some activity the boys had planned for the day.

When he told Kevin that he didn't want to go, Kevin went nuts. The two of them had a huge fight. Kevin laid it all out in front of him, once and for all. He gave Alex an ultimatum. All of the boys knew what was going on. It was up to Alex to fix the problem or they would throw him out of the group.

That was Alex's bottom. Reality had finally struck. He was scared to death that if he did not do something immediately he would not live through the tour. He actually feared for his life!

At that point, I wondered if there was more to the story than he was telling me. Had he been arrested? Was he someplace other than his hotel room and afraid to return? In an instant, all sorts of horrible scenarios played out in my head. It seemed too simple. Could a fight with Kevin really have shone the light on Alex's tunnel of darkness? I just could not believe him anymore.

I told him that I thought coming home was not the answer unless I could find a place that would take him in for treatment right away. After making that statement, it dawned on me that I had absolutely no clue where to start to even find a place like that. I told him to hang up and I would ask Vicki and Marcus to come to his room. I would call him back as soon as a plan could be put into place. Alex agreed.

Vicki was not in her room when I called, so I tracked down Marcus, who was able to locate her. Together, they put a plan into motion. Vicki was much more emotionally and mentally equipped to deal with finding a treatment facility than I was, so she immediately suggested a few places that she felt would get the job done and protect Alex's privacy as a celebrity.

Countless telephone calls later, we reached a decision about where to put Alex for treatment. That meant that it would be necessary to postpone the next leg of the tour. That task was put on The Firm's shoulders. We all had to focus on getting Alex the help he needed. Arrangements were made for Alex and Marcus to fly out that night to the treatment center in Arizona.

Once I knew my son was headed for the safety and treatment he needed with Marcus by his side, I realized that there was one more telephone call I had to make. I knew Kevin well enough to know that he was probably feeling pretty rotten about himself. I needed to set the record straight. I found Kevin in his room. We had a very good heart-to-heart about the day's events. I thanked him for the intervention that saved my son's life. He was very emotional on the telephone and kept repeating that the boys were behind Alex one hundred percent. They would make certain that he got everything he needed to get better. They would postpone the tour and wait for him to heal. He needed to just get better and not worry about anything else. Later that week, the boys went on MTV and announced that Alex had gone into rehab for treatment involving depression and excessive use of alcohol.

I spoke to Alex the next day. He had settled into the treatment center and he sounded really calm. He told me he felt safe, that he would get what he needed there and work at getting better. It was a short, tearful conversation, but at least it left me with the hope that my son was back on the right path and now had a future. I cried a lot that day. I probably ran the entire gamut of emotions. I went from anger to frustration to helplessness to relief to final tears of joy that my son was on the road to recovery.

The following twenty-eight days were monumental. We learned a lot about each other and ourselves. The therapy sessions were rough on Alex. When he started to talk about his childhood, things came up that even he had not realized were buried deep in his heart and soul. He had underlying issues with my divorce from his father and feelings of abandonment that had never been addressed.

Then came the issues that involved his grandmother and, of course, her death. Those were things that we would discuss later during the family sessions. There were issues that he had within himself, like his personality flaws, his inability to handle confrontation and his constant need to always please others. Alex was always so concerned with what everyone thought about him that he never did things for the simple pleasure of doing them. Also discussed in therapy was his exorbitant spending.

They tested Alex for all sorts of things during the first week. He came up negative for most. He did test positive for post-traumatic stress syndrome, as well as a mild attention deficit disorder (ADD). The stress issue I understood. The business he was in constantly put him in the position that demanded that he deal with things he was not equipped to handle. But the ADD was a bit bewildering to me, until they explained how common that was with addicts. That did better explain his frenetic behavior. It was a behavior that had definitely increased over the last couple of years. Perhaps it could be attributed to the erratic lifestyle he had lived for so long.

The real kicker was the last issue that surfaced. It floored us all. My son had not really felt like he was Alex since he was eight years old. The persona of AJ and all that it stood for had grown up to envelop the little boy he had left behind. He really felt that he had had no childhood. AJ had taken it away from him.

In my mind, that was the root of the problem. He had developed a split personality of sorts. It was as though good and evil lived in the same body. The good one hung around with family and friends at home and showed up during the holidays. But as the bad one, the AJ persona, grew and became the popular one, Alex disappeared. The stage persona won the battle and took over my son.

I went with the flow those first few days. I bided my time until I could get there and talk to some of the therapists myself. After all, most of what I was hearing came from Alex and I was still reluctant to believe everything he had to say. As the week wore on, I became more anxious to see him. He sounded better each time we spoke on the telephone and he said he felt stronger everyday.

Finally, I was told that I could visit him for a brief time at the end of the first week. Sundays were family and friends visiting day. I was eager to hold my child in my arms again and give him the hugs and kisses he deserved for being so brave. I had actually been able to regain some of the faith I had lost in him. The road ahead was going to be a difficult one, but at least it would be a healthier one.

Over the course of the days leading up to the trip, I faxed letters to Alex every morning. I tried to be as supportive and as upbeat as I could. At night we would speak. I would ask about his day and kiss him good-night over the telephone. The new world he had brought me into had me scared to death. What was I going to learn about my son and myself during the coming weeks? I was unsure if I was fully prepared to hear the things that he was going to say or what the doctors would uncover about him.

Again the protective nature of being a parent came into the picture. In some ways, I was just as eager to please people as Alex was at times. While I needed approval, I never felt that I went to the extreme. There came a point when I just knew there were people I would not get along with no matter what. In those instances, I would resign myself to that and move on. Alex had never been able to cope with the moving-on part. People hung onto him like leeches. He never knew how or when to pull them off.

All of that, plus the fake friends who had ingratiated themselves with him, had gotten him to the place where he now found himself. Therein lay the next big fear. How was he going to cope with the real world after having been sequestered in such a safe place? Would they be able to help him become stronger and face his fears or would he sink back into the same hole? My anxieties grew day after day.

So many questions went through my head that it began to swim in fog. I slept that night wrapped in the warmth of the lovely thought of seeing Alex the next day and holding him close. At that moment, it was enough.

———

MY BROTHER AND I flew out that Friday and rented a truck at the airport. The facility was miles from the city in the middle of the desert. Sarah and Marcus drove from Los Angeles to meet us on Sunday morning before we all set out to see Alex. We registered at a motel and went to our rooms, filled with anticipation over the next day's meeting. My brother and I had dinner together that night and spoke of the events that had led us there.

I was glad that my brother was with me since I really needed his strength to help me through the coming day. He was as apprehensive as I about seeing Alex. Neither of us knew what to expect, or for that matter, what to say to him. I had spoken a few times to Vicki about Alex's progress. She thought he was doing very well. She had the inside scoop on him from the doctors at the center and told me everything Alex was doing. I just wanted to make sure he was getting the proper care and progressing with his treatment.

The next morning, I awoke early and made coffee in my room. As I looked outside my window and sipped my wake-up juice, I marveled at the serenity that surrounded my motel. I had always liked that part of the country, with its beautiful desert vastness shadowed by majestic mountain ranges.

I had visited Arizona a couple of times before, once with the boys when they were on tour, and again with a friend for a five-day spa vacation. Both times I was impressed by the waves of positive energy I felt as we walked the hiking trails or sat high on a horse plodding through the rocky terrain. The boys and I had experienced a genuine cowboy campfire barbeque and hayride during our visit. We had had a wonderful time.

Who could have known during those happy times that I would some-day be standing on a balcony, looking at the same beautiful scenery and breathing in the wonderful smells of nature, but with a looming dark cloud in the background? I understood why they would build a sub-stance abuse treatment center out in the middle of nowhere; it was also in the middle of ultimate tranquility.

At breakfast, my brother sensed my nervousness and tried to console me. He told me it would all be okay. I should just focus on reuniting with my son. If Alex felt comfortable sharing his experiences, then so be it. If not, that could wait for another day. I agreed, but deep inside I had questions about everything. I focused on the happiness I knew I would feel when I saw my son again.

As we drove into the parking lot, I was struck by how quiet and peace-ful the surroundings were. The entrance to the facility had a lovely circu-lar fountain and everything was terra-cotta. Lots of cactus and desert plants filled the pathways. It reminded me of a park until we entered the lobby.

We were greeted by several people who made us sign in for our visi-tors' badges. Our bags were also examined. They had to know what we were bringing onto the premises. Certain things, we later found out, were permitted. Other items they kept for the patients until after their visitors left.

Sarah and Marcus met us in the lobby and we exchanged hugs and kisses. Sarah seemed very nervous but happy. There were a lot of people in the lobby—other relatives and friends of patients just like my son. From that area, we could see down a long, well-lit hallway that we were told led to the main building and dining room.

I went to use the restroom. Off to the sides were some small class-rooms with couches and chairs. As I walked back to join my brother and the others, I asked if Alex had been told that we were there. The answer was yes.

Journal Entry, July 15, 2001: *As we stood there waiting for him, my heart pounded. I shifted my weight from one foot to the other in anticipation. Then, suddenly, Alex appeared and my heart jumped to a new place. Our eyes filled with tears as I ran to grab onto him. He held me and cried into my shoulder as he said hello.*

After what seemed like a very long hug, I let him go and we walked back to greet everyone else. He kissed Sarah and gave Marcus and my brother long hearty hugs. Then he took us on a tour of his temporary home. As we made our way around the entire facility, Alex talked about everything there was to do. He told us about the classes and the horses and just expounded on tale after tale of his first week.

I listened to his every word and my insides danced with glee as we followed along behind him. There was a genuine bounce in his step that I had not seen in a long time. His skin glowed with health and he was very relaxed. Those were all of the things that had been missing from him for a long time. I was happy to see that they had returned. I was also greatly comforted by the fact that my most pressing question had been answered. Alex was safe, getting the help he needed and in the right place.

Alex was learning a lot about nutrition, exercise and discipline. He talked about having to do all the normal everyday stuff that I realized he had probably never done for himself, things as mundane as laundry. Between his grandmother, his girlfriends and me, there had always been someone around to do it for him. When they were on the road, a staff member collected his laundry from him and returned it clean.

At the treatment center, Alex experienced some aspects of life in the real world that he probably would not have encountered for years had it not been for his addiction. Not that I was going to start a plus list for that. There is no upside to addiction, just a very long downside.

Alex told us that he had made some new friends in his therapy group. They had learned a lot about each other during the therapy sessions, and that had brought them together as a group. There was a young man in his group named Barkley who suffered from a similar addiction to Alex, but for much different reasons. He came from a well-to-do family of professionals. Barkley had some issues from his childhood that were being addressed and he really got along well with Alex. He was a very likeable young man. We all developed a fondness for him during that month.

Alex asked me two questions when I arrived: "How are the boys?" and "What are the fans saying about me?" I told him what the boys had done on MTV and he was relieved that they had broken the ice for him. Then I relayed to him how the fans had reacted. We had gotten so many letters, calls and e-mails of support that we were completely overwhelmed.

I told him that we would have to do something nice for them when he got out and we would talk about it later. He was so relieved. He said he thought people would hate him for what he had done and how he had screwed up the tour. I said no, just the opposite. Everyone was behind him and he should not give it a second thought.

Alex told me that he had spoken to Kevin, who informed him that some of the boys planned to visit him over the coming weeks. They really needed to see for themselves that he was okay—especially Kevin, who still felt bad about the fight they had had before Alex left the tour. I told Alex that I had thanked Kevin for what he had done. Alex said he felt the same way. He felt that Kevin had saved his life.

After we walked the grounds, we sat in the dining room and talked more about his experiences since he had arrived. He told us about the coyotes he heard at night and about a certain type of wild boar that wandered around right outside the fence of the facility. He had even seen a couple of tarantulas. They were very large and furry and could jump up to six feet. He and I agreed we were not fond of them.

While we were there, Alex was called to a class. We walked around outside for a while longer and then later met him for dinner. There was a small gift shop stocked with books about addiction, stuffed toys and all sorts of staples like toiletries and such. It was fascinating to look at all the information on addiction. I purchased a couple of books to read on the flight home. I also bought a stuffed toy for Alex as a memento from his loving mom.

Dinner was very pleasant in the airy dining room. I learned how the food was prepared with the addict in mind. They served very plain food because even certain types of spices could be triggers to an addict. There were also patients there with eating disorders and they were served first. That way, their choices were fewer and their diets could be overseen. It was an interesting lesson.

To be honest, I wasn't interested in the food. I was too busy relishing the fact that I was sitting across from my son as he ate his dinner with more gusto and happiness than I had seen in a long time. The day passed much too quickly. Before we knew it, we were hugging our tearful good-byes. We watched as he retreated down the hallway to his room. I think he was crying when he walked away. That was difficult to see.

I took heart in the fact that I would see him again in a couple of weeks for family week, and in that I would be able to speak to him more frequently on the telephone until then. Alex told us more about family week in the phone conversations that followed. For the first few days, we would not be able to have any contact with him. We had to stay within our group of other parents and spouses. Then, during the last couple of days, we would come together as one large group to do some exercises and therapy sessions. It sounded like it was going to be very intense, but it needed to be done. That seemed frightening in a way, but my brother and Sarah were coming back with me, so at least I would not be alone.

DURING THE NEXT SEVERAL WEEKS, Alex called me to talk about his father. He had discussed him in therapy and it brought up some very raw anger issues. The therapist had him beat a pillow with some type of stick to help release his anger. He broke the stick. He spoke a lot about the divorce and the abandonment issues he was working through.

The main reason for Alex's call was to ask if I thought it would all right for him to have his father come to family week. That would allow them to work out some of their stuff. I said definitely not. It was not okay with me. I had been there for Alex all of his life and was now going through all of this as well.

I would have felt very betrayed if his father had waltzed into the picture at that point and stole the show. There were too many unresolved things between us that had to be dealt with before he started with his father. After I had said my piece, Alex agreed. To my relief, we ended the call on a happy and loving note.

I told my brother what Alex had suggested. He felt I said exactly the right thing. My brother would have felt uncomfortable as well if my ex-husband had been sitting there listening to all of us bare our souls in therapy. He had not been a part of our family for over twenty years. That gave him zero right to be involved in the healing process. It was too important for those of us who really loved Alex to help him work through that time in his life. His father had long ago given up any right to be there.

I proceeded to read as much as I could over the next several days about addiction. I also had to fill out several questionnaires in preparation for family week. We had an entire workbook to go through during that time. When I showed it to my brother, he was amazed. "That's heavy-duty stuff," he said.

It was a necessary evil, though. It was that bare-bones work that brought out all of the feelings and emotions it would take to begin the healing process. It was a large learning curve for me. I had never dealt with therapy before. The closest thing I had done was go to a marriage counselor. We all know how that turned out.

When the time finally arrived to fly out for family week, I was filled with excitement at the prospect of seeing Alex again. At the same time, I was fearful of the unknown, though I had prepared myself mentally for the week and had gone through the entire workbook several times over. I was as ready as I would ever be.

My brother was also nervous, even though he found comfort in the fact that he would be seeing Alex again and would be helping him work through his issues. He was also using this time as a healing point in his own life. Her confided to me that he had never really confronted his own drinking issues. He felt that this would be a good time to learn more about his own demons.

The week started out on a silly note. When we arrived at the center, Alex was bopping around with a bandana on his head and smiling like a loon. It was obvious that something was up with him. It was not until he took off the bandana at dinnertime and peeked at us from the hallway that his little surprise was revealed.

Alex had shaved his head!

I have to say, at that moment he looked like a real mental patient. Since he knew we were not allowed to make any physical contact with him for the first few days, I knew he had done it for shock value. We just laughed it off.

As the week progressed, we went through some pretty intense emotions. The group sessions revealed a lot about our family dynamics. We learned who had been the strong influences on Alex while he was growing up. It was mostly Mom and me, with Dad and my brother running a close second. Mom's influence on him did not really surprise me since she had been the family icon.

There was also a lot of discussion about Alex and his intense desire, from a young age, to please everyone. It was enlightening for all of us. We learned a lot more about Sarah and her family during that week. She had her own issues, given the recent passing of her sister.

We also learned about other patients' situations from their parents, siblings and spouses. The group counselors were more like mediators than therapists; they only joined the conversations if we reached a question or stumbling block. At first, everyone was rather timid about sharing information. As we grew to know each other better, the tenseness in the room eased. We were all there for the same reason.

We talked about why and how we believed our loved one had become an addict. Then we focused on how to cope with the disease. That was a revelation for me. Before that time, I had never really thought of addiction as a disease. They gave us many statistics for different levels of addiction and recovery. The odds were really kind of depressing. Many addicts relapse during their first year of recovery.

The key to recovery was to follow the twelve-step program established by Alcoholics Anonymous. They believed that by following those steps and focusing every day on that day's recovery, an addict could live his or her life free from substance abuse. There were other groups that were specific to each type of addiction. Whether it was cocaine addiction or teenagers with addictions, every disease had a program geared toward that specific problem.

The concept for each group is essentially the same. It is based on the belief that everyone has the capacity to be healed by a Higher Power. Alcoholics Anonymous has always defined that Higher Power as God, but some treatment programs have redefined it as whatever the addict chooses his or her Higher Power to be. At Alex's treatment center, some people went with nature, energy or, in one case, electricity. That person actually wore an electrical-outlet cover on a neck chain; it was proof of their devotion to the Higher Power of electricity. That was kind of weird, I thought, but whatever works, I guess.

Other steps in the AA recovery program required Alex to acknowledge that his life was unmanageable and that he was powerless over alcohol. He was also asked to admit to himself, his higher power and others who knew him the exact nature of what he had done wrong in his life. Finally, he was asked to make amends to those he had harmed and to seek a spiritual awakening.

With each day, we moved closer to the therapy sessions, which were the final step in the process. We learned increasingly more about the disease that had taken hold of our loved one and how we would be making a very important decision in their recovery. That decision was whether or not to continue to be their enabler. That was key. I learned how I had enabled Alex to manipulate my family and me over the past several years. How our concern and ultimatums were not really the right course of action.

One of the main revelations was how I was supposed to tend to my own needs first whenever he and I came to an impasse. In other words, if I saw Alex falling back into his addictive behavior, I simply walked away and healed myself. That was a hard pill to swallow.

During the last few sessions, Sarah, my brother and I sat in a circle with a group of other patients and family members. In the center of the circle were two chairs. The idea was for the family members and friends to take turns sitting in the chairs to tell the addict exactly how he or she had made them feel about issues dealing with anger, love, disappointment and pain.

The sessions, which proved to be very revealing, were split into two days. On the first day, Sarah, my brother and I made a list of specific incidents and went over them, telling Alex what he had done to hurt us or to make us angry. He sat in one chair; we took turns sitting in the other chair, going through our list of concerns. He had to sit there and take it. He was not allowed to respond to our statements.

I began with, "When you went to New York and had me plan a birthday party for your cousin Kathy and you did not show up because you claimed to miss three flights, I felt angry, hurt, sad and frustrated."

Alex took it on the chin.

"When you are on the road touring and I try to call you and you rush me off the phone and promise to call me back, but never do, that makes me feel very hurt and lonely," I continued. "You only call me when you need something—or want to buy something."

Alex had never heard me talk to him that way. I could tell by his facial expressions that my words were having an impact on him.

I pressed on: "When you were in Los Angeles on a video shoot and you told me that you had tried cocaine but would not do it again, you lied—and that made me feel hurt and sad. I feel the same way when you are away from home and never call your family to find out how we are or what is going on."

The following day, it was Alex's turn to face me in the circle and read off his list of concerns about his relationship with me. I was apprehensive, to say the least—not just because of what I feared he might say, but because I was surrounded by people whom, with the exception of Sarah and my brother, I had never met until that week. I had to reach down real deep to hold on for that ride.

Alex's first item on the list was one that was a sore spot with me, not just because it burrowed to the core of my motherhood, but because it had been an issue in our disagreements over Donna's influence in his life.

"When you try to control my life and not let me make my own decisions," Alex said, sitting face-to-face with me, "it makes me feel sad, hurt and angry."

Ouch! I had a response, but I was not allowed to open my mouth.

Alex continued: "When you act like a business manager, instead of my mom, it makes me feel lonely and afraid."

Alex's representation of his life before rehab

My representation of life before rehab

Alex's representation of his life after rehab

My representation of life after rehab

Believe me, there was nothing easy about those therapy sessions. They were very intense and emotional for all of us. Alex brought up some things that really made me think, like how he felt I was too controlling and did not let him run his own life. That one struck a chord. Alex also told my brother how Bill's drinking and sometimes fighting while Alex was growing up scared him and made him angry. That gave my brother something to think about. It was a very soul-cleansing experience.

One of the things that struck me was how Alex had seen the transformation into AJ taking place but chose to hold onto it instead of seeking help. He had become the stage persona to such an extent that Alex really was hidden from everyone, even Sarah and his own family.

It was clear that he tried to escape by sleeping during the day. The pressures of his career and the group had just become too much for him to deal with. He became AJ-the-party-animal to escape from all of that. I felt so sorry for him. However, once we discovered more about how the insidious disease works, we realized that we had been enabling Alex to keep up that game.

Time and again, we had made excuses for him to the other boys and to his family. I felt very stupid for allowing that to happen, but I realized that I was in a form of denial myself at the time, so it was easier for me to make the excuses rather than face the alternative that my child was an addict.

One of the main things we walked away with from those sessions was an understanding of the skills needed to react to Alex's manipulations. If we saw him fall back into old habits, we knew there were things we could do to deal with it. Just knowing that made us feel better about our ability to cope with his disease. His recovery wouldn't be easy, but at least we were now armed with the knowledge that we needed to help him.

I wrote volumes of notes during that week and saved them to refer to if I needed them. The other things I saved were pictures. We were asked to draw pictures for each other that represented how we saw ourselves with Alex, before rehab and after.

Alex drew a lovely picture of him and me. There was a big red heart between us as we held hands with the word "real" underneath the heart. It made me cry when he gave it to me and explained it in his own words. He wanted desperately to get back to a good place, where we were both happy and trusting of each other again. So did I.

At one point that week, I was asked to write a description of what I would consider a perfect day with Alex. I wrote: "To be with my son where no one knows who we are—no bodyguards, no fans—just us at an amusement park where there are all of our favorite rides and no lines. Water rides, roller coasters, haunted houses. An entire day of fun, where when we want or need anything it appears and we are happy and laughing all day long."

The Sunday before we left for home, some of the boys came to see Alex. Not all of them showed up—and that was disappointing—but Kevin and Brian tried to make him feel better and gave him all of their support. He was grateful for that and probably quite relieved. He was still very concerned about the fans and the tour, but he knew that his focus must remain on his recovery.

They talked behind closed doors for a long time. Alex told me later that they tried to figure out a game plan for when he was released. They asked him to think about what he intended to do about the rest of the tour and then they left on a happy note.

The last day of family week was amazing. Everyone sat in a circle in a large room that was illuminated with bright lights. There were no shadows in which to seek refuge or solace. We each got up to tell the other person what he or she had gained from the week and what their hopes were for the future.

When the patients spoke to their families, they gave them a gold token and held their hand. It was a very joyful but emotional time.

I rose and faced Alex with tears in my eyes.

"Hello, my name is Denise and I have learned about addiction, love and my son's disease," I said, touching his cheek. "I prayed that when he came here I would get back the son I lost to this terrible disease. I believe that to be true. Thank you for giving me my son back."

Alex and I hugged, tears streaming down our cheeks.

Then it was Alex's turn. He gave me my token and said, "Hello, my name is Alex and I have also learned a lot about my disease and myself. I am grateful for having been here and . . . Mom, you have your son back."

Again, we hugged and wept.

—————

WE RETURNED TO THE REHAB CENTER a week-and-a-half later to take Alex home. Nicole went with me, as did Andre. Once Alex was released, we drove back to Los Angeles, where he had rented an apartment before all of the rehab began so that he would not have to fly all the way across the country just to have a place to hang his hat. For the time being, he planned to keep his house in Orlando. The L.A. apartment seemed the logical thing to do, given that the boys were spending more time on the West Coast.

Before going back on tour, Alex decided to take ten additional days off. Everyone agreed with that. The booking agents and promoters were given a green light to announce new concert dates based on his anticipated return.

While he was in Los Angeles that first week, Andre took some pictures for me to use on postcards to send to the fans who had written to Alex to offer their support. By then, magazines were calling for interviews and the media was buzzing about Alex coming out of rehab. Since he was not ready to face that yet, I stayed with him for a couple of weeks before returning home.

The first day back from rehab, Alex and I went to his apartment and then walked to a nearby town square. As we walked, I saw the happiness on his face when passersby recognized him. Many of the people we met on the sidewalk shook his hand and congratulated him on his recovery.

Before we reached the street corner, we passed a homeless man on a bench. It was hard to tell how old the man was since he was covered in layers of clothing from head to toe and had long hair and a long beard. I did not see much gray in his hair, so I figured he was still young. He looked right at Alex as we passed.

"Hello," he said.

"Hello," we both responded.

We continued walking until we reached a coffee shop, not giving much thought to the homeless man. It is the sort of thing that you run into on any big-city street. Later, as we walked back from the coffee shop, I noticed that the bench where the homeless man had been sitting was empty.

We took a different route back to Alex's apartment so that he could take in the air and sunshine a bit more. He stopped at a record shop on the corner and looked around for a bit. He bought a few CDs and we continued on our way.

We walked another block and noticed the same homeless man sitting on another bench in our path. As we approached, he looked right at Alex and said, "It's a real bear when you stray off the path sometimes, isn't it, son? But now that you're back on it, you'll be fine."

Alex and I looked at each other in amazement and continued walking. After several steps, we turned around and saw that the homeless man was gone. He was nowhere in sight! I turned to my son and said, "You know who that was, right?"

Alex looked into my eyes, smiled and answered, "Yes, Mom, it was an angel."

I smiled back and we continued home.